PHILIP'S FAMILY WORLD ATLAS

Contents

CITY CENTRE MAPS – KEY TO SYMBOLS

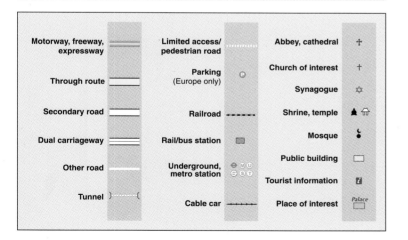

Motorway, freeway, expressway	Limited access/pedestrian road	Abbey, cathedral ✝
Through route	Parking (Europe only) ⓟ	Church of interest ✝
Secondary road	Railroad	Synagogue ✡
Dual carriageway	Rail/bus station	Shrine, temple
Other road	Underground, metro station	Mosque
Tunnel	Cable car	Public building
		Tourist information
		Place of interest *Palace*

Philip's World Atlases are published in association with The Royal Geographical Society (with The Institute of British Geographers).

The Society was founded in 1830 and given a Royal Charter in 1859 for 'the advancement of geographical science'. It holds historical collections of national and international importance, many of which relate to the Society's association with and support for scientific exploration and research from the 19th century onwards. It was pivotal in establishing geography as a teaching and research discipline in British universities close to the turn of the century, and has played a key role in geographical and environmental education ever since.

Today the Society is a leading world centre for geographical learning – supporting education, teaching, research and expeditions, and promoting public understanding of the subject.

The Society welcomes those interested in geography as members. For further information, please visit the website at: www.rgs.org

CITY CENTRE MAPS – Cartography by Philip's
Page iii, Dublin: The town plan of Dublin is based on Ordnance Survey Ireland by permission of the Government Permit Number 7617. © Government of Ireland.

Ordnance Survey® Page iii, Edinburgh, and page iv, London: This product includes mapping licensed from Ordnance Survey® with the permission of the Controller of Her Majesty's Stationery Office. © Crown copyright 2003. All rights reserved. Licence number 100011710.

Vector data: Courtesy of Gräfe and Unser Verlag GmbH, München, Germany (city centre maps of Bangkok, Mexico City, Singapore, Sydney and Tokyo).

Published in Great Britain in 2003 by Philip's, a division of Octopus Publishing Group, 2–4 Heron Quays, London E14 4JP

Copyright © 2003 Philip's

Cartography by Philip's

ISBN 0–540–08411–5

A CIP catalogue record for this book is available from the British Library.

Printed in Hong Kong

Details of other Philip's titles and services can be found on our website at: www.philips-maps.co.uk

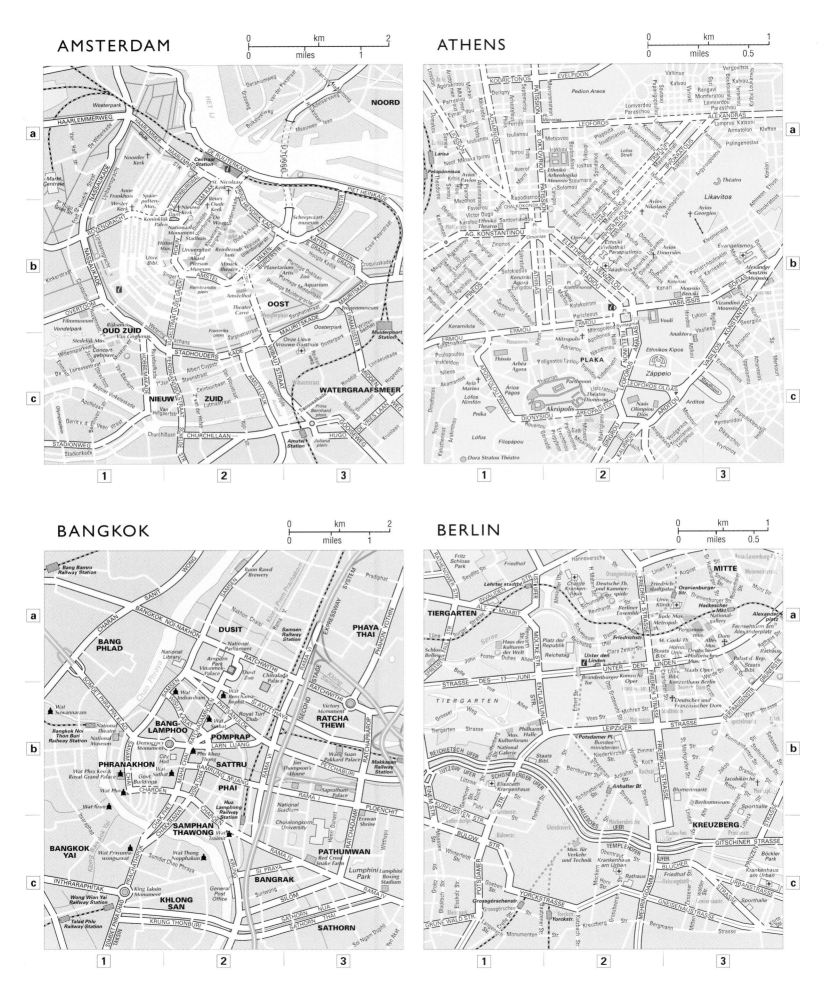

AMSTERDAM

ATHENS

BANGKOK

BERLIN

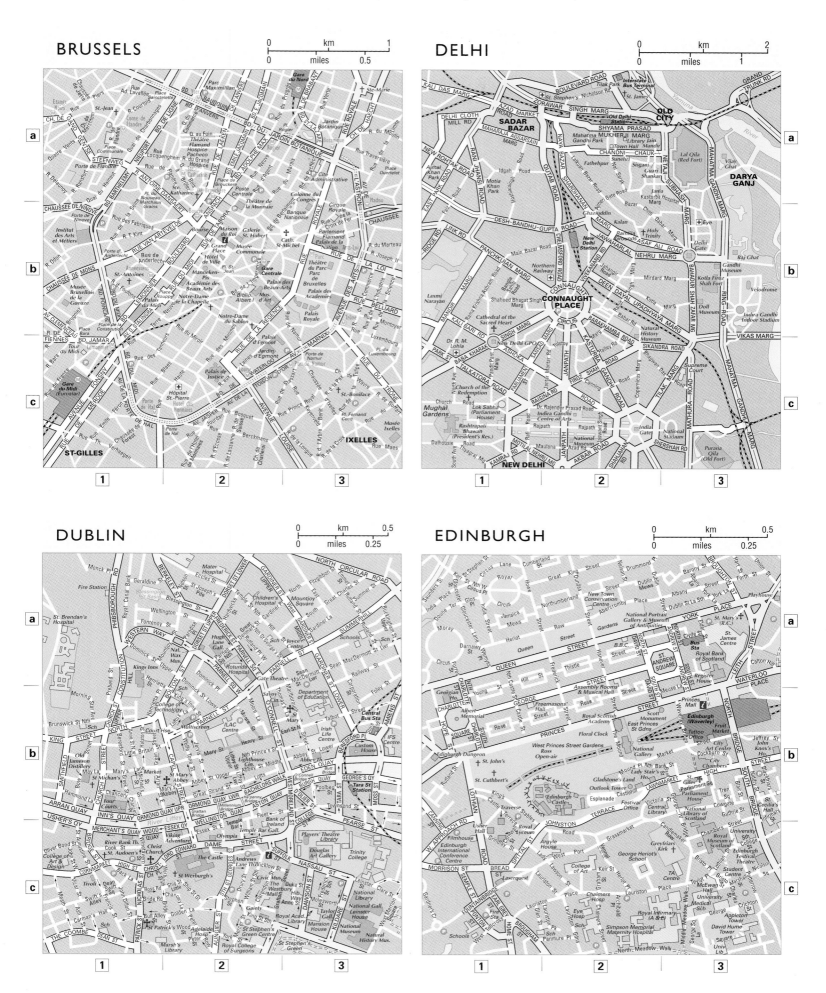

BRUSSELS

DELHI

DUBLIN

EDINBURGH

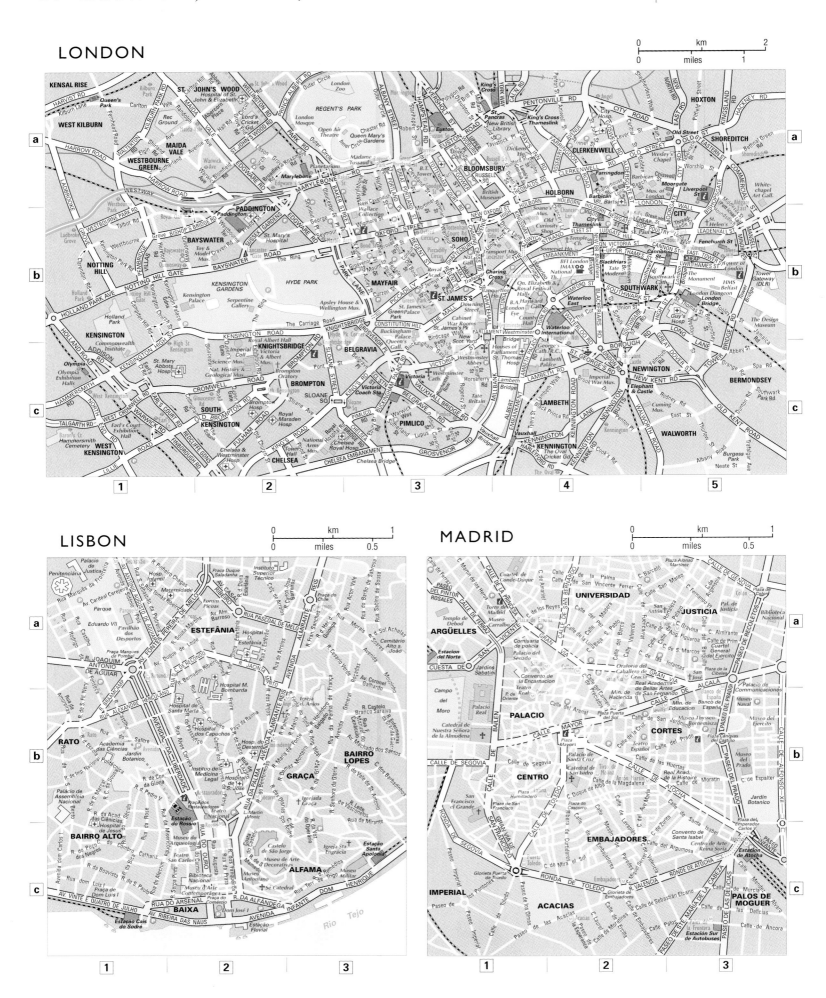

LONDON

LISBON

MADRID

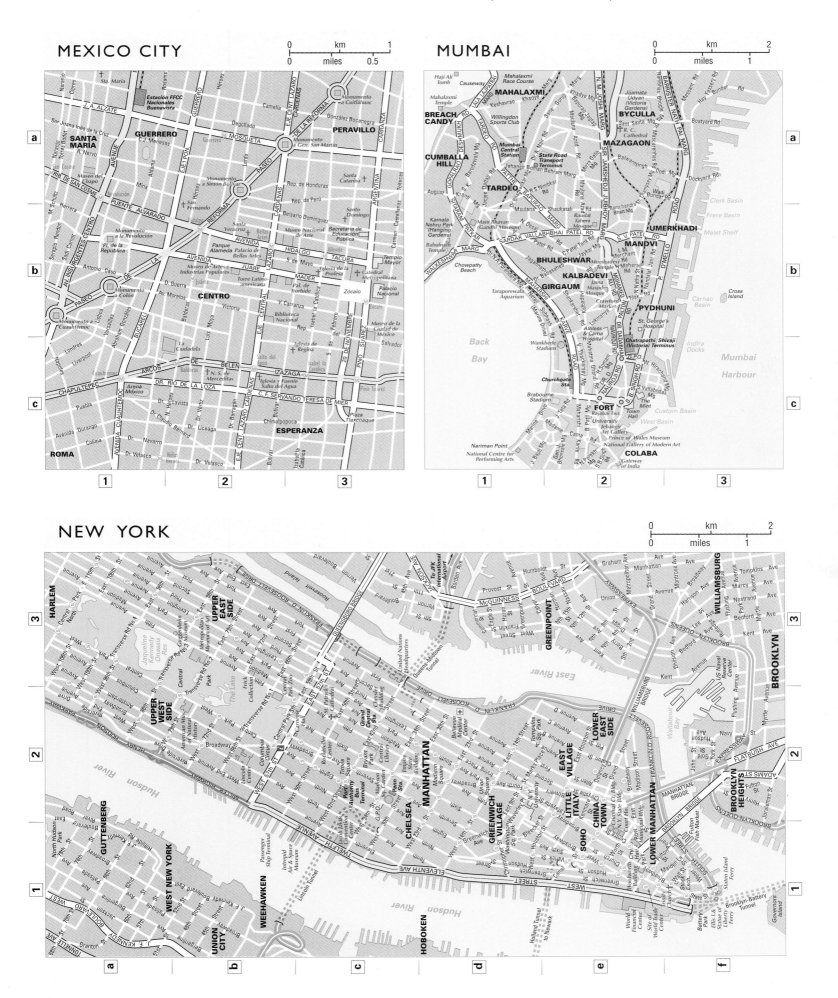

MEXICO CITY

MUMBAI

NEW YORK

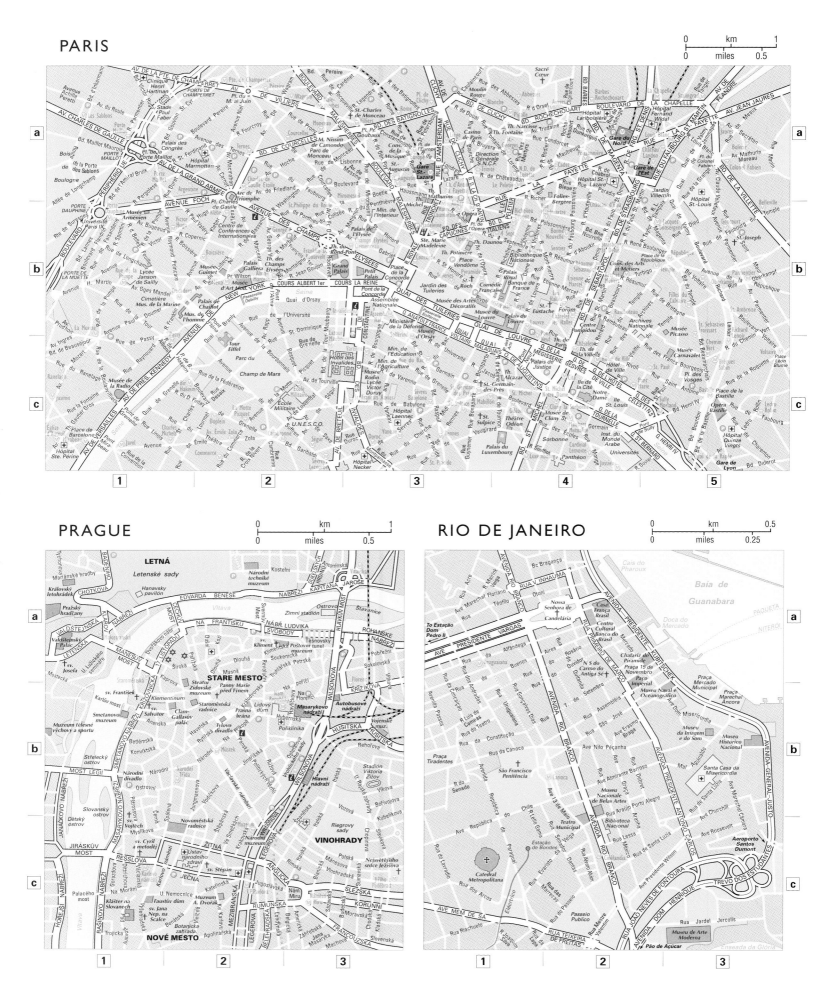

PARIS

PRAGUE

RIO DE JANEIRO

VIII WORLD CITIES: DISTANCES

The table shows air distances in miles and kilometres between 24 major cities. Known as 'Great Circle' distances, these measure the shortest routes between the cities, which aircraft use wherever possible. The maps show the world centred on six cities, and illustrate, for example, why direct flights from Japan to northern America and Europe are across the Arctic regions. The maps have been constructed on an Azimuthal Equidistant projection, on which all distances measured through the centre point are true to scale. The red lines are drawn at 5,000, 10,000 and 15,000 km from the central city.

Kms (upper right triangle) / **Miles** (lower left triangle)

	Beijing	Bombay (Mumbai)	Buenos Aires	Cairo	Calcutta (Kolkata)	Caracas	Chicago	Hong Kong	Honolulu	Johannesburg	Lagos	London	Los Angeles	Mexico City	Moscow	Nairobi	New York	Paris	Rio de Janeiro	Rome	Singapore	Sydney	Tokyo	Wellington	
Beijing	Beijing	2956	11972	4688	2031	8947	6588	1220	5070	7276	7119	5057	6251	7742	3600	5727	6828	5106	10773	5049	2783	5561	1304	6700	Beijing
Bombay (Mumbai)	4757	Bombay (Mumbai)	9275	2706	1034	9024	8048	2683	8024	4334	4730	4467	8700	9728	3126	2816	7793	4356	8332	3837	2432	6313	4189	7686	Bombay (Mumbai)
Buenos Aires	19268	14925	Buenos Aires	7341	10268	3167	5599	11481	7558	5025	4919	6917	6122	4591	8374	6463	5298	6867	1214	6929	9867	7332	11410	6202	Buenos Aires
Cairo	7544	4355	11814	Cairo	3541	6340	6127	5064	8838	3894	2432	2180	7580	7687	1803	2197	5605	1994	6149	1325	5137	8959	5947	10268	Cairo
Calcutta (Kolkata)	3269	1664	16524	5699	Calcutta (Kolkata)	9609	7978	1653	7048	5256	5727	4946	8152	9494	3438	3839	7921	4883	9366	4486	1800	5678	3195	7055	Calcutta (Kolkata)
Caracas	14399	14522	5096	10203	15464	Caracas	2502	10166	6009	6847	4810	4664	3612	2228	6175	7173	2131	4738	2825	5196	11407	9534	8801	8154	Caracas
Chicago	10603	12953	9011	3206	12839	4027	Chicago	7783	4247	8689	5973	3949	1742	1694	4971	8005	711	4132	5311	4809	9369	9243	6299	8358	Chicago
Hong Kong	1963	4317	18478	8150	2659	16360	12526	Hong Kong	5543	6669	7360	5980	7232	8775	4439	5453	8047	5984	11001	5769	1615	4582	1786	5857	Hong Kong
Honolulu	8160	12914	12164	14223	11343	9670	6836	8921	Honolulu	11934	10133	7228	2558	3781	7036	10739	4958	7437	8290	8026	6721	5075	3854	4669	Honolulu
Johannesburg	11710	6974	8088	6267	8459	11019	13984	10732	19206	Johannesburg	2799	5637	10362	9063	5692	1818	7979	5426	4420	4811	5381	6860	8418	7308	Johannesburg
Lagos	11457	7612	7916	3915	9216	7741	9612	11845	16308	4505	Lagos	3118	7713	6879	3886	2366	5268	2929	3750	2510	6925	9643	8376	9973	Lagos
London	8138	7190	11131	3508	7961	7507	6356	9623	11632	9071	5017	London	5442	5552	1552	4237	3463	212	5778	889	6743	10558	5942	11691	London
Los Angeles	10060	14000	9852	12200	13120	5812	2804	11639	4117	16676	12414	8758	Los Angeles	1549	6070	9659	2446	5645	6310	6331	8776	7502	5475	6719	Los Angeles
Mexico City	12460	15656	7389	12372	15280	3586	2726	14122	6085	14585	11071	8936	2493	Mexico City	6664	9207	2090	5717	4780	6365	10321	8058	7024	6897	Mexico City
Moscow	5794	5031	13477	2902	5534	9938	8000	7144	11323	9161	6254	2498	9769	10724	Moscow	3942	4666	1545	7184	1477	5237	9008	4651	10283	Moscow
Nairobi	9216	4532	10402	3536	6179	11544	12883	8776	17282	2927	3807	6819	15544	14818	6344	Nairobi	7358	4029	5548	3350	4635	7552	6996	8490	Nairobi
New York	10988	12541	8526	9020	12747	3430	1145	12950	7980	12841	8477	5572	3936	3264	7510	11842	New York	3626	4832	4280	9531	9935	6741	8951	New York
Paris	8217	7010	11051	3210	7858	7625	6650	9630	11968	8732	4714	342	9085	9200	2486	6485	5836	Paris	5708	687	6671	10539	6038	11798	Paris
Rio de Janeiro	17338	13409	1953	9896	15073	4546	8547	17704	13342	7113	6035	9299	10155	7693	11562	8928	7777	9187	Rio de Janeiro	5725	9763	8389	11551	7367	Rio de Janeiro
Rome	8126	6175	11151	2133	7219	8363	7739	9284	12916	7743	4039	1431	10188	10243	2376	5391	6888	1105	9214	Rome	6229	10143	6127	11523	Rome
Singapore	4478	3914	15879	8267	2897	18359	15078	2599	10816	8660	11145	10852	14123	16610	8428	7460	15339	10737	15712	10025	Singapore	3915	3306	5298	Singapore
Sydney	8949	10160	11800	14418	9138	15343	14875	7374	8168	11040	15519	16992	12073	12969	14497	12153	15989	16962	13501	16324	6300	Sydney	4861	1383	Sydney
Tokyo	2099	6742	18362	9571	5141	14164	10137	2874	6202	13547	13480	9562	8811	11304	7485	11260	10849	9718	18589	9861	5321	7823	Tokyo	5762	Tokyo
Wellington	10782	12370	9981	16524	11354	13122	13451	9427	7513	11761	16050	18814	10814	11100	16549	13664	14405	18987	11855	18545	8526	2226	9273	Wellington	Miles

MEXICO CITY
19 26°N 99 4°W

LONDON
51 28°N 0 27°W

TOKYO
35 33°N 139 46°E

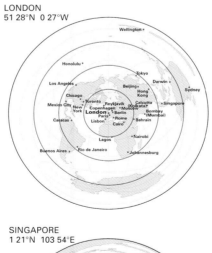

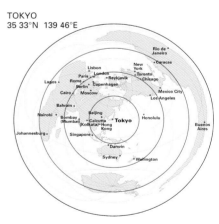

RIO DE JANEIRO
22 50°S 43 15°W

SINGAPORE
1 21°N 103 54°E

SYDNEY
33 56°S 151 10°E

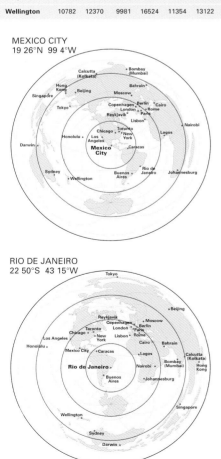

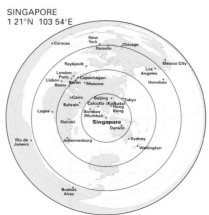

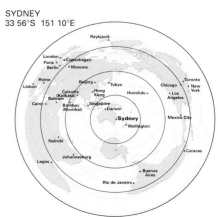

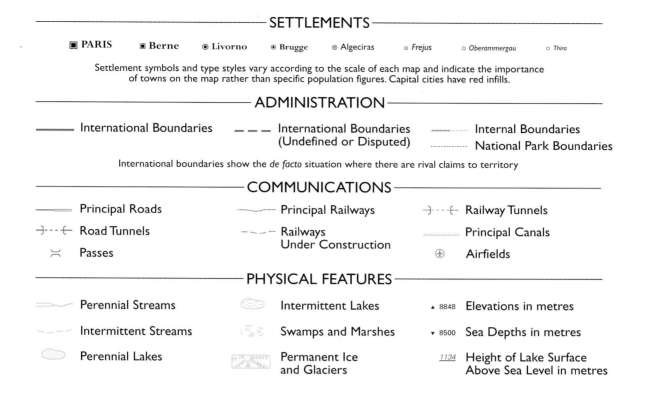

SETTLEMENTS

■ PARIS ■ Berne ◉ Livorno ◉ Brugge ◎ Algeciras ○ Frejus ○ Oberammergau ○ Thira

Settlement symbols and type styles vary according to the scale of each map and indicate the importance of towns on the map rather than specific population figures. Capital cities have red infills.

ADMINISTRATION

——— International Boundaries

– – – International Boundaries (Undefined or Disputed)

······ Internal Boundaries

··········· National Park Boundaries

International boundaries show the *de facto* situation where there are rival claims to territory

COMMUNICATIONS

——— Principal Roads

⊣···⊢ Road Tunnels

⨆ Passes

——⌢—— Principal Railways

– –⌢– – Railways Under Construction

⊣···⊢ Railway Tunnels

··········· Principal Canals

⊕ Airfields

PHYSICAL FEATURES

～～ Perennial Streams

-- Intermittent Streams

▱ Perennial Lakes

▱ Intermittent Lakes

Swamps and Marshes

Permanent Ice and Glaciers

▲ 8848 Elevations in metres

▼ 8500 Sea Depths in metres

1134 Height of Lake Surface Above Sea Level in metres

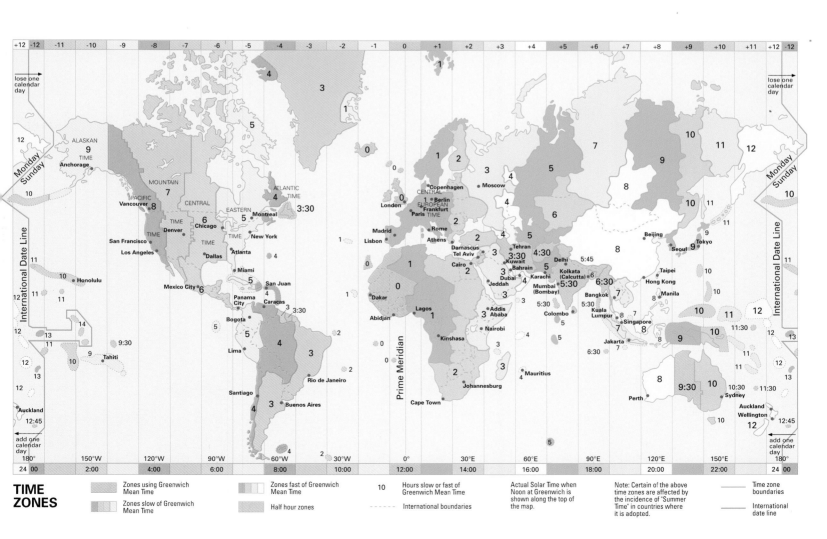

TIME ZONES

▨ Zones using Greenwich Mean Time	▨ Zones fast of Greenwich Mean Time	10 Hours slow or fast of Greenwich Mean Time
▨ Zones slow of Greenwich Mean Time	▨ Half hour zones	--- International boundaries

Actual Solar Time when Noon at Greenwich is shown along the top of the map.

Note: Certain of the above time zones are affected by the incidence of "Summer Time" in countries where it is adopted.

——— Time zone boundaries

——— International date line

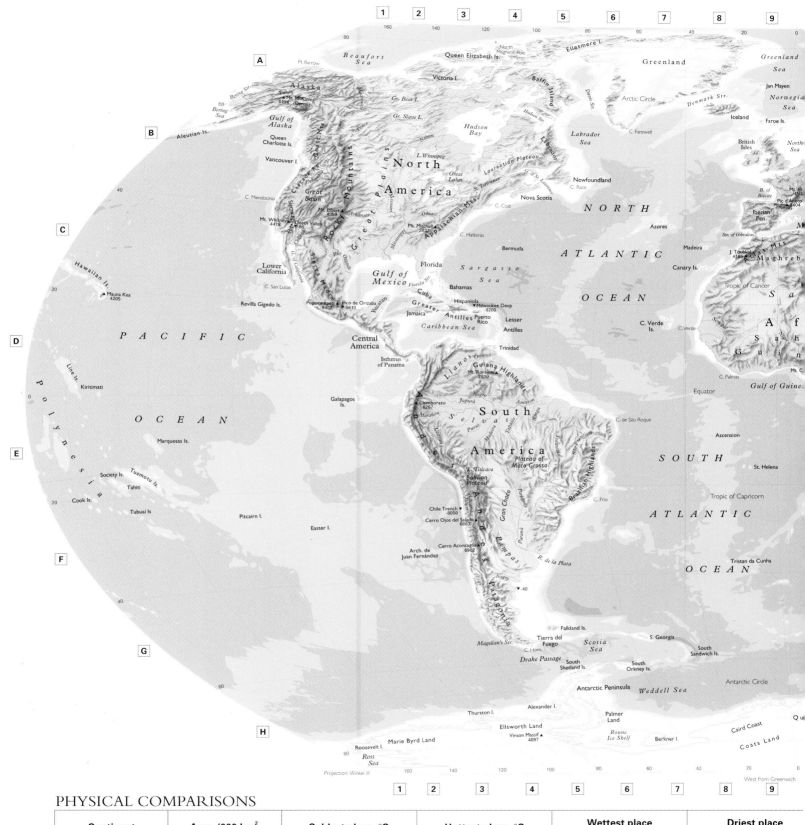

PHYSICAL COMPARISONS

Continent	Area, '000 km²	Coldest place, °C	Hottest place, °C	Wettest place (average annual rainfall, mm)	Driest place (average annual rainfall, m
Asia	44 500	Verkhoyansk, Russia -68°C	Tirat Zevi, Israel 54°C	Cherrapunji, India 11 430	Aden, Yemen 46
Africa	30 302	Ifrane, Morocco -24°C	El Azizia, Libya 58°C	Debundscha, Cameroon 10 290	Wadi Halfa, Sudan 2
North America	24 241	Snag, Yukon -63°C	Death Valley, California 57°C	Henderson Lake, Canada 6 500	Bataques, Mexico 30
South America	17 793	Sarmiento, Argentina -33°C	Rivadavia, Argentina 49°C	Quibdó, Colombia 8 990	Quillagua, Chile 0.6
Antarctica	14 000	Vostok -89°C	Vanda Station 15°C		
Europe	9 957	Ust'Shchugor, Russia -55°C	Seville, Spain 50°C	Crkvice, Serbia & M. 4 650	Astrakhan, Russia 160
Oceania	8 557	Charlotte Pass, Australia -22°C	Cloncurry, Australia 53°C	Tully, Australia 4 550	Mulka, Australia 100

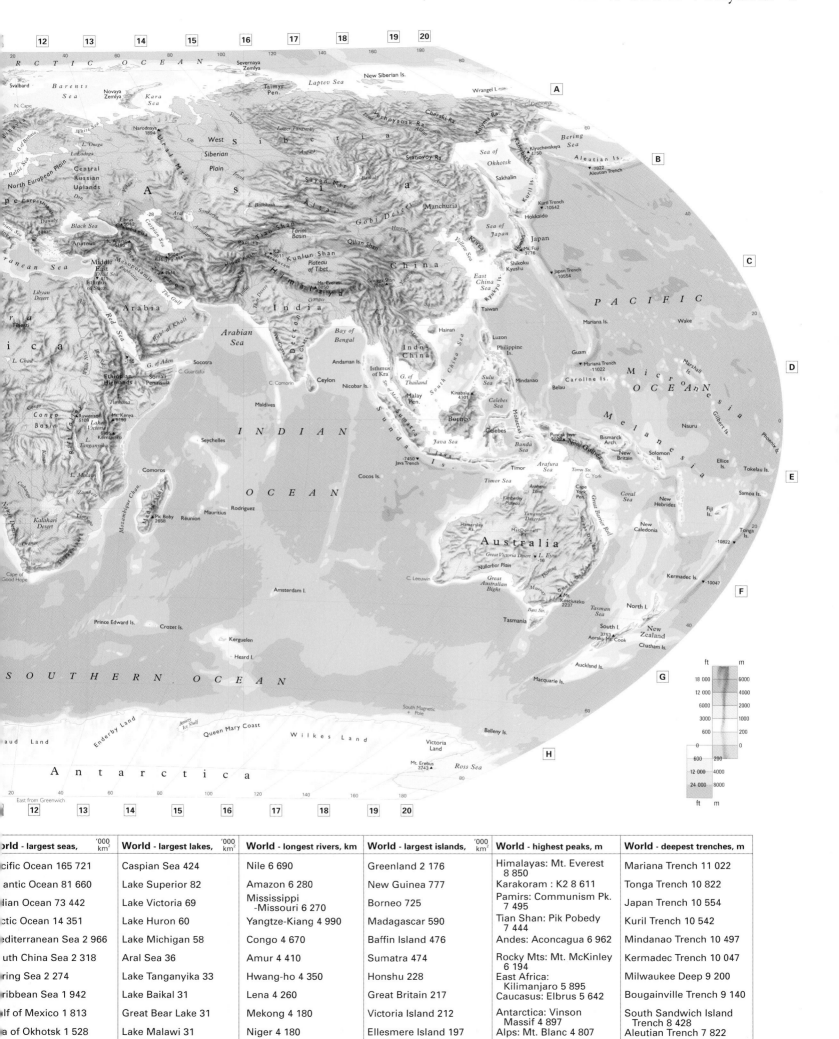

World - largest seas,	'000 km²	World - largest lakes,	'000 km²	World - longest rivers,	km	World - largest islands,	'000 km²	World - highest peaks,	m	World - deepest trenches,	m
cific Ocean 165 721		Caspian Sea 424		Nile 6 690		Greenland 2 176		Himalayas: Mt. Everest 8 850		Mariana Trench 11 022	
antic Ocean 81 660		Lake Superior 82		Amazon 6 280		New Guinea 777		Karakoram : K2 8 611		Tonga Trench 10 822	
dian Ocean 73 442		Lake Victoria 69		Mississippi -Missouri 6 270		Borneo 725		Pamirs: Communism Pk. 7 495		Japan Trench 10 554	
ctic Ocean 14 351		Lake Huron 60		Yangtze-Kiang 4 990		Madagascar 590		Tian Shan: Pik Pobedy 7 444		Kuril Trench 10 542	
editerranean Sea 2 966		Lake Michigan 58		Congo 4 670		Baffin Island 476		Andes: Aconcagua 6 962		Mindanao Trench 10 497	
uth China Sea 2 318		Aral Sea 36		Amur 4 410		Sumatra 474		Rocky Mts: Mt. McKinley 6 194		Kermadec Trench 10 047	
ring Sea 2 274		Lake Tanganyika 33		Hwang-ho 4 350		Honshu 228		East Africa: Kilimanjaro 5 895		Milwaukee Deep 9 200	
ribbean Sea 1 942		Lake Baikal 31		Lena 4 260		Great Britain 217		Caucasus: Elbrus 5 642		Bougainville Trench 9 140	
lf of Mexico 1 813		Great Bear Lake 31		Mekong 4 180		Victoria Island 212		Antarctica: Vinson Massif 4 897		South Sandwich Island Trench 8 428	
a of Okhotsk 1 528		Lake Malawi 31		Niger 4 180		Ellesmere Island 197		Alps: Mt. Blanc 4 807		Aleutian Trench 7 822	

Equatorial Scale 1:95 000 000

COUNTRY COMPARISONS

Country	Population in thousands 2001 estimate	Area in thous' km²	Country	Population in thousands 2001 estimate	Area in thous' km²	Country	Population in thousands 2001 estimate	Area in thous' km²	Country	Population in thousands 2001 estimate	Area in thous' km²	Country	Population in thousands 2001 estimate	Area in thous' km²
China	1 280 200	9 598	Mexico	99 600	1958	France	59 200	552	Argentina	37 500	2 767	Venezuela	24 600	
India	1 033 000	3 288	Germany	82 200	357	Italy	57 800	301	Tanzania	36 200	945	Uganda	24 000	
United States	284 500	9 373	Vietnam	78 700	332	Congo, Dem. Rep.	53 600	2 345	Sudan	31 800	2 506	Iraq	23 600	
Indonesia	206 100	1 905	Philippines	77 200	300	Ukraine	49 100	604	Algeria	31 000	2 382	Nepal	23 500	
Brazil	171 800	8 512	Egypt	69 800	1 001	Korea, South	48 800	99	Canada	31 000	9 976	Malaysia	22 700	
Pakistan	145 000	796	Turkey	66 300	779	Burma (Myanmar)	47 800	677	Kenya	29 800	580	Taiwan	22 500	
Russia	144 400	17 075	Iran	66 100	1 648	South Africa	43 600	1 220	Morocco	29 200	447	Romania	22 400	
Bangladesh	133 500	144	Ethiopia	65 400	1 128	Colombia	43 100	1 139	Afghanistan	26 800	652	Korea, North	22 000	
Japan	127 100	378	Thailand	62 400	513	Spain	39 800	505	Peru	26 100	1 285	Saudi Arabia	21 100	2
Nigeria	126 600	924	United Kingdom	60 000	243	Poland	38 600	313	Uzbekistan	25 100	447	Ghana	19 900	

Projection : Hammer Equal Area

Equatorial Scale 1:95 000 000

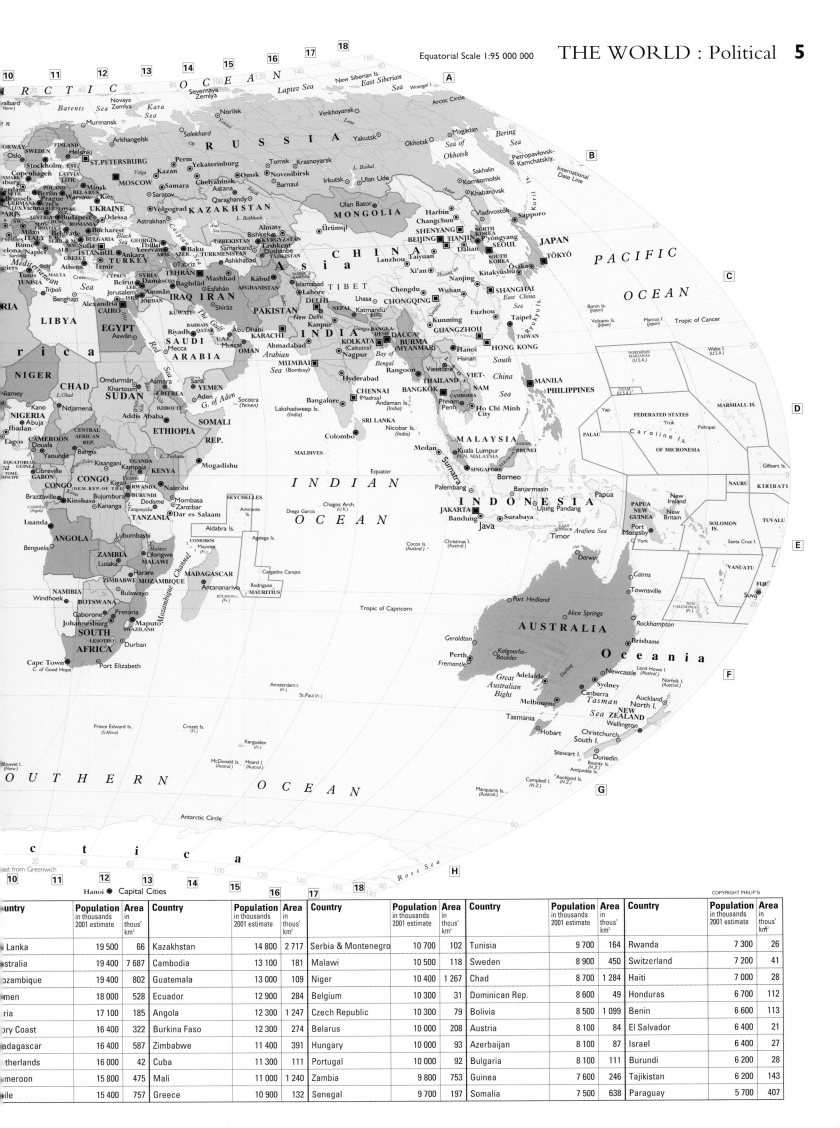

Hanoi ■ Capital Cities

COPYRIGHT PHILIP'S

Country	Population in thousands 2001 estimate	Area in thous' km²	Country	Population in thousands 2001 estimate	Area in thous' km²	Country	Population in thousands 2001 estimate	Area in thous' km²	Country	Population in thousands 2001 estimate	Area in thous' km²	Country	Population in thousands 2001 estimate	Area in thous' km²
...Lanka	19 500	66	Kazakhstan	14 800	2 717	Serbia & Montenegro	10 700	102	Tunisia	9 700	164	Rwanda	7 300	26
...stralia	19 400	7 687	Cambodia	13 100	181	Malawi	10 500	118	Sweden	8 900	450	Switzerland	7 200	41
...ozambique	19 400	802	Guatemala	13 000	109	Niger	10 400	1 267	Chad	8 700	1 284	Haiti	7 000	28
...men	18 000	528	Ecuador	12 900	284	Belgium	10 300	31	Dominican Rep.	8 600	49	Honduras	6 700	112
...ria	17 100	185	Angola	12 300	1 247	Czech Republic	10 300	79	Bolivia	8 500	1 099	Benin	6 600	113
...ry Coast	16 400	322	Burkina Faso	12 300	274	Belarus	10 000	208	Austria	8 100	84	El Salvador	6 400	21
...adagascar	16 400	587	Zimbabwe	11 400	391	Hungary	10 000	93	Azerbaijan	8 100	87	Israel	6 400	27
...therlands	16 000	42	Cuba	11 300	111	Portugal	10 000	92	Bulgaria	8 100	111	Burundi	6 200	28
...meroon	15 800	475	Mali	11 000	1 240	Zambia	9 800	753	Guinea	7 600	246	Tajikistan	6 200	143
...ile	15 400	757	Greece	10 900	132	Senegal	9 700	197	Somalia	7 500	638	Paraguay	5 700	407

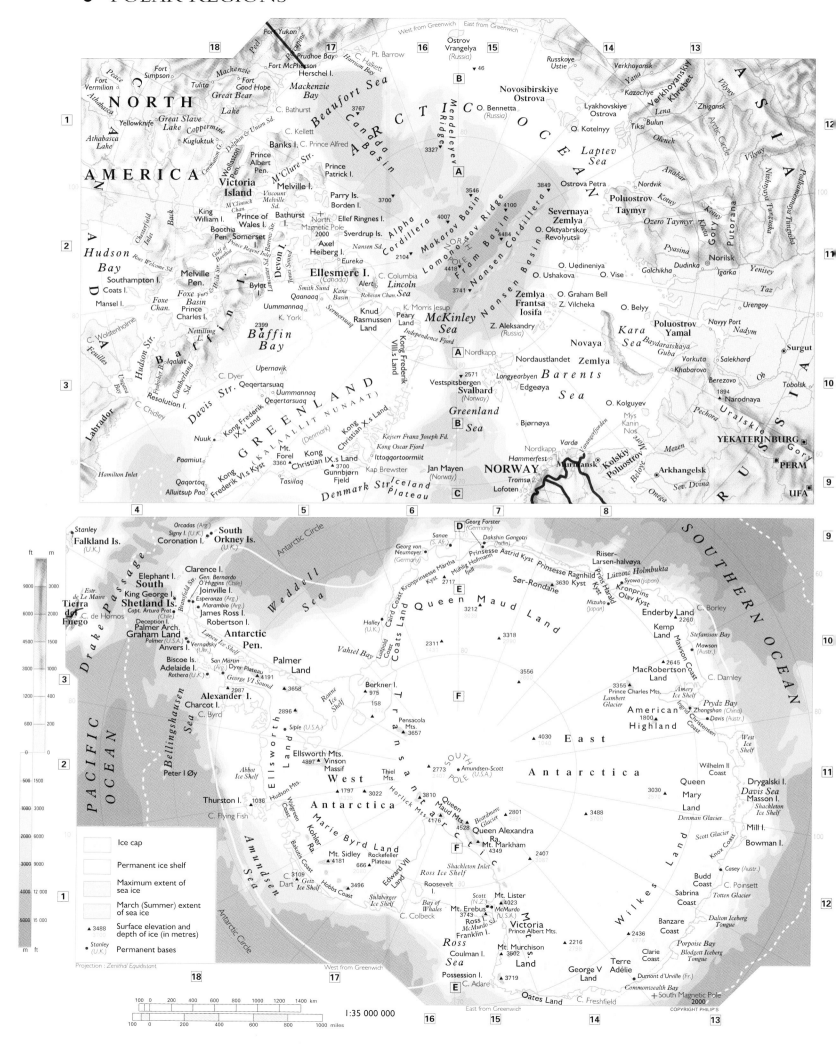

Projection : Zenithal Equidistant

1:35 000 000

COPYRIGHT PHILIP'S

Legend:
- Ice cap
- Permanent ice shelf
- Maximum extent of sea ice
- March (Summer) extent of sea ice
- ▲3488 Surface elevation and depth of ice (in metres)
- • Stanley (U.K.) Permanent bases

1:10 000 000

50 0 100 200 300 400 km
50 0 50 100 150 200 250 miles

ICELAND

West from Greenwich

Arctic Circle

Ísafjörður · Húnaflói · Siglufjörður · Húsavík
Breiðafjörður · Sauðárkrókur · Akureyri · Seyðisfjörður
Faxaflói · Hofsjökull · Langjökull 1355 · 1765 · 2000 · Vatnajökull
Akranes · Reykjavik · Keflavík · Mýrdalsjökull 1450 · Öræfajökull 2119
Heimaey · Surtsey

ICELAND on same scale

NORWEGIAN SEA

Arctic Circle

BARENTS SEA

Nordkapp · Sørøya · Hammerfest · Varanger-halvøya · Vardø
Senja · Tromsø · Varangerfjorden · Vadsø
Halta 1328 · Inarijärvi · Rybachiy Poluostrov · Pechenga · Kolskiy Zaliv
Narvik · Lappland · Inari · Zapolyarnyy · Port-Vladimir · Polyarny
Vesterålen · Torneträsk 2117 · Porttipahtan tekojärvi · Kola · Severomorsk · Murmansk
Lofoten · Kebnekaise · Kiruna · Lokkan tekojärvi · Monchegorsk · Olenegorsk · Kolskiy Poluostrov
Vestfjorden · Stora Lulevatten · Gällivare · Torne älv · Alakurtti · Koydor · Ozero Imandra 1191 · Kirovsk · Apatity · Kuzomen
Bodø · 1913 · Rovaniemi · Kemijärvi · Kuusamo · Kandalaksha · Kandalakshskiy Zaliv · Ponoy · Ponoy
Mo i Rana · Horna-van · Luleå älv · Kemijoki · Pya-ozero · Kestenga · Top-ozero · Umba · Beloye More (White Sea) · Dvinskaya Guba · Arkhangelsk
Vega · Mosjøen · Storavan · Boden · Haparanda · Tornio · Kemi · Kuusamo · Kem · Severodvinsk
Vikna · Storuman · Skellefte älv · Piteå · Luleå · Oulu · Kem · Belomorsk · Onega
Folda · Vilhelmina · Umeå älv · Hailuoto · Raahe · Oulujärvi · Kajaani · KARELIA · Onezhskaya Guba · Obozerskiy
Kristiansund · Levanger · Kallsjön · Vännäs · Umeå · Kokkola · Iisalmi · Pielinen · Segezha · Nadvoitsy · Vyg-ozero
Molde · Trondheim · Östersund · Örnsköldsvik · Vaasa · Seinäjoki · Kuopio · Joensuu · Medvezhyegorsk · Povenets · Plesetsk
Ålesund · Snøhetta 2286 · Bräcke · Härnösand · Jyväskylä · Savonlinna · Suoyarvi · Kondopoga · Konevo · Kargopol
Florø · Dovrefjell · Ånge · Sundsvall · Pori · Tampere · Imatra · Sortavala · Petrozavodsk · Ozero Vozhe · Ozero Beloye
Galdhøpiggen 2469 · Indalsälven · Hudiksvall · Rauma · Lahti · Kouvola · Priozersk · Olonets · Svir · Voznesenye
Høyanger · Jotunheimen · Storsjön · Söderhamn · Hämeenlinna · Vyborg · Ladozhskoye Ozero · Podporozhye · Lodeynoye Pole · Belozersk
Bergen · Sognefjorden · Flåm · Lillehammer · Mora · Falun · Gävle · Uusikaupunki · Turku · Vantaa · Novaya Ladoga · Kirillov
Hardangerfjorden · 1719 · Hønefoss · Hamar · Mjøsa · Avesta · Sala · Uppsala · Åland · Espoo · Helsinki · Kronshtadt · Kolpino · Tikhvin · Cherepovets
Haugesund · Oslo · Svealand · Dalälven · Västerås · Hanko · Gulf of Finland · SANKT-PETERBURG (St. Petersburg) · Malaya Vishera
Stavanger · Drammen · Karlstad · Örebro · Eskilstuna · STOCKHOLM · Hiiumaa (Dagö) · Tallinn · Narva · Kohtla-Järve · Gdov · Borovichi · Rybinsk Res.
Kristiansand · Skien · Larvik · Fredrikstad · Halden · Vänern · Norrköping · Gotland · Saaremaa (Ösel) · Pärnu · Tartu · ESTONIA · Ozero Chudskoye · Novgorod · Ozero Ilmen · Bologoye · Vyshniy Volochek
Mandal · Lindesnes · Skagerrak · Trollhättan · Götaland · Linköping · Västervik · Visby · Gulf of Riga · Valga · Pskov · Dno · Staraya Russa · Valdayskaya Vozvyshennost · Tver · Kimry
Göteborg (Gothenburg) · Skogen · Borås · Jönköping · Oskarshamn · Öland · Ventspils · Rīga · LATVIA · Valka · Rēzekne · Velikiye Luki · Rzhev · Zelenograd
Frederikshavn · Alborg · Kattegat · Varberg · Halmstad · Kalmar · Liepāja · Jelgava · Daugava · Daugavpils · Nevel · MOSKVA (Moscow) · Odintsovo
Holstebro · Jylland · Randers · Helsingborg · Karlskrona · BALTIC SEA · Šiauliai · Panevėžys · Polatsk · Vitsyebsk · Vyazma · Kaluga
Esbjerg · Århus · DENMARK · KØBENHAVN (Copenhagen) · Lund · Malmö · Bornholm · Klaipėda · LITHUANIA · Nemunas · Lyepyel · Orsha · Smolensk · Roslavl · Belev
Helgoland · Odense · Fyn · Sjælland · Gedser · Rügen · Sassnitz · Kaliningrad (Russia) · Kaunas · Vilnius · Barysaw · Mahilyow · Seltso
Flensburg · Kiel · Lübeck · Stralsund · Rostock · Gdynia · Gdańsk · Elblag · Suwałki · Hrodna · MINSK · Babruysk · Bryansk · Orel
Emden · Bremen · HAMBURG · Świnoujście · Szczecin · Koszalin · Olsztyn · Łomża · Białystok · BELARUS · Baranavichy · Slutsk · Zhlobin · Homyel · Novhorod-Siverskyy
Osnabrück · Hannover · Potsdam · BERLIN · Bydgoszcz · Toruń · Płock · Hrodna · Pinsk · Brest · Pripet Marshes · Mazyr · Chernihiv · Konotop
Münster · Braunschweig · Magdeburg · Frankfurt · Poznań · WARSZAWA (Warsaw) · Pripyat · Korosten · Chornobyl · Nizhyn · Pryluky · Okhtyrka
Dortmund · GERMANY · Kassel · Halle · Leipzig · Görlitz · Legnica · Kalisz · Łódź · Radom · Lublin · Kovel · Rivne · Zhytomyr · KYYIV (Kiev) · Sumy
Frankfurt · Fulda · Erfurt · Chemnitz · Dresden · Wrocław · Opole · Kielce · Lutsk · Chervonohrad · Berdychiv · Bila Tserkva · Poltava
Darmstadt · Würzburg · Thüringer Wald · Plauen · 1602 Śnieżka · Wałbrzych · Częstochowa · Chorzów · Katowice · Kraków · Rzeszów · Lviv · Pereyaslav-Khmelnytskyy · UKRAINE · Cherkasy
Heidelberg · Nürnberg · PRAHA · Plzeň · Hradec Králové · Ostrava · Tychy · Tarnów · Przemyśl · Cieszyn · Żilina 2655 · CZECH REP.

East from Greenwich

Projection: Conical with two standard parallels

COPYRIGHT PHILIP'S

1:2 000 000

Key to English unitary authorities on map

25 HARTLEPOOL
26 DARLINGTON
27 STOCKTON-ON-TEES
28 MIDDLESBROUGH
29 REDCAR AND CLEVELAND
30 BLACKPOOL
31 BLACKBURN WITH DARWEN
32 HALTON
33 WARRINGTON
34 KINGSTON UPON HULL
35 NORTH EAST LINCOLNSHIRE
36 STOKE-ON-TRENT
37 TELFORD AND WREKIN
38 DERBY CITY
39 CITY OF NOTTINGHAM
40 LEICESTER CITY
41 RUTLAND
42 PETERBOROUGH
43 MILTON KEYNES
44 LUTON
45 NORTH SOMERSET
46 CITY OF BRISTOL
47 BATH AND NORTH EAST SOMERSET
48 SWINDON
49 READING
50 WOKINGHAM
51 WINDSOR AND MAIDENHEAD
52 SLOUGH
53 BRACKNELL FOREST
54 THURROCK
55 SOUTHEND-ON-SEA
56 MEDWAY
57 PLYMOUTH
58 TORBAY
59 POOLE
60 BOURNEMOUTH
61 SOUTHAMPTON
62 PORTSMOUTH
63 BRIGHTON AND HOVE

Key to Welsh unitary authorities on map

15 SWANSEA
16 NEATH PORT TALBOT
17 BRIDGEND
18 RHONDDA CYNON TAFF
19 MERTHYR TYDFIL
20 CAERPHILLY
21 BLAENAU GWENT
22 TORFAEN
23 CARDIFF
24 NEWPORT

NORTH SEA

IRISH SEA

North Channel

NORTHERN IRELAND

SCOTLAND

SCOTTISH BORDERS

SOUTHERN UPLANDS

DUMFRIES & GALLOWAY

SOUTH AYRSHIRE

NORTH AYRSHIRE

EAST AYRSHIRE

SOUTH LANARKSHIRE

NORTHUMBERLAND

CUMBRIA

DURHAM

TYNE & WEAR

NORTH YORKSHIRE

NORTH YORK MOORS

YORKSHIRE DALES

LAKE DISTRICT

LANCASHIRE

GREATER MANCHESTER

MERSEYSIDE

CHESHIRE

EAST RIDING OF YORKSHIRE

LINCOLNSHIRE

NORTH LINCOLNSHIRE

LINCOLNSHIRE WOLDS

WEST YORKSHIRE

SOUTH YORKSHIRE

DERBYSHIRE

NOTTS

STAFFORDSHIRE

WREXHAM

FLINTSHIRE

DENBIGHSHIRE

CONWY

GWYNEDD

ISLE OF ANGLESEY

ISLE OF MAN

The Wash

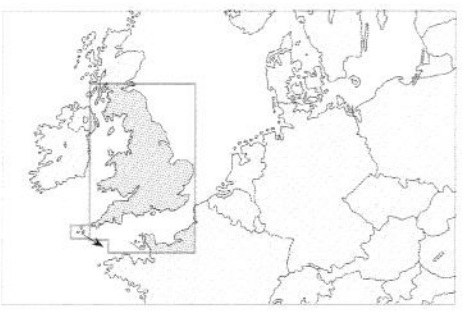

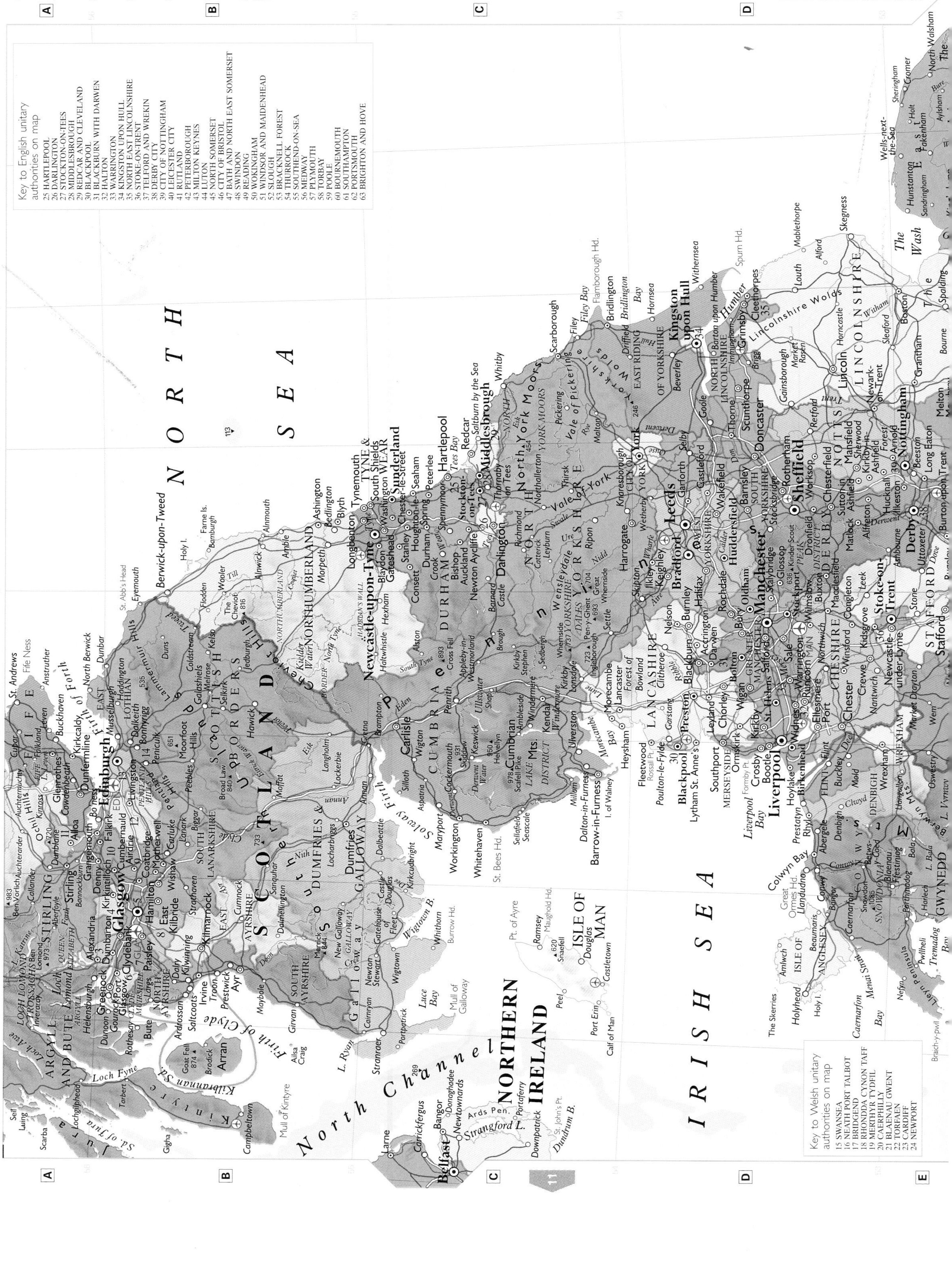

ENGLISH CHANNEL

FRANCE

HAUTE-NORMANDIE

SEINE-MARITIME

Le Havre

Rouen

Dieppe

Boulogne-sur-Mer

Calais

Strait of Dover

CALVADOS

Caen

Cherbourg

MANCHE

Baie de la Seine

Baie de la Somme

CHANNEL ISLANDS (U.K.)

Jersey   St. Helier

Guernsey   St. Peter Port

Alderney   Herm   Sark

WALES

ENGLAND

LONDON

Birmingham

Coventry

Cardiff

Swansea

Bristol

Bath

Bournemouth

Southampton

Portsmouth

Brighton

Plymouth

Exeter

Cardigan Bay

Bristol Channel

Lyme Bay

CORNWALL

DEVON

SOMERSET

DORSET

WILTSHIRE

HAMPSHIRE

WEST SUSSEX

EAST SUSSEX

KENT

SURREY

BERKSHIRE

OXFORDSHIRE

GLOUCS

HEREFORD

SHROPSHIRE

POWYS

CEREDIGION

PEMBROKESHIRE

CARMARTHENSHIRE

GLAMORGAN

VALE OF GLAMORGAN

MONMOUTHSHIRE

WORCESTER

WARWICK

NORTHAMPTON

BEDFORD

BUCKS

HERTS

ESSEX

SUFFOLK

NORFOLK

CAMBRIDGESHIRE

RUTLAND

GREATER LONDON

ISLE OF WIGHT

Isle of Portland

Portland Bill

Land's End

Lizard Pt.

Projection : Lambert's Conformal Conic

East from Greenwich

West from Greenwich

ISLES OF SCILLY on same scale

Isles of Scilly

St. Mary's

Tresco

m ft
−50 150
100 300
200 600

1:2 000 000

10 0 10 20 30 40 50 60 70 80 km
10 0 10 20 30 40 50 miles

Key to Scottish unitary authorities on map
1 CITY OF ABERDEEN
2 DUNDEE CITY
3 WEST DUNBARTONSHIRE
4 EAST DUNBARTONSHIRE
5 CITY OF GLASGOW
6 INVERCLYDE
7 RENFREWSHIRE
8 EAST RENFREWSHIRE
9 NORTH LANARKSHIRE
10 FALKIRK
11 CLACKMANNANSHIRE
12 WEST LOTHIAN
13 CITY OF EDINBURGH
14 MIDLOTHIAN

ORKNEY IS. on same scale
ORKNEY
North Ronaldsay
Papa Westray
Westray
Eday
Sanday
Rousay
Stronsay
Brough Hd.
Mainland
Shapinsay
Stromness
Kirkwall
Scapa Flow
St. Mary's
Burray
Hoy
South Ronaldsay
Dunnet Hd. Stroma
Duncansby Head
John o' Groats
Thurso
Pentland Firth
Sinclair's Bay

SHETLAND IS. on same scale
Muckle Flugga
Unst
Haroldswick
Esha Ness
Fetlar
Yell Sound
Yell
Ulsta
Out Skerries
St. Magnus Bay
Sullom Voe
Voe
Whalsay
Papa Stour
Walls
Mainland
Scalloway
SHETLAND
Lerwick
Foula
Bressay
West Burra
Boddam
Sumburgh Hd.

ATLANTIC OCEAN

WESTERN ISLES
Butt of Lewis
Flannan Is.
Gallan Hd.
Stornoway
Broad Bay
Eye Peninsula
Lewis
Scarp
Taransay
Clisham 799
Harris
Toe Hd.
L. Seaforth
Tarbert
Pabbay
Berneray
North Uist
Lochmaddy
Baleshare
Grimsay
Benbecula
Ardivachar Pt.
South Uist
Ben Mhor 620
Lochboisdale
Eriskay
Barra
Castlebay
Vatersay
Sandray
Barra Hd. 268

Outer Hebrides
Sea of the Hebrides
North Minch
Little Minch
Sound of Harris
Wiay

C. Wrath
Durness
L. Eriboll
Strathy Pt.
Dounreay
Dunnet Hd. Stroma
John o' Groats
Thurso
Pentland Firth
Scapa Flow
Hoy 481
Burwick
L. Laxford
Reay Forest
Ben Hope 927
Tongue
Naver
Halkirk
Caithness
Sinclair's Bay
Noss Hd.
Wick
Eddrachillis B.
Pt. of Stoer
Sutherland
961
705
Lybster
Enard B.
Rubha Coigeach
L. Assynt
Ben More Assynt 998
L. Shin
Lairg
Brora
Ord of Caithness
Helmsdale
Golspie
Gruinard B.
Greenstone Pt.
L. Broom
Ullapool
Oykel
Bonar Bridge
Dornoch
Dornoch Firth
Tarbat Ness
Tain
Moray Firth
L. Ewe
Gairloch
L. Maree 1053
L. Fannich
Ben Wyvis 1045
Alness
Invergordon
Cromarty
Lossiemouth
Burghead
Elgin
Portknockie
Portsoy
Rosehearty
Kinnairds Hd.
Fraserburgh
Rattray Hd.
Rubha Hunish
Uig
L. Gairloch
Strathpeffer
Dingwall
Fortrose
Nairn
Forres
MORAY
Buckie
Cullen
Banff
Macduff
Aberchirder
Turriff
Peterhead
Skye
Portree
Raasay
Rona
Sound of Raasay
Inner Sound
L. Torridon
1081
Ben Dearg
1109
L. Monar
Muir of Ord
Beauly
Inverness
Rothes
Charlestown of Aberlour
Keith
Huntly
Deveron
BUCHAN
Buchan Ness
Cruden Bay
Dunvegan
Scalpay
L. Carron
Stromeferry
Carn Eige 1182
1083
Beauly
HIGHLAND
Dufftown
Tomintoul
Aberchirder
Oldmeldrum
Ellon
Cuillin Hills
Kyleakin
Kyle of Lochalsh
Dornie
1068
Glen Affric
992
Glen Moriston
Fort Augustus
Loch Ness
Grantown-on-Spey
Aviemore
GLEN MORE
Cairn Gorm 1309
ABERDEENSHIRE
Alford
Inverurie
Kintore
Don
Dyce
1
Westhill
Aberdeen
Girdle Ness
Peterculter
Cuillin Sound
Sd. of Sleat
Mallaig
Glen Garry
1342
Spean
Spean Bridge
Monadhliath Mts.
941
Kingussie
Carn Ban
Newtonmore
Cairn Toul
Ben Macdhui 1309
Braemar
Ballater
Aboyne
Banchory
Dee
Canna
Rhum (Rùm)
Eigg
Arisaig
L. Morar
L. Arkaig
Loch Lochy 1128
Glen Spean
1148
CAIRNGORMS
Cairngorm Mts.
Lochnagar
N. Esk
Stonehaven
Muck
L. Moidart
L. Shiel
Lochaber
Ben Nevis 1342
Fort William
Kinlochleven
Glen Coe
Rannoch Moor
1148
Forest of Atholl 1121
Blair Atholl
Garry
ANGUS
Laurencekirk
Brechin
Inverbervie
Pt. of Ardnamurchan
Coll
Tobermory
Morvern
Sound of Mull
Lismore
Ballachulish
L. Linnhe
L. Leven
L. Etive
Ben Cruachan 1126
1148
Rannoch
L. Rannoch
Pitlochry
PERTH AND
TAY
Dunkeld
Kirriemuir
Forfar
Arbroath
NORTH SEA
Tiree
Staffa
Ulva
Mull
Ben More 966
Iona
Kerrera
Oban
Lorn
ARGYLL
Crianlarich
1174
Ben Lawers 1214
Aberfeldy
Dunkeld
Blairgowrie
455
Sidlaw Hills
Strathmore
S. Esk
Carnoustie
Monifieth
Firth of Tay
Colonsay
Oronsay
Scarba
Luing
Seil
Firth of Lorn
Loch Awe
L. Fyne
Inveraray
LOCH LOMOND TROSSACHS
983
Ben Vorlich 1174
Crieff
Earn
Auchterarder
Scone
Perth
KINROSS
Dundee
Tayport
Leuchars
St. Andrews
Fife Ness
SCOTLAND
Islay
Bowmore
Port Ellen
Rhinns Pt.
Mull of Oa
Jura
Sd. of Jura
Gigha
Lochgilphead
Tarbert
Kintyre
Loch Fyne
Dunoon
Greenock
Gourock
Helensburgh
Alexandria
Dumbarton
Clydebank
Glasgow
Paisley
Ben Lomond 973
Aberfoyle
Callander
Dunblane
Stirling
Alloa
Dunfermline
Cowdenbeath
Kirkcaldy
Glenrothes
Buckhaven
Leven
Anstruther
Cupar
Auchtermuchty
Falkland
Kinross
Ochil Hills
FIFE
L. Leven
Firth of Forth
North Berwick
Dunbar
St. Abb's Head
Eyemouth
Berwick-upon-Tweed
Holy I.
Campbeltown
Mull of Kintyre
Firth of Clyde
Rothesay
Bute
Largs
NORTH AYRSHIRE
Ardrossan
Saltcoats
Irvine
Troon
Prestwick
Ayr
Goat Fell 874
Brodick
Arran
Kilbrannan Sd.
Dalry
Kilwinning
Kilmarnock
EAST AYRSHIRE
Maybole
Cumnock
Ailsa Craig
Girvan
SOUTH AYRSHIRE
Merrick 844
Dalmellington
Sanquhar
Moffat
Broad Law 840
Peebles
Moorfoot Hills
Galashiels
Melrose
SCOTTISH BORDERS
Selkirk
Kelso
Coldstream
Jedburgh
Hawick
The Cheviot 816
Cheviot Hills
Alnwick
Amble
Alnmouth
New Galloway
Newton Stewart
733
Nith
Lockerbie
Langholm
Gretna
ENGLAND
Newcastle-upon-Tyne
Blaydon
Gateshead
Stranraer
Portpatrick
Wigtown
Whithorn
GALLOWAY
DUMFRIES & GALLOWAY
Dumfries
Lochmaben
Locharbriggs
Annan
Carlisle
Brampton
Haltwhistle
Hexham
Alston
893
Cross Fell
Penrith
CUMBRIA
DURHAM
Crook
Bishop Auckland
Barnard Castle
Wigtown B.
Luce Bay
Mull of Galloway
Burrow Hd.
L. Ryan
Cairnryan
Gatehouse of Fleet
Castle Douglas
Dalbeattie
Kirkcudbright
Solway Firth
Silloth
Maryport
Workington
Whitehaven
St. Bees Hd.
Cockermouth
Keswick
Derwent Water
931 Skiddaw
950 Helvellyn
Ullswater
Appleby-in-Westmorland
Consett
Stanley

NORTHERN IRELAND
Larne
Carrickfergus
Belfast
Bangor
Donaghadee
Newtownards
North Channel
Garron Pt.
269

Projection : Lambert's Conformal Conic

West from Greenwich

COPYRIGHT PHILIP'S

m ft
0
50 150
100 300
200 600
500 1500
1000 3000

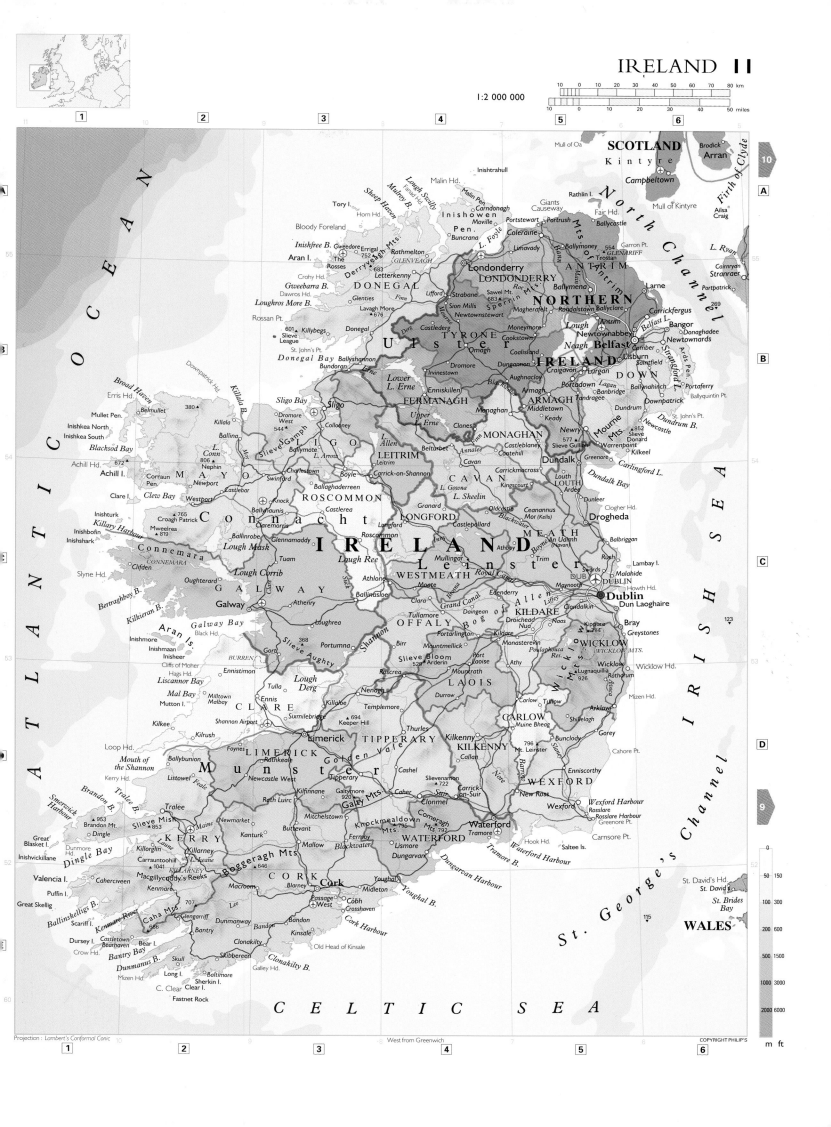

1:2 000 000

Projection : Lambert's Conformal Conic

West from Greenwich

COPYRIGHT PHILIP'S

1:5 000 000

50 ... 0 25 50 75 100 125 150 175 km

50 ... 0 25 50 75 100 125 miles

Corse (Corsica)

MEDITERRANEAN SEA

Projection: Conical with two standard parallels

COPYRIGHT PHILIP'S

West from Greenwich | East from Greenwich

1:5 000 000

Projection: Conical with two standard parallels

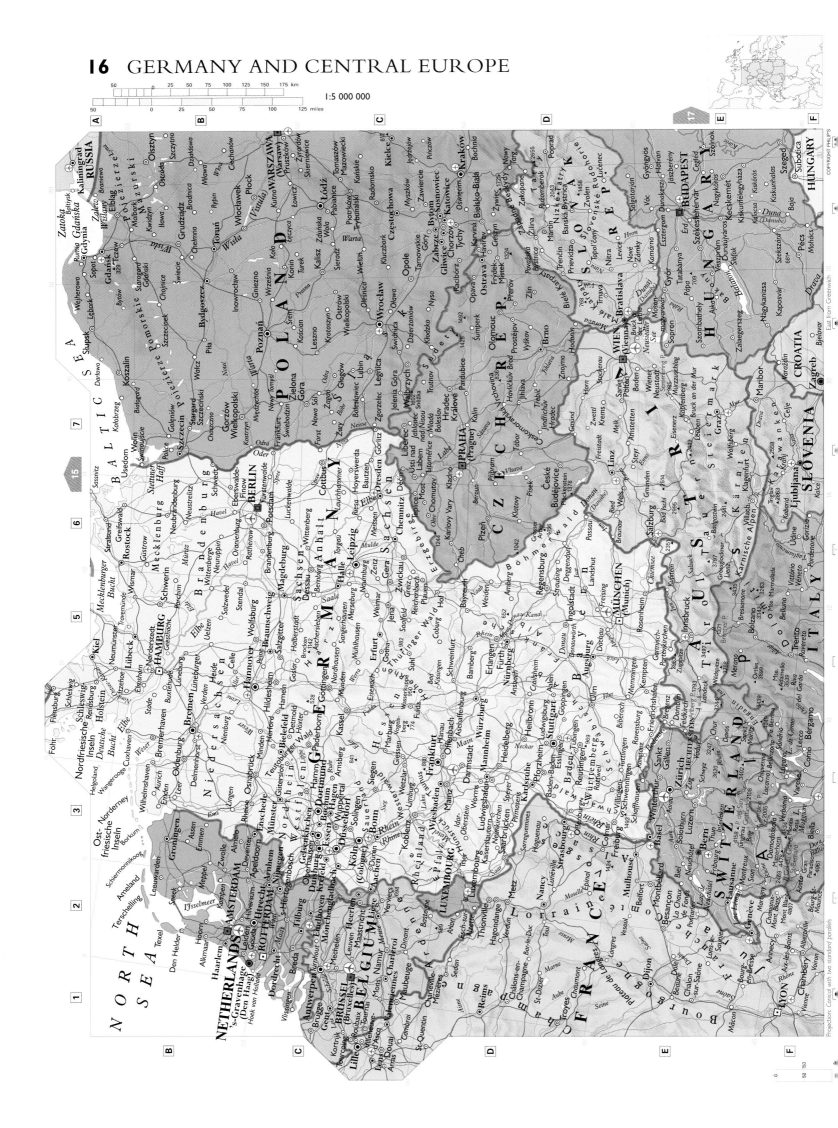

1:10 000 000

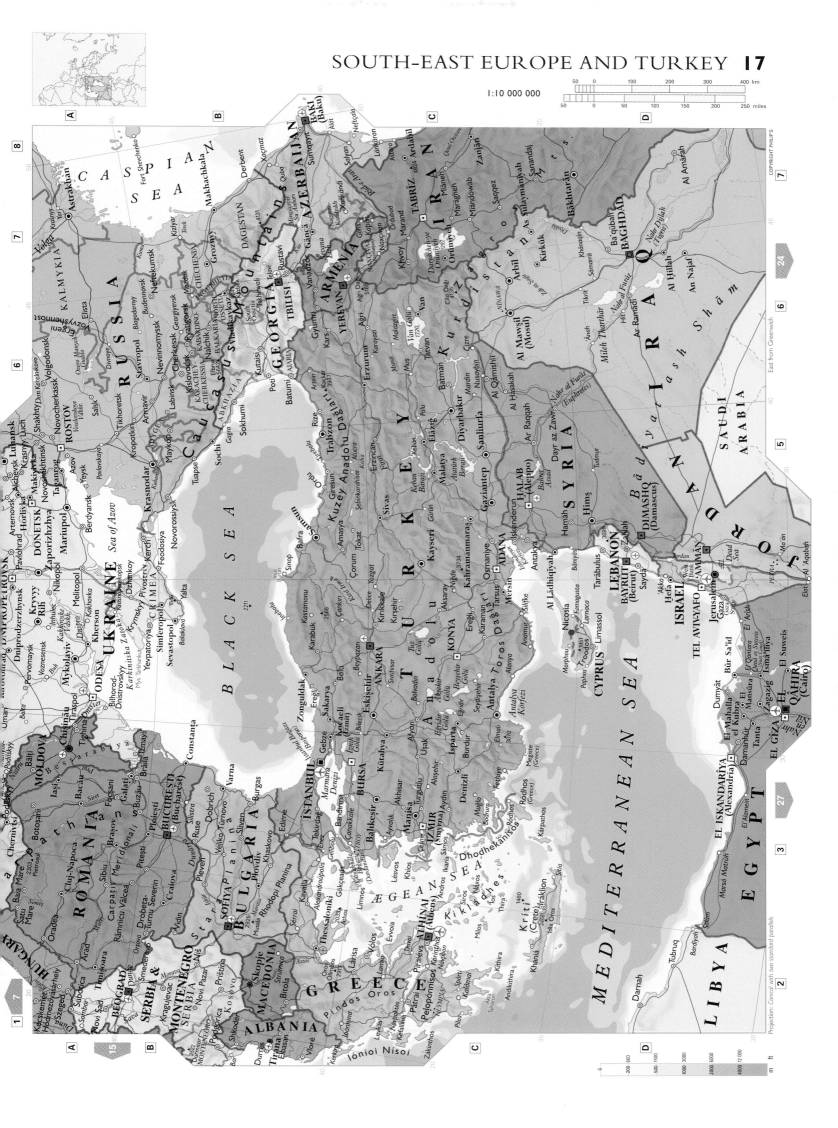

100 0 100 200 300 400 500 600 700 800 km
1:20 000 000
100 0 100 200 300 400 500 miles

D   C   B

RUSSIA
1 Adygea
2 Karachey-Cherkessia
3 Kabardino-Balkaria
4 North Ossetia
5 Ingushetia
6 Chechenia
7 Dagestan
8 Mordvinia
9 Chuvashia
10 Mari El
11 Tatarstan
12 Udmurtia
13 Khakassia

AZERBAIJAN
14 Naxçivan

GEORGIA   UKRAINE
15 Ajaria   17 Crimea
16 Abkhazia

Projection: Conical Orthomorphic with two standard parallels   East from Greenwich

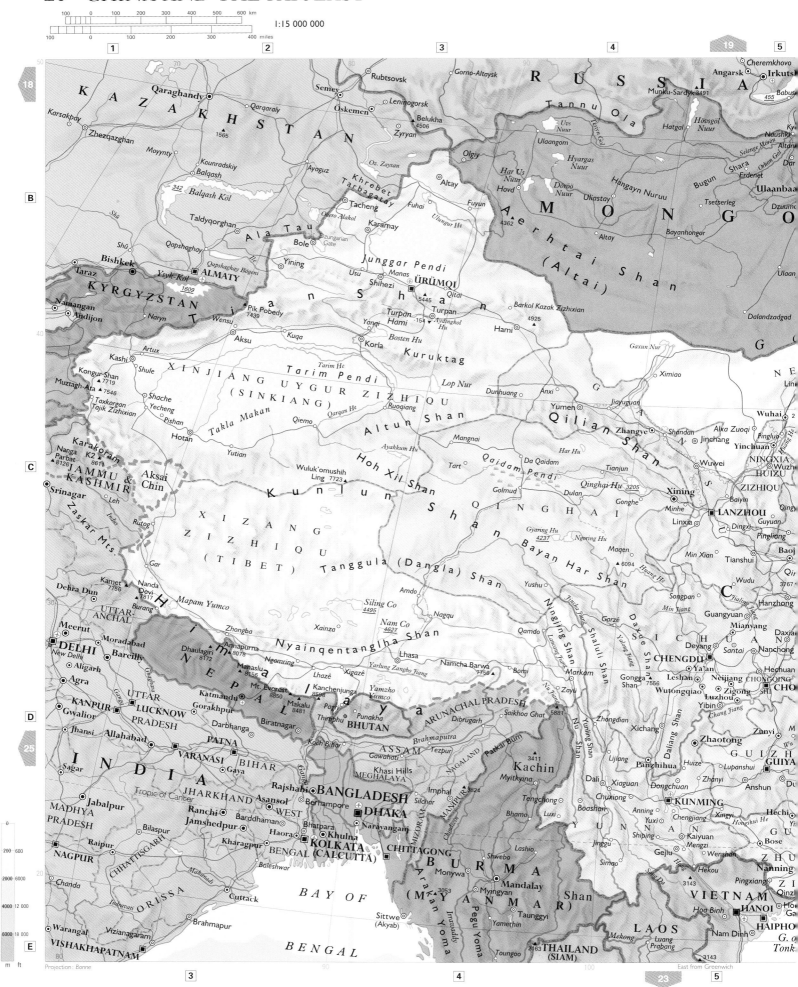

1:15 000 000

Projection: Bonne

East from Greenwich

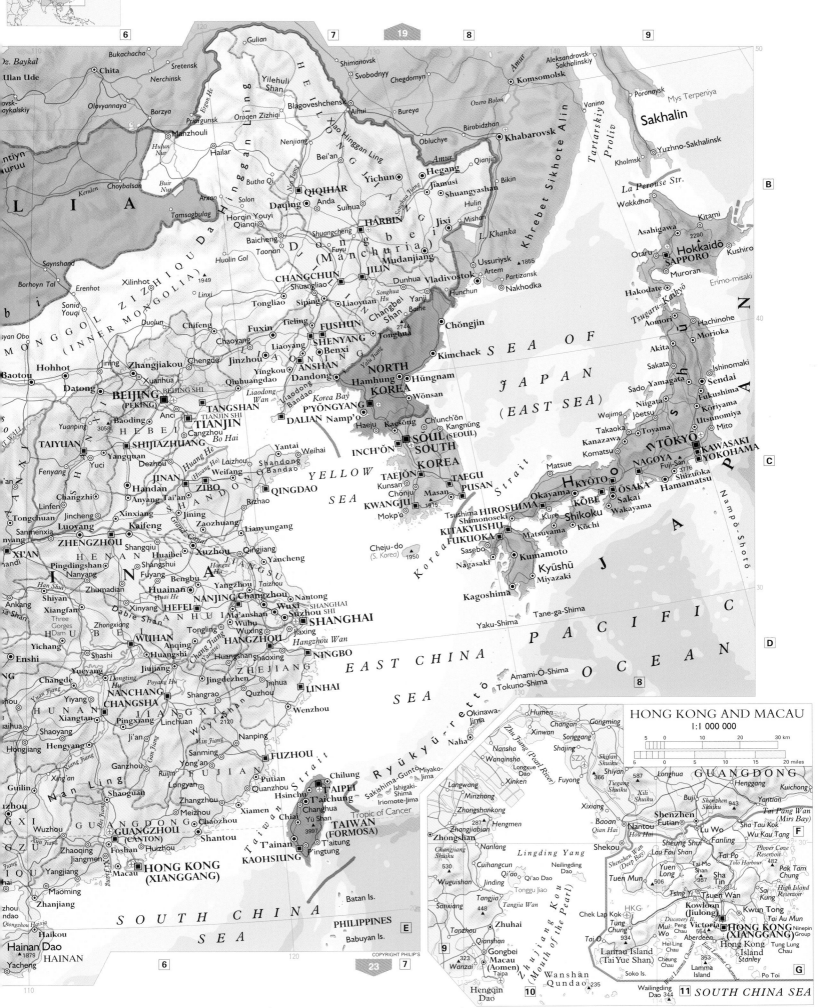

1:6 400 000

50 25 0 25 50 75 100 125 150 175 km
50 25 0 25 50 75 100 125 miles

CHINA

RUSSIA

Linkou
Novokachalinsk
Kamen-Rybolov
Spassk Dalniy
Lipovcy
Manzovka
Suifenhe
Ussuriysk
1498
Trudovoye
Vladivostok
Slavyanka
Nakhodka
Khasan
Najin
Chŏngjin

NORTH KOREA

SOUTH KOREA
Pohang
Ullŭng-do (S. Korea)
Tok-do

Lesozavodsk
Rakitnoye
Kirovskiy
Ariadnoye
Gornyy
Yakovleyka
Arsenev
Kavalerovo
1855
Lazo
Margaritovo
Preobrazheniye

Terney
Plastun
Dalnegorsk
Sikhote Alin Ra.

SEA OF JAPAN (EAST SEA)

JAPAN

Korea Strait
Tsushima (Japan)

Wakkanai
Rebun-Tō
Rishiri-Tō
Esashi
Teshio
Otoineppu
Ōmu
Mombetsu
Yūbetsu
Abashiri-Wan
Rausu-Dake 1661
Embetsu
Nayoro
Engaru
Abashiri
Kitami
Shari
Nakashibets
Haboro
Shibetsu
Rumoi
Takikawa
Asahigawa
Daisetsu-Zan 2290
2077
Honbetsu
Shibecha
Akkeshi
Kushiro
Nemur
Kunasi

HOKKAIDŌ

Ishikari-Wan
Otaru
Atsuta
Bibai
Iwamizawa
Ebetsu
SAPPORO
Iwanai
Suttsu
Setana
Toya-Ko
Tomakomai
Poroshiri-Dake 2052
Obihiro
Hiroo
Kamui-Misaki
Sikotu-Ko
Uchiura-Wan
Muroran
Samani
Erimo-misaki
Okushiri-Tō
Yakumo
Esashi
Hakodate
Matsumae
Shiragami-Misaki
Ohata
Mutsu
Tsugaru Strait
Esan-Misaki
Shiriya-Zaki
Kanagi
Mutsu-Wan
Goshogawara
Aomori
Towada
Hachinohe
Henashi-Misaki
Towada-Ko
Hirosaki
Ōdate
Kuji
Noshiro
Oga
Iwaizumi
Oga-Hantō
Iwate-San 2041
Morioka
Miyako
Akita
Ōmagari
1914
Kamaishi
Honjō
Hanamaki
Kesennuma
Sakata
2230
Ichinoseki
Furukawa
Ishinomaki
Tsuruoka
Mogami-Gawa 1980
Yamagata
Sendai
Sendai-Wan

HONSHŪ

Sado
Ryōtsu
Niigata
Shibata
Sōma
Haranomachi
Aikawa
Niitsu
Fukushima
Sanjo
Higashijima-San 2024
Nagaoka
Aizuwakamatsu
Kōriyama
Iwaki
8412
Suzu-Misaki
Tōkamachi
Sukagawa
Tajima
Tanakura
Kitaibaraki
Wajima
Suzu-Wan
Takada
2578
Hitachi
Nanao
Toyama-Wan
Nagano
Mito
Himi
Toyama
Maebashi
Kiryū
Utsunomiya
Takaoka
Hodaka-Dake 3190
Takasaki
Oyama
Kanazawa
Takayama
Matsumoto
Kumagaya
Kawagoe
Komatsu
3063
Ina
Kōfu
TŌKYŌ
Funabashi
Chiba
Fukui
2782
Kiso-Gawa
3192
KAWASAKI
Ichihara
Takefu
Gifu
Iida
Fuji-San 3776
Odawara
YOKOHAMA
Tsuruga
Ōgaki
Ichinomiya
NAGOYA
Toyota
Fuji
Numazu
Yokosuka
Kyō-ga-Saki
Maizuru
Ayabe
Ōtsu
Yokkaichi
Shizuoka
Itō
Tateyama
Wakasa-Wan
Toyooka
Fukuchiyama
KYŌTO
Suruga-Wan
Ō-Shima
Nojima-Zaki
Tottori
Tsuyama
Biwa-Ko
Okazaki
Toyohashi
Iwata
Nii-Jima
Izu-Shoto
Matsue
Yonago
Himeji
Amagasaki
Higashiōsaka
Hamamatsu
Izumo
1712
KOBE
OSAKA
Matsusaka
Irō-Zaki
Miyake-Jima
Ōda
Chugoku-Sanchi
Fuchū
Izumi-Sano
Ise-Wan
9076
Hamada
Okayama
Wakayama
Daiō-Misaki
Masuda
Fukuyama
Takamatsu
Awaji-Shima
Owase
Hagi
HIROSHIMA
Kure
Marugame
Naruto
1915
Yamaguchi
Iwakuni
Imabari
Tokushima
Tanabe
Shingū
Ube
Tokuyama
Ikeda
Anan
Kushimoto
Shimonoseki
Hōfu
Matsuyama
1955
Mugi
Shio-no-Misaki
Iki
Nōgata
KITAKYŪSHŪ
Kōchi
Muroto
Hachijō-Jima
FUKUOKA
Buzen
Yawatahama
Muroto-Misaki
Karatsu
Saga
Kurume
Ōita
Uwajima
SHIKOKU
Imari
Ōmuta
Beppu
1787
Nakamura
Aoga-Shima
Sasebo
Kumamoto
Saiki
Sukumo
Nagasaki
Isahaya
Nobeoka
Ashizuri-Zaki
Fukue-Shima
Amakusa-Shotō
Minamata
Hyūga
Gotō-Rettō
Ushibuka
KYŪSHŪ
Miyazaki
Koshikijima-Rettō
Miyakonojō
Kagoshima
Nichinan
Makurazaki
Kanoya
Ibusuki
Sata-Misaki

SEA OF JAPAN

PACIFIC OCEAN

Nampō Shotō

ft m
0
600 200
6000 2000
12 000 4000
18 000 6000
24 000 8000

Projection: Conical with two standard parallels   East from Greenwich

1:20 000 000

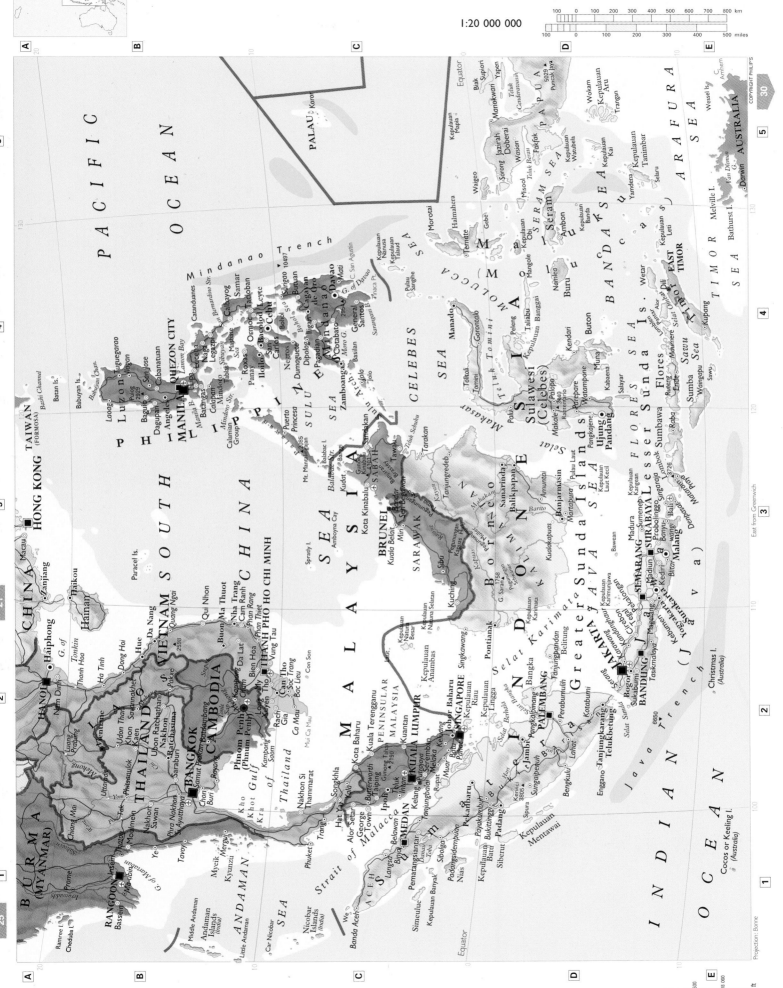

1:17 500 000

Projection: Alber's Equal Area with two standard Parallels

East from Greenwich

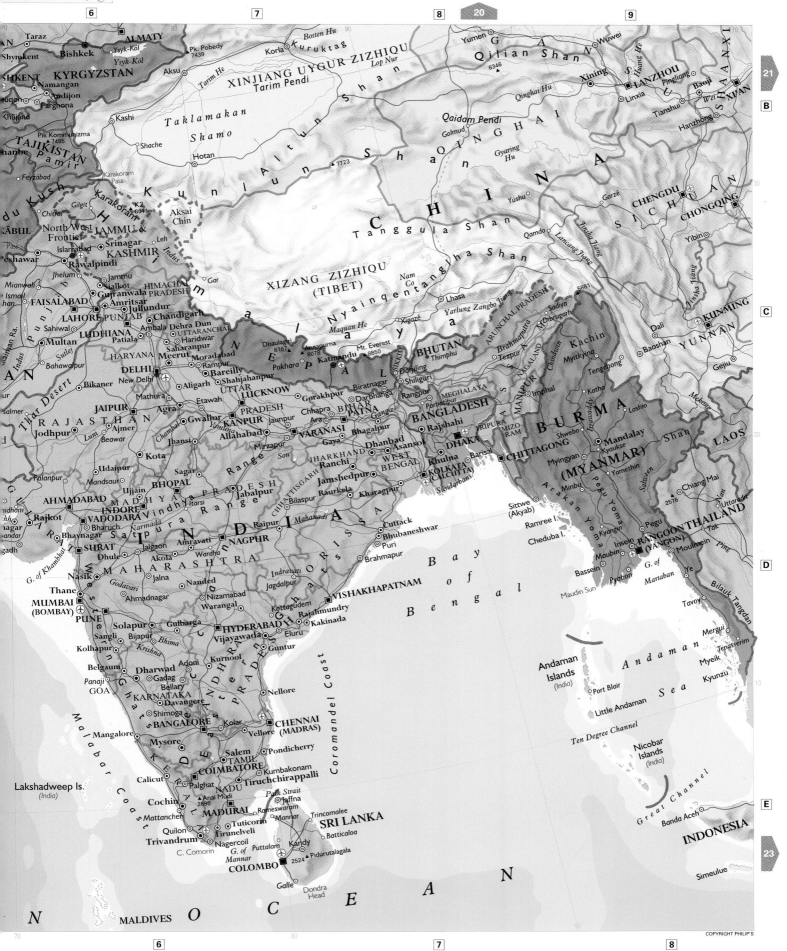

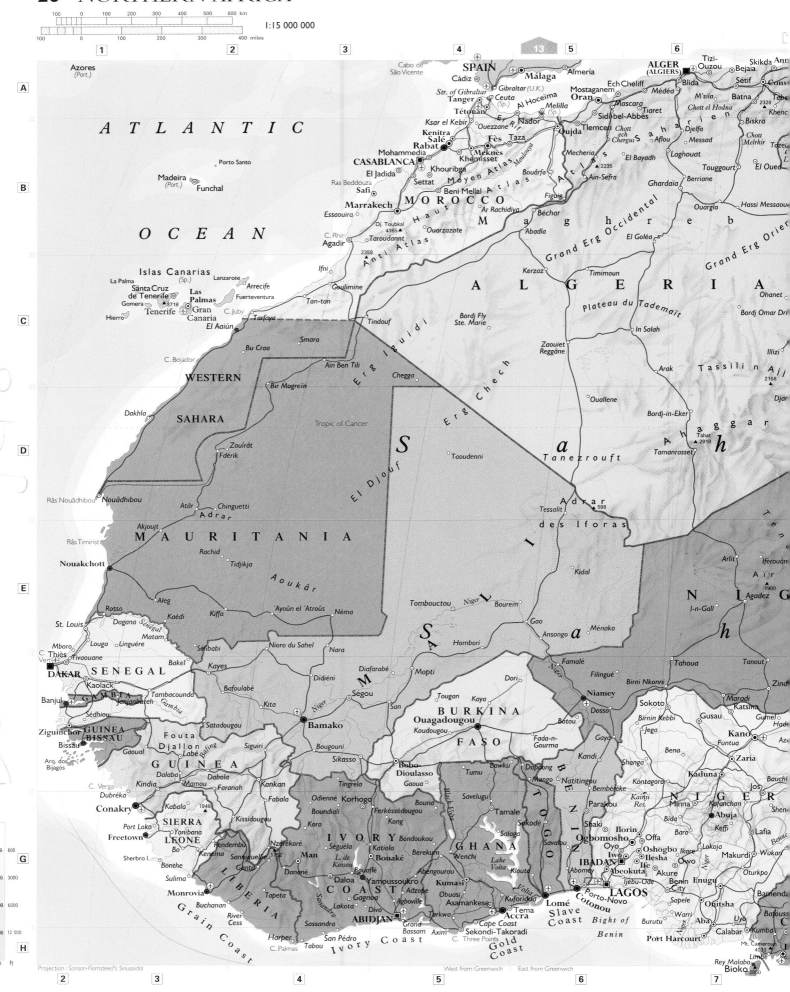

100 0 100 200 300 400 500 600 km
100 0 100 200 300 400 miles
1:15 000 000

| 1 | | 2 | | 3 | | 4 | 13 | 5 | | 6 |

ATLANTIC

OCEAN

Azores
(Port.)

Cabo de
São Vicente

SPAIN

Cádiz Gibraltar (U.K.) **Málaga** Almería
Str. of Gibraltar Ceuta Al Hoceima
Tanger (Sp.) Mostaganem Oran Ech Cheliff **ALGER** Tizi-
Tétouan Melilla (ALGIERS) Ouzou Bejaïa Skikda Ann
Ksar el Kebir (Sp.) Nador Sidi-bel-Abbès Médéa Blida Sétif
Ouezzane Mascara Tiaret S a h a r i e n Batna 2328
Kenitra Taza Tlemcen Chott Djelfa M'sila Chott el Hodna Biskra Khenc
Rabat Salé Fès Oujda ech Chergui Aflou Messad Chott
Mohammedia Meknès Chergui Laghouat Melrhir Touggourt

Madeira
(Port.) Funchal

Porto Santo

CASABLANCA Khémisset El Bayadh
El Jadida Khouribga Moyen Atlas Moulouya Aïn-Sefra Ghardaïa Berriane El Oued
Ras Beddouza Settat Béni Mellal Bouârfa M a g h r e b
Safi **MOROCCO** M Figuig Ouargla
Marrakech Haut Atlas Ar Rachidia Béchar Hassi Messaoud

Essaouira Dj. Toubkal 4165 Abadla Grand Erg Occidental
4165 Beni Mellal El Goléa Grand Erg Orien
C. Rhir Taroudannt Ouarzazate Kerzaz Timimoun Ohanet
Agadir Anti Atlas 2359 Tindouf Bordj Fly Ste. Marie In Salah Bordj Omar Dri
Ifni Goulimine I g u i d i Zaouiet Reggâne Illizi
Tan-tan Arak Tassili n Ajj
Islas Canarias 2158
(Sp.) El Aaiún Smara Chegga Ouallene Bordj-in-Eker Djar
La Palma Lanzarote Arrecife Tarfaya Erg Ain Ben Tili Erg Chech A h a g g a r
Santa Cruz Fuerteventura **WESTERN** Bu Craa I Tamanrasset Tahat
de Tenerife **Las** C. Juby C. Bojador Bir Mogrein g u e c h 2918
Gomera **Palmas** Tropic of Cancer S a
3718 **Gran** **SAHARA** Zouîrât E El Djouf Taoudenni Tanezrouft
Hierro Tenerife **Canaria** Dakhla Fdérik l D Adrar 598
Tessalit d e s   I f o r a s

Râs Nouâdhibou Nouâdhibou Atâr Chinguetti Adrar Arlit Iferouâ
Râs Timirist Akjoujt **MAURITANIA** Kidal Aïr Agadez 1900
Rachid Aoukâr I **N** **I**
Nouakchott Tidjikja l I-n-Gali
Rosso Aleg Kiffa 'Ayoûn el 'Atroûs Néma Tombouctou Bourem a Ménaka **h**
St. Louis Kaédi Niger Gao Tahoua Tanout
Dagana Sénégal 'Ayoûn el 'Atroûs Ansongo Famalé Filingué Birni Nkonni
Mboro Matam Sélibabi Nioro du Sahel Nara Hombori S A Niamey Dosso Sokoto Maradi
Louga Linguère Kayes Didiéni Diafarabé Mopti M Gaya Birnin Kebbi Gusau Katsina
C. Vert Tivaouane Bakel Kita Ségou San Tougan Kaya Botou Jega Gumel
DAKAR Kaolack **SENEGAL** Bafoulabé Niger **BURKINA** Dori Kano
Thiès Tambacounda Satadougou **Bamako** Bougouni **Ouagadougou** Fada-n- Bena Funtua Zaria
GAMBIA Janjanbereh Gambia Koudougou **FASO** Gourma Kandi Shanga Kaduna
Banjul Sédhiou Siguiri Sikasso Bobo- Bawku Mango Kontagora Bauchi
Ziguinchor **GUINEA** Fouta Dabola Kankan Dioulasso Tumu Natitingou Bembéréke Minna **NIGER** Jos
Bissau Djallon Bafing Siguiri Gaoua Dapaong Parakou Kaïnji **Abuja** Kafanchan
GUINEA-BISSAU Labé Mamou Faranah Fabala Tingrela Odienné Korhogo Bouna Savelugu Kontagora Minna Kafanchan
Arq. dos Gaoual Dalaba Dabola Bondoukou Savalou Lafia
Bijagós C. Verga Kindia Mamou Faranah Fabala Ferkéssédougou Kong Tamale Salaga Shaki Ilorin Keffi
Dubréka Kissidougou Boundiali   B Sokodé Oyo Offa Baro Lokoja Owo Turkpo
Conakry Kabala Koro Séguéla Katiola Berekum **GHANA** E Ogbomosho Oshogbo Ilesha Benin Onitsha
Port Loko 1948 Nzérékoré Man Bouaké Wenchi Kumasi N Oyo **IBADAN** Iwo Ife Akure City Enugu
SIERRA Yonibana L. de Bouaflé Abengourou Lake I Iseyin Abeokuta Ijebu-Ode Sapele Aba
Freetown **LEONE** Kenema Kossou **Yamoussoukro** Obuasi Volta N Iwo Warri Uyo
Sherbro I. Bo Sanniquellie 1752 Daloa Adzopé Asamankese Kuforida Porto-Novo Ikare Calabar Bafouss
Bonthe Kenema Gagnoa Agboville Obuasi Kloutou **LAGOS** Benin Burutu Kumba
Sulima **LIBERIA** Danané Divo Volta **Lomé** **Cotonou** Bight of Port Harcourt
Monrovia Tapeta Sassandra Lakota Tema Kpalimé Slave Benin Mt. Cameroun
Buchanan River Gagnoa **ABIDJAN** **Accra** Coast 4010
Cess Grand Cape Coast Bois Rey Malabo
Harper Bassam Axim Sekondi-Takoradi **Bioko** 2850
C. Palmas Ivory Coast C. Three Points Gold Limbe
Grain Coast Tabou Coast

West from Greenwich | East from Greenwich

0
200 600
1000 3000
2000 6000
4000 12 000
m ft

Projection : Sanson-Flamsteed's Sinusoidal

| 2 | | 3 | | 4 | | 5 | | 6 | | 7 |

A B C D E G H

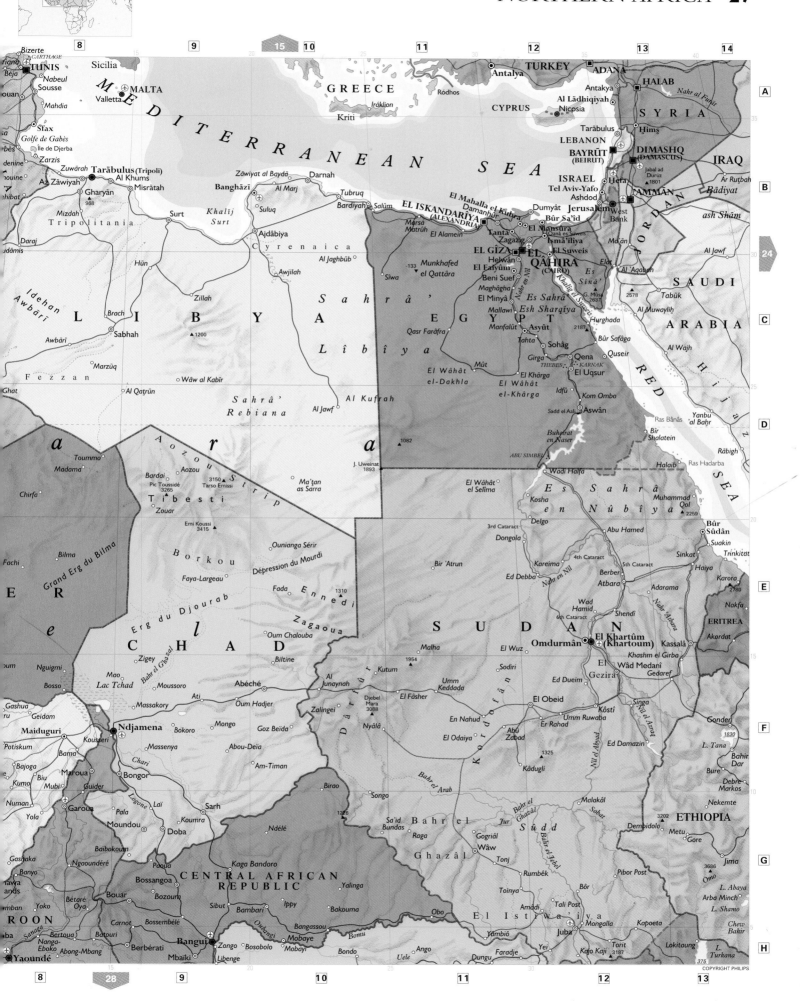

1:15 000 000

INDIAN OCEAN

ATLANTIC OCEAN

MADAGASCAR
on same scale

Tropic of Capricorn

COPYRIGHT PHILIPS

Projection : Sanson-Flamsteed's Sinusoidal

East from Greenwich

100 0 100 200 300 400 500 600 700 800 km
1:20 000 000
100 0 100 200 300 400 500 miles

Projection: Lambert's Equivalent Azimuthal   East from Greenwich

m ft

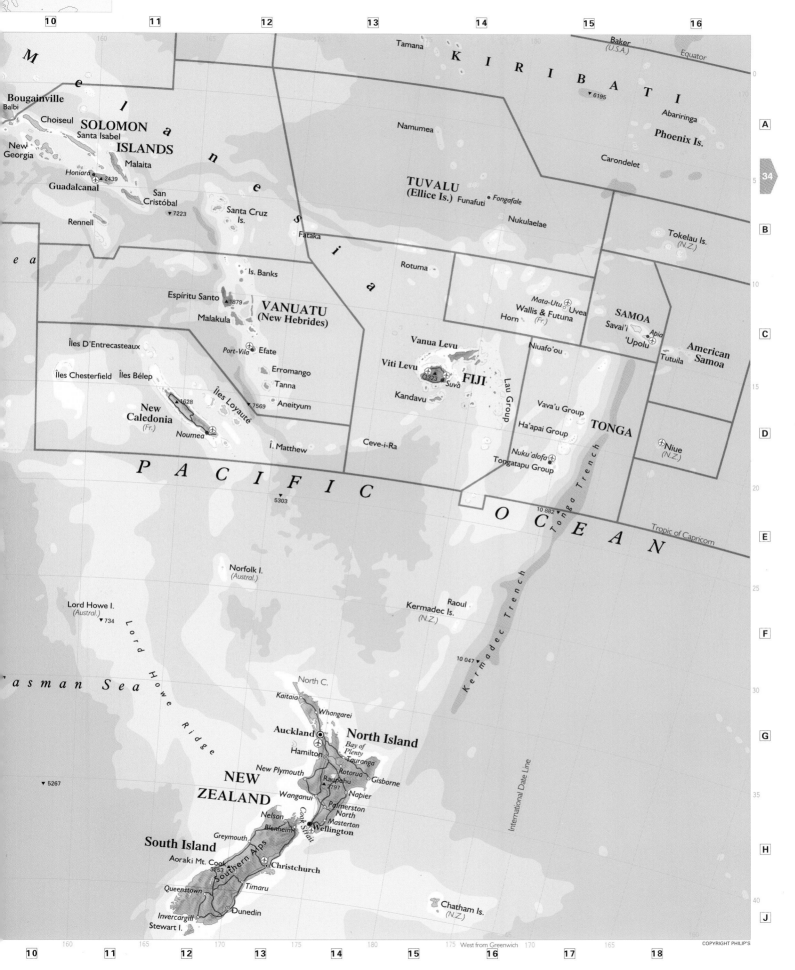

Tamana

K I R I B A T I

Baker
(U.S.A.)

Equator

Bougainville
Balbi

Choiseul

SOLOMON

Santa Isabel

ISLANDS

New
Georgia

Malaita

Honiara ▲ 2439

Guadalcanal

San
Cristóbal

▼ 7223

Rennell

Namumea

Abariringa

Phoenix Is.

Carondelet

TUVALU
(Ellice Is.)

Funafuti • Fongafale

▼ 6195

Tokelau Is.
(N.Z.)

Santa Cruz
Is.

Fataka

Nukulaelae

M
e
l
a
n
e
s
i
a

Rotuma

Is. Banks

Espíritu Santo

▲ 1879

VANUATU
(New Hebrides)

Malakula

Mata-Utu ⊕ Uvea
Wallis & Futuna
Horn   (Fr.)

SAMOA
Savai'i

'Upolu

Apia ⊕

American
Samoa

Tutuila

Îles D'Entrecasteaux

Port-Vila ⊕ Efate

Erromango

Tanna

Vanua Levu

Viti Levu

Niuafo'ou

Îles Chesterfield   Îles Bélep

Îles Loyauté

⊙
▲ 1323 ▾
Suva

FIJI

Vava'u Group

New
Caledonia
(Fr.)

▲ 1628

Noumea ⊕

▼ 7569

Aneityum

Kandavu

Ha'apai Group

TONGA

Î. Matthew

Ceve-i-Ra

Nuku'alofa ⊕
Tongatapu Group

Niue
(N.Z.)

P   A   C   I   F   I   C

▾ 5303

10 882 ▾

Tropic of Capricorn

O   C   E   A   N

Lau Group

Tonga Trench

Norfolk I.
(Austral.)

Lord Howe I.
(Austral.)   ▾ 734

Raoul

Kermadec Is.
(N.Z.)

10 047 ▾

Kermadec Trench

T a s m a n   S e a

North C.

Kaitaia

Whangarei

Lord Howe Ridge

Auckland ⊚

North Island

Hamilton

Bay of
Plenty

Tauranga

▾ 5267

New Plymouth

Rotorua

Gisborne

NEW

Raupahu
▲ 2797

Napier

ZEALAND

Wanganui

Palmerston
North

Nelson

Masterton

International Date Line

South Island

Greymouth

Blenheim

Cook Strait

Wellington ⊙

Aoraki Mt. Cook
▲ 3753

Southern Alps

Christchurch

Queenstown

Timaru

Invercargill
Stewart I.

Dunedin

Chatham Is.
(N.Z.)

West from Greenwich

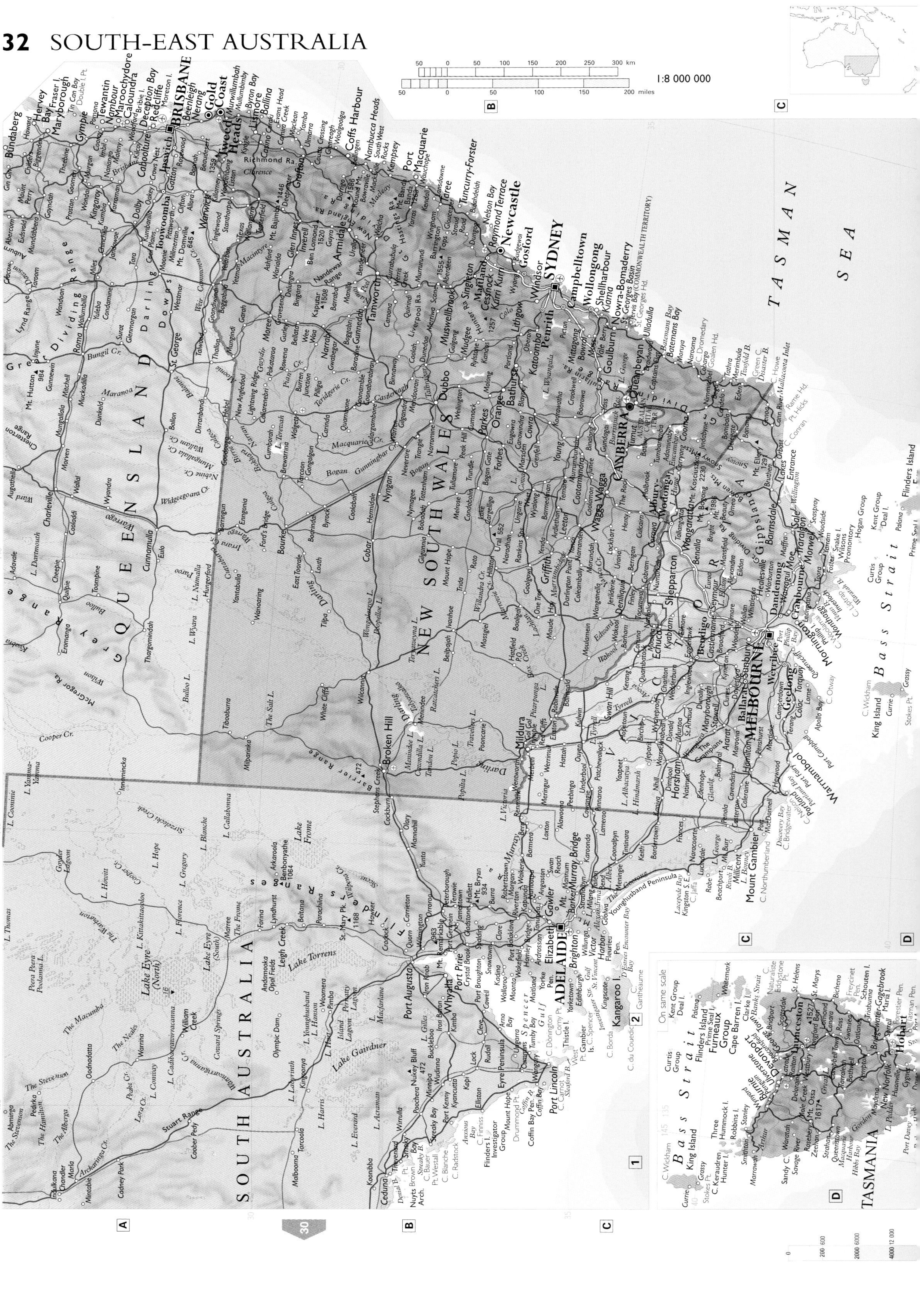

1:8 000 000

50 0 50 100 150 200 250 300 km
50 0 50 100 150 200 miles

QUEENSLAND

NEW SOUTH WALES

SOUTH AUSTRALIA

VICTORIA

TASMANIA

TASMAN SEA

Bass Strait

BRISBANE
Gold Coast
Newcastle
SYDNEY
Gosford
Wollongong
CANBERRA
Broken Hill
ADELAIDE
MELBOURNE
Geelong
Ballarat
Hobart
Launceston

Great Dividing Range

Darling Downs

Grey Range

Barrier Range

Flinders Ranges

Lake Eyre (North)
Lake Eyre (South)
Lake Torrens
Lake Gairdner
Lake Frome
Lake Blanche

Murray R.
Darling R.

Spencer Gulf
Gulf St. Vincent

Kangaroo I.
Yorke Peninsula
Eyre Peninsula

King Island
Flinders Island

Cooper Cr.

1:6 000 000

50 0 50 100 150 200 km
50 0 50 100 150 miles

31
34

North Island

TASMAN SEA

South Island

PACIFIC OCEAN

C. Reinga
C. Maria van Diemen
North C.
Houhora Heads
Rangaunu B.
Doubtless B.
Mongonui
Whangaroa Harb.
Ahipara B.
Kaitaia
Tauroa Pt.
Okaihau
C. Brett
Rawene
Opua
B. of Islands
Hokianga Harbour
Kaikohe
Hikurangi
Donnelly's Crossing
Whangarei
Dargaville
Whangarei Harb.
Bream Hd.
Waipu
Bream B.
Little Barrier I.
Great Barrier I.
Warkworth
C. Rodney
C. Colville
Cuvier I.
Kaipara Harbour
Helensville
Hauraki Gulf
Coromandel
Whitianga
Takapuna
AUCKLAND
Manukau
Papakura
Thames
Mayor I.
Waiuku
Pukekohe
Mercer
Waihi
Waikato
Paeroa
Tauranga Harb.
Huntly
Te Aroha
Mount Maunganui
White I.
C. Runaway
Morrinsville
Bay of Plenty
East C.
Hamilton
Tauranga
Te Puke
Raglan
Cambridge
Whakatane
Opotiki
Te Awamutu
Kawerau
Raukumara Ra.
Hikurangi 1753
Kawhia Harbour
Otorohanga
Putaruru
Rotorua
Rotorua
Taneatua
Motu
Waipiro
Te Kuiti
Kinleith
L. Tarawera
Murupara
UREWERA
Mokau
Mokau
Tokoroa
Mangakino
Wairakei
Ongarue
Taupo
Rangitaiki
Waikaremoana
Ormond
North Taranaki Bight
Waitara
L. Taupo
Taumarunui
WHANGANUI
Turangi
Kaimanawa Mts.
Gisborne
Poverty Bay
New Plymouth
Inglewood
Whangamomona
Tarawera
Nuhaka
Waikokopu
Mt. Taranaki 2518
EGMONT
Stratford
Eltham
Ruapehu 2797
TONGARIRO
Waiouru
Wairoa
Mahia Pen.
C. Egmont
Mt. Egmont
Opunake
Kaponga
Ohakune
Raetihi
Bay View
Hawke Bay
Hawera
Waverley
Taihape
Ruahine Ra.
Napier
C. Kidnappers
South Taranaki Bight
Patea
Mangaweka
Hastings
Wanganui
Hunterville
Waipawa
Marton
Halcombe
Waipukurau
Bulls
Feilding
Dannevirke
Palmerston North
Woodville
Pahiatua
Foxton
Shannon
Levin
Eketahuna
Otaki
Tararua Ra.
Masterton
Paraparaumu
Kapiti I.
Carterton
Greytown
Upper Hutt
Martinborough
C. Turnagain
C. Farewell
Petone
Lower Hutt
Wairarapa
Golden B.
ABEL TASMAN
D'Urville I.
Eastbourne
WELLINGTON
Collingwood
Tasman B.
Cook Strait
KAHURANGI
Tasman Mts.
Motueka
Picton
Karamea
Karamea Bight
Matiri Ra.
Nelson
Havelock
Richmond
Wakefield
Blenheim
Seddonville
Granity
Murchison
NELSON LAKES
Wairau
Seddon
Ward
Westport
Lyell
Inangahua
L. Rotoiti
Awatere
Tapuaenuku 2885
PAPAROA
Reefton
Mt. Travers 2338
Spenser Mts.
Clarence
Kaikoura
Blackball
Grey
Lewis Pass
Hanmer Springs
Runanga
Stillwater
Waiau
Greymouth
Kumara
L. Brunner
Jacksons
ARTHUR'S PASS
Culverden
Hokitika
Waikari
Hurunui
Ross
Arthur's Pass
Waiau
Amberley
Waipara
Pegasus Bay
Abut Hd.
Coleridge
Rangiora
Oxford
WESTLAND
Aoraki
Mt. Cook 3753
MT. COOK
Springfield
Whitecliffs
Kaiapoi
New Brighton
Christchurch
Okuru
Haast
Southern Alps
Methven
Staveley
Riccarton
Lincoln
Lyttelton
Banks Pen.
Jackson B.
Mount Cook
L. Tekapo
Fairlie
Canterbury Plains
Rakaia
Southbridge
Little River
Akaroa
MOUNT ASPIRING
Mt. Aspiring 3027
L. Ohau
L. Pukaki
Geraldine
Temuka
Ashburton
Canterbury Bight
Milford Sd.
Sutherland Falls
Bligh Sound
George Sound
Mt. Earnslaw 2818
Milford Sound
Wanaka
L. Hawea
Waitaki
St. Andrews
Timaru
Secretary I.
Doubtful Sd.
Te Anau
Arrowtown
Cromwell
Kurow
Waimate
Breaksea Sd.
FIORDLAND
Queenstown
Wakatipu
Naseby
Tokarahi
Oamaru
Resolution I.
Dusky Sd.
Manapouri
Clyde
Alexandra
Dunstan Mts.
Kakanui Mts.
Maheno
Hampden
Danback
Chalky Inlet
Preservation Inlet
Te Anau
Kingston
Eyre Mts.
Garvie Mts.
Roxburgh
Waikouaiti
Palmerston
Port Chalmers
Clifden
Manapouri
Mossburn
Nightcaps
Otago
Kelso
Lawrence
Mosgiel
Otago Harbour
Tuatapere
Lumsden
Southland
Edievale
Milton
Fairfield
Saunders C.
Dunedin
Ohai
Winton
Gore
Clinton
Balclutha
Orepuki
Mataura
Kaitangata
Riverton
Wyndham
Owaka
Invercargill
South Invercargill
Tokanui
Bluff
Ruapuke I.
Foveaux Str.
Halfmoon Bay
Stewart I.
Southwest C.
Port Pegasus

Projection : Conical with two standard parallels
East from Greenwich

SAMOAN ISLANDS
1:12 000 000

SAMOA
AMERICAN SAMOA
Savai'i
Apia
Upolu
Pago Pago
Tutuila
West from Greenwich

Wallis & Futuna (Fr.)
Futuna
Niuafo'ou (Tonga)
Thikombia
Labasa
Vanua Levu
Taveuni
Koro
Yasawa Group
FIJI
Vanua Balavu
Lautoka
Levuka
Ovalau
Nandi
Viti Levu 1323
Koro Sea
Lau Group
Lakeba
Suva
Gau
Moala
Kandavu
Vatoa
Vava'u
Tofua
TONGA (Friendly Is.)
Tongatapu
Nuku'alofa

FIJI AND TONGA
1:12 000 000
50 0 50 100 150 200 km
50 0 50 100 150 miles

m ft
200 600
2000 6000
4000 12 000
6000 18 000

7   8   9

6

1   2   3   4   5

B

R   U   S   S   I   A

Yekaterinburg
Tomsk
MOSKVA
Volga
Novosibirsk
Irkutsk
Lena
Chita
Ob'
Oz. Baykal
Blagoveshchensk
Amur
Khabarovsk
Sakhalin
Sea of Okhotsk
Okhotsk
Poluostrov Kamchatka
Komandorskiye Ostrova *(Russia)*
Near Is. *(U.S.A.)*
Andreano... *(U.S.A.)*
Petropavlovsk-Kamchatskiy
Aleutia...
7822
Aleutian Trench
Ber... Se...

C

Astana (Aqmola)
Semey
KAZAKHSTAN
Aral Sea
Balqash Köl
Almaty
ÜRÜMQI
MONGOLIA
Ulaanbaatar
Altai
Harbin
Changchun
SHENYANG
Sapporo
Vladivostok
Hakodate
Sea of Japan
La Pérouse Str.
Kurilskiye Ostrova *(Russia)*
10,542
Kuril Trench
Emperor Seamount Chain

Toshkent
KYRGYZSTAN
TAJIKISTAN

D

AFGHANISTAN
Kabul
Srinagar
Indus
PAKISTAN
Lahore
DELHI
Kanpur
Ganga
CHINA
Kunlun Shan
XIZANG
Lanzhou
Chang J.
Xi'an
CHONGQING
Wuhan
Nanjing
Huang He
TIANJIN
BEIJING
Taiyuan
Dalian
Yellow Sea
NORTH KOREA
SOUTH KOREA
SŎUL
Qingdao
Kitakyūshū
Kyōto
Osaka
Nagoya
Fuji-San 3776
TŌKYŌ
Yokohama
JAPAN
Shikoku
Kyūshū
10,554
Japan Trench
Ogasawara Gunto *(Japan)*
Midway Is. *(U.S.A.)*
Ho...

E

Himalaya
NEPAL
8855 Mt. Everest
Brahmaputra
Lhasa
Irrawaddy
Kunming
Changsha
HANGZHOU
SHANGHAI
East China Sea
Fuzhou
Taipei
TAIWAN
Ryūkyū-rettō (Japan)
South Honshu Ridge
Kazan-Rettō *(Japan)*
Minami-Tori-Shima *(Japan)*
Lisianski I. *(U.S.A.)*
Necker Ridge

BANGLADESH
KOLKATA (Calcutta)
DHAKA
Mandalay
BURMA
GUANGZHOU
HONG KONG
Macau
Wake I. (U.S.A.)

F

INDIA
Hyderabad
Bay of Bengal
Rangoon
Salween
Mekong
LAOS
Hanoi
Hainan
C. Engano
Luzon
Paracel Is.
MANILA
PHILIPPINES
NORTHERN MARIANAS *(U.S.A.)*
Saipan
GUAM *(U.S.A.)* 11,022
Yap
Caroline Is.
MARSHALL IS.
Bikini Atoll
Enewetak Atoll
Dalap-Uliga-Darrit
P   A

CHENNAI (Madras)
THAILAND
BANGKOK
Andaman Is. *(India)*
South China Sea
Mindoro
Samar 10,497
Mariana Trench
M i c r o n e s i a

G

SRI LANKA
Colombo
Nicobar Is. *(India)*
CAMBODIA
Phnom Penh
G. of Thailand
Thanh Pho Ho Chi Minh
Palawan
Sulu Sea
Mindanao
Mindanao Trench
Koror
PALAU
Yap
Truk
Pohnpei
Palikir
FEDERATED STATES OF MICRONESIA
Jaluit I.
Butaritari
Howland I. Baker I.
M e l a n e s i a

MALAYSIA
4101
BRUNEI
SABAH
Celebes Sea
Banda Sea 4101
Maluku
Tarawa
Gilbert Is.
Banaba
Phoenix Is.
Abariri... Enderbu...
O
K I...

H

Sumatera
Kuala Lumpur
PEN. MALAYSIA
SARAWAK
Borneo
Sulawesi
Buru
Seram
Halmahera
PAPUA NEW GUINEA
Admiralty Is.
New Ireland
NAURU
SOLOMON IS.
Fongafale
TUVALU
Tokela... (N.Z.)

SINGAPORE
Java Sea
Palembang
Ujung Pandang
Puncak Jaya 5029
PAPUA
New Guinea
Bismarck Arch.
Rabaul
New Britain
Bougainville
Lae
Honiara
Guadalcanal
Santa Cruz I. 9165
Rotuma
Is. Wallis & Futuna *(Fr.)*
SAMO...
Api...

INDONESIA
JAKARTA
Surabaya
Jawa
Selat Sunda
Java Trench
Bali
Flores Sea
Flores
7440
EAST TIMOR
Timor
Sumbawa
Sumba
Arafura Sea
Torres Strait
C. York
Port Moresby
Louisiade Arch.
Coral Sea
Espíritu Santo
Is. Chesterfield
Vanua Levu
VANUATU
Port Vila
Viti Levu
Suva
FIJI
Nuku'alofa
TONG...

L

Cocos Is. *(Austral.)*
Christmas I. *(Austral.)*
INDIAN
OCEAN
Mid-Indian Ridge
C. Arnhem
Darwin
Gulf of Carpentaria
Broome
North West C.
Cairns
Townsville
Mount Isa
AUSTRALIA
Alice Springs
Great Barrier Reef
Great Dividing Ra.
Rockhampton
Brisbane
NEW CALEDONIA *(Fr.)*
Nouméa
Is. Loyauté
7570
10,822
Tonga Trench
Norfolk I. *(Austral.)*
Kermadec Is. *(N.Z.)*
Kermadec Trench 10,047

Geraldton
L. Eyre
Great Australian Bight
Albany
Perth
Adelaide
Murray
Canberra
Sydney
Mt. Kosciuszko 2237
Lord Howe I. *(Austral.)*
NEW ZEALAND
Auckland
Nuku'alofa
Tasman Sea

M

Indian Ridge
Nouvelle Amsterdam *(Fr.)*
I. St. Paul *(Fr.)*
Is. Crozet *(Fr.)*
Kerguelen *(Fr.)*
Darling
Melbourne
Bass Str.
Tasmania
Hobart
Aoraki Mt. Cook 3753
Christchurch
Chatha... (N.Z.)
Dunedin
Invercargill
Wellington
Cook Strait
Bounty Is. (N.Z.)
Antipodes Is. (N.Z.)

N

Heard I. *(Austral.)*
Auckland Is. (N.Z.)
Macquarie Is. *(Austral.)*
Campbell I. (N.Z.)

Projection: Mollweide's Homolographic   East from Greenwich

ft   m
12 000   4000
9000   3000
6000   2000
3000   1000
1500   500
600   200
0   0
200   600
1000   3000
2000   6000
4000   12 000
6000   18 000
8000   24 000
m   ft

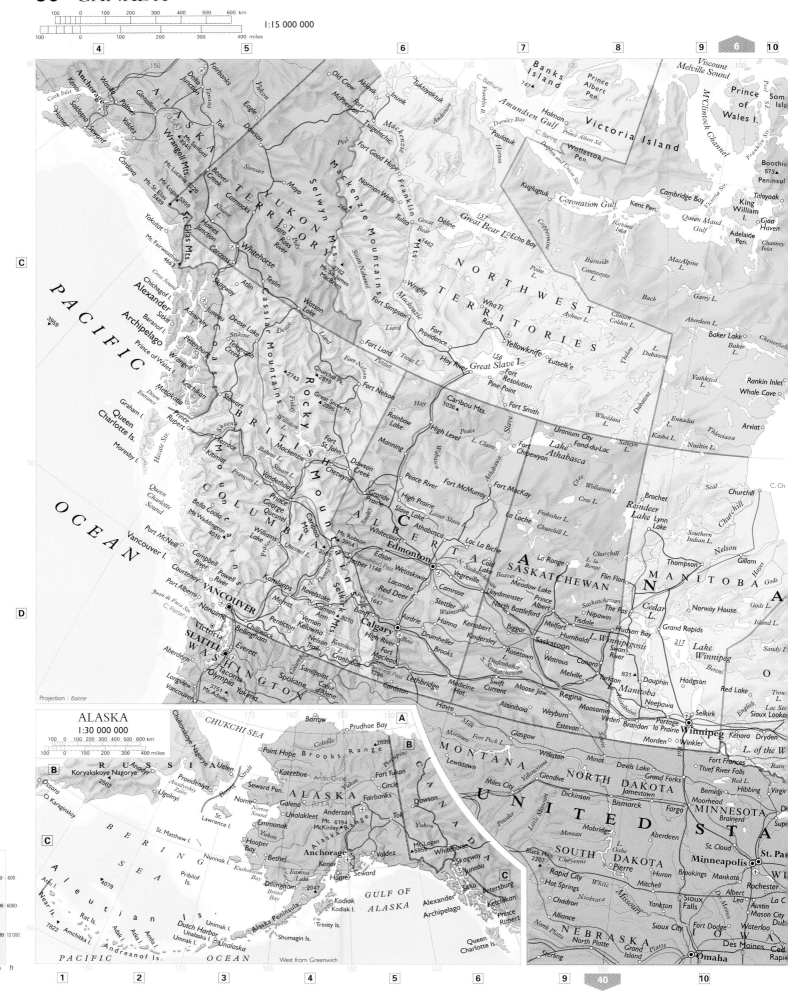

100 0 100 200 300 400 500 600 km

1:15 000 000

100 0 100 200 300 400 miles

Projection : Bonne

ALASKA
1:30 000 000

100 0 100 200 300 400 500 600 km

100 0 100 200 300 400 miles

West from Greenwich

Devon I.
Lancaster Sound
Arctic Bay
Nanisivik
1890
Bylot I.
Borden
Pen.
Eclipse
Sd.
Pond Inlet
rodeur
Peninsula
C. Adair
Baffin Bay
Nunavut
Uummannaq
Ahmassalik

G R E E N L A N D
(KALAALLIT NUNAAT)
(Denmark)

A T L A N T I C

B a f f i n   I s l a n d

Qeqertarsuaq
Qeqertarsuaq
Qasigiannguit
Ilulissat
Kong Frederik VI's Kyst

Davis Strait
C. Raper
Clyde River
Home B.
Qikiqtarjuaq
C. Dyer
Sisimiut
Kangerlussuaq
Monitsoq
Nuuk
Arsuk
Qeqertarsuatsiaat
Allitsup Paa
Nunarsuit
Paamiut
Nunap Isua

Fury and Hecla Str.
Igloolik
mpson
Pen.
Melville
Hall Beach
Air
Force
Prince
Charles
I.
2591
Cumberland
Peninsula
Pangnirtung
Hoare B.
C. Mercy
Cumberland Sd.

N U N A V U T
Foxe
Basin
Foxe
Pen.
Meta
Iqaluit
Hall
Peninsula

C. Dorchester
Amadjuak
Foxe Channel
Cape Dorset
Incognita
Kimmirut
Peninsula
Frobisher Bay
Resolution I.

Rae Isthmus
Repulse
Bay
Southampton
Coral
Harbour
Bell
Pen.
Nottingham
Salisbury I.
Hudson   Strait
Ivujivik
Salluit
Quaqtaq
Akpatok I.
C. Chidley

Labrador
Sea

3809

Coats
I.
Mansel
I.
Kangiqsujuaq
Kangirsuk
Ungava Bay
Hebron
Kangiqsualujjuaq
1652
Nain

H u d s o n
Péninsule
d'Ungava
Puvirnituq
Arnaud
Payne
Feuilles
Baleine
George
Hopedale
C. Harrison

Ottawa Is.
257
Inukjuak
L. Minto
Rigolet
Cartwright
NEWFOUNDLAND &

B a y
Sleeper Is.
King George Is.
Baker's
Dozen
Is.
Sanikiluaq
Belcher Is.
Kuujjuarapik
Grande Baleine
L. à l'Eau
Claire
Scheffeville
Smallwood
Res.
North West River
Churchill
Falls
Churchill
Port Hope Simpson
Belle Isle
C. Bauld
St. Anthony

Peawanuck
Winisk
C. Henrietta
Maria
Pte. Louis
XIV
Chisasibi
Kanaaupscow
La Grande
L. Bienville
Petitsikapau L.
Esker
Labrador
City
Fermont
Ashuanipi
Happy Valley-
Goose Bay
L A B R A D O R
St-Augustin
Str. of Belle Isle
Baie
Verte
Lewisporte
Gander
Bonavista

Q U É B E C
1135
Gagnon
Manic
St-Augustin
Deer
Lake
Grand Falls-
Windsor
Carbonear
St. John's

Big
Trout L.
Attawapiskat
Akimiski I.
Wemindji
Eastmain
L. Sakami
Mistassini
Rés.
Manicouagan
Havre-
St-Pierre
I. d'Anticosti
814
Corner Brook
Newfoundland
Placentia
C. Race

James Bay
Attawapiskat
Charlton
I.
Eastmain
Waskaganish
Rupert
L. Albanel
Sept-Îles
Port-Cartier
Gulf of
St. Lawrence
Ray
C. North
Channel-Port
aux Basques
Marystown
Placentia B.

O N T A R I O
Fort Albany
Moosonee
Harricana
Nottaway
Chibougamau
Baie-Comeau
St. Lawrence
St-Matane
Pen. de la
Gaspésie
Gaspé
Îles de la Madeleine

Albany
St. Joseph
Nakina
Kenogami
Hearst
L. Matagami
Matagami
Dolbeau-
Mistassini
St-Jean
Chicoutimi
Rimouski
Campbellton
Bathurst
PR. EDWARD I.
Cape Breton I.
Sydney
Glace Bay

Greenstone
Marathon
Oba
Kapuskasing
Cochrane
Amos
Rés. Gouin
Roberval
Jonquière
Rivière-du-Loup
Edmundston
Chatham
Summerside
Charlottetown
Northumberland Str.
Port Hawkesbury
Antigonish

L.
ipigon
Nipigon
Timmins
Kirkland
Lake
New
Liskeard
Val-d'Or
1190
Grand Falls
NEW
BRUNSWICK
Moncton
New Glasgow
Truro
N O V A   S C O T I A

Thunder Bay
Rouyn-
Noranda
La Tuque
Québec
Lévis
Woodstock
Fredericton
Amherst
Kentville
Digby
Dartmouth

Lake Superior
Houghton
183
Wawa
Chapleau
Mont-
Laurier
Rés.
Cabonga
Shawinigan
Trois-Rivières
Thetford
Mines
MAINE
Saint
John
B. of Fundy
Bridgewater
Liverpool
Halifax
Sable I.
(Nova Scotia)

M-I-C-H-I-G-A-N
Marquette
Sault Ste.
Marie
Elliot
Lake
Sudbury
North
Bay
Pembroke
MONTRÉAL
Hull
Ottawa
St-Hyacinthe
Sherbrooke
Bangor
Yarmouth
C. Sable
6309

ronwood
Manistique
Sault Ste.
Marie
L. Nipissing
Manitoulin
Parry
Sound
Georgian
Bay
Huntsville
Cornwall
Burlington
Champlain
Montpelier
VERMONT
NEW
HAMPSHIRE
Concord
Augusta
Lewiston
Portland

Escanaba
Menominee
Petoskey
Traverse City
Cadillac
Lake
Huron
Barrie
Owen Sound
Peterborough
Belleville
Kingston
25
Albany
Springfield
MASS.
BOSTON
C. Cod

W-I-S-C-O-N-S-I-N
Wausau
Green
Bay
Appleton
Sheboygan
Lansing
Flint
London
Saginaw
Kitchener
Hamilton
TORONTO
L. Ontario
Oshawa
Rochester
Syracuse
Hartford
CONN.
Providence
R.I.
New Haven

Milwaukee
Madison
Racine
Kenosha
Rockford
Grand
Rapids
177
Lake Michigan
Sarnia
Niagara
Falls
Buffalo
L. Erie
Elmira
Binghamton
Scranton
Bridgeport
NEW YORK

CHICAGO
Gary
DETROIT
Windsor
South Bend
Toledo
CLEVELAND
174
Erie
Jamestown
NEW YORK
PENNSYLVANIA
Newark
N.J.
Allentown
Trenton

ILINOIS
INDIANA
OHIO

West from Greenwich
COPYRIGHT PHILIP'S

1:6 000 000

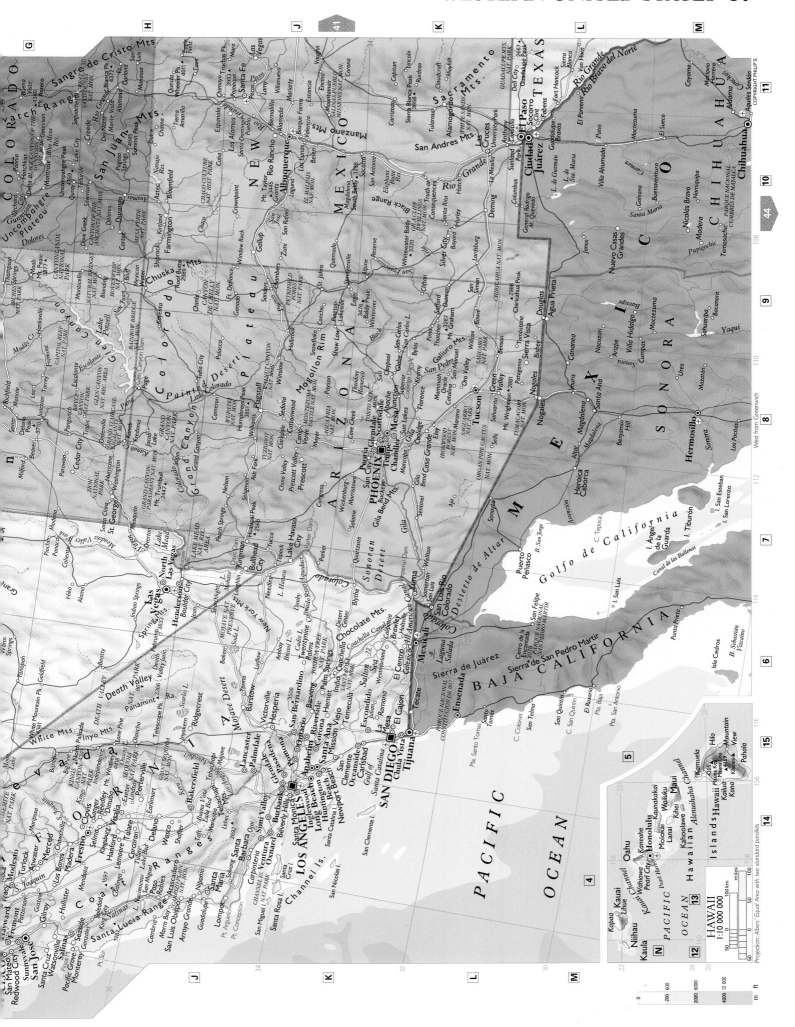

1:6 000 000

50 0 50 100 150 200 km
50 0 50 100 150 miles

A major reference map of the Middle United States showing the states of Minnesota, Wisconsin, Michigan (upper), North Dakota, South Dakota, Nebraska, Iowa, Illinois, Missouri, Kansas, Colorado (eastern), Montana (eastern), and Wyoming (eastern), with Lake Superior, Lake Michigan, and portions of Canada.

Selected major features and place names:

CANADA — Lake of the Woods, Rainy Lake, Voyageurs Nat. Park, Isle Royale, Isle Royale Nat. Park

LAKE SUPERIOR — Apostle Islands, Keweenaw Pen., Thunder Bay, Marquette

MICHIGAN — Iron Mountain, Menominee, Escanaba

WISCONSIN — Superior, Duluth, Ashland, Eau Claire, La Crosse, Wausau, Green Bay, Appleton, Oshkosh, Fond du Lac, Madison, Milwaukee, Kenosha, Racine, Beloit, Janesville

MINNESOTA — International Falls, Bemidji, Brainerd, St. Cloud, Minneapolis, St. Paul, Rochester, Mankato, Winona, Moorhead, Fergus Falls, Willmar

NORTH DAKOTA — Williston, Minot, Bismarck, Mandan, Jamestown, Grand Forks, Fargo, Dickinson, Devils Lake

SOUTH DAKOTA — Aberdeen, Watertown, Huron, Pierre, Rapid City, Mitchell, Sioux Falls, Yankton, Black Hills, Mt. Rushmore, Badlands Nat. Park, Wind Cave Nat. Park, Lake Oahe, Deadwood, Sturgis

IOWA — Sioux City, Fort Dodge, Mason City, Waterloo, Cedar Rapids, Dubuque, Iowa City, Davenport, Des Moines, Council Bluffs, Ottumwa, Burlington

NEBRASKA — Omaha, Lincoln, Grand Island, Norfolk, Kearney, North Platte, Scottsbluff, Sand Hills

ILLINOIS — Rockford, Chicago, Cicero, Evanston, Waukegan, Aurora, Joliet, Peoria, Bloomington, Springfield, Decatur, Champaign, Urbana, Quincy

MISSOURI — St. Louis, Kansas City, Columbia, Jefferson City, Hannibal, St. Joseph, Independence

KANSAS — Kansas City, Topeka, Lawrence, Atchison, Leavenworth, Manhattan, Junction City, Salina, Smoky Hills

COLORADO — Denver, Boulder, Longmont, Fort Collins, Greeley, Aurora, Lakewood, Englewood, Colorado Springs, Pueblo, Castle Rock

WYOMING — Cheyenne, Laramie, Laramie Mountains, Douglas

MONTANA — Wolf Point, Glendive, Miles City, Fort Peck L.

Rivers: Missouri, Mississippi, Red, Platte, North Platte, South Platte, Republican, James, Cheyenne, White, Niobrara, Illinois

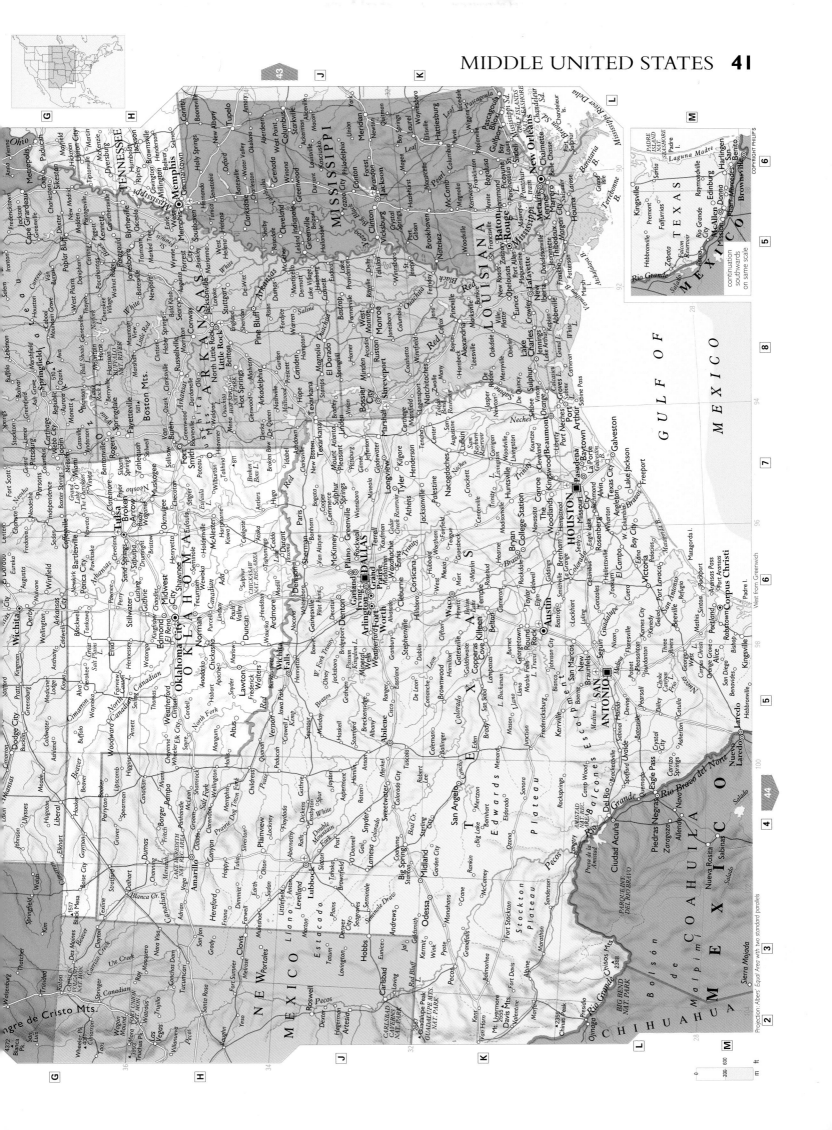

1:6 000 000

continuation eastwards on same scale

ATLANTIC

OCEAN

BAHAMAS

A T L A N T I C

O C E A N

M A I N E

NEW HAMPSHIRE

C A N A D A

NORTH CAROLINA

SOUTH CAROLINA

G E O R G I A

TENNESSEE

A L A B A M A

MISSISSIPPI

F L O R I D A

G U L F   O F

M E X I C O

West from Greenwich

Projection: Albers' Equal Area with two standard parallels

COPYRIGHT PHILIP'S

1:15 000 000

UNITED STATES

SAN DIEGO
Tijuana
Ensenada
Mexicali
Yuma
PHOENIX
Tucson
Roswell
3659
Lubbock
Wichita Falls
Little Rock
Huntsville

San Felipe
3078
San Quintín
Nogales
Douglas
Deming
Las Cruces
Ciudad Juárez
El Paso
Carlsbad
Odessa
Abilene
Sherman
Birmingham
Tuscaloosa
Montgomery

I. Ángel de la Guarda
Caborca
Sonoyta
Cananea
Nacozari
Agua Prieta
Nuevo Casas Grandes
Ahumada
Ojinaga
Fort Stockton
San Angelo
Waco
Austin
FORT WORTH
DALLAS
Shreveport
Monroe
Jackson
Meridian
Dothan

I. Tiburón
Magdalena
Chihuahua
Cuauhtémoc
Delicias
Río Grande
Del Rio
SAN ANTONIO
Bryan
HOUSTON
Beaumont
Lake Charles
Lafayette
Mobile
Pensacola

Hermosillo
Guaymas
Empalme
Ciudad Obregón
Navojoa
Huatabampo
El Fuerte
Hidalgo del Parral
3150
Jiménez
Ciudad Camargo
Piedras Negras
Eagle Pass
Nueva Rosita
Sabinas
Nuevo Laredo
Laredo
Victoria
Corpus Christi
Port Arthur
NEW ORLEANS

GULF OF MEXI

Bahía Sebastián Vizcaíno
El Rosarito
Santa Rosalía
Los Mochis
Guasave
Guamúchil
Gómez Palacio
Torreón
Monclova
San Pedro de las Colonias
Sabinas Hidalgo
Reynosa
MONTERREY
Matamoros
Brownsville
Matagorda I.
Padre I.
Laguna Madre
Mississippi River Delta

Culiacán
B. de La Paz
La Paz
2090
Durango
El Salto
Concepción del Oro
Saltillo
Linares
Montemorelos
San Fernando
Falcon Res.
Cabo San Lucas
C. San Lucas

C. San Lázaro

Mazatlán
Rosario
Sombrerete
Matehuala
Charcas
4054
Ciudad Victoria
3664
Tropic of Cancer

Escuinapa
Acaponeta
Jerez
Fresnillo
Zacatecas
3353
San Luis Potosí
Ciudad Mante
Ciudad Madero
Tampico
Yucatán

Islas Marías
Tuxpan
Tepic
Rio Grande de Santiago
Aguascalientes
Guanajuato
Ciudad de Valles
C. Rojo
Magosal
Tuxpan
Poza Rica
Papantla
Progreso
Tizimín
C. Catoche

Is. de Revillagigedo (Mex.)
Puerto Vallarta
C. Corrientes
Ameca
GUADALAJARA
León
Irapuato
Celaya
Querétaro
Pachuca
Tulancingo
Mérida
Motul
Peto
Valladolid
Cancún
Cozumel I. de Cozumel

Ciudad Guzmán
Zamora
L. de Chapala
Morelia
MÉXICO
Toluca
Popocatépetl
Xalapa
Veracruz
Campeche
Yucatán

Nevado de Colima
4339
Colima
Uruapan
Cuernavaca
Pico de Orizaba
5610
Córdoba
Orizaba
Champotón
Golfo de Campeche
Ciudad del Carmen
Laguna de Términos
Felipe Carrillo Puerto

Manzanillo
Tecomán
Lázaro Cárdenas
Balsas
Iguala
PUEBLA
Tlapa
Minatitlán
Coatzacoalcos
Villahermosa
Escárcega
Chetumal
Corozal
Ambergris Cay

Chilpancingo
3703
Balsas
Chilapa
3395
Istmo de Tehuantepec
Tuxtla Gutiérrez
San Cristóbal de las Casas
Belize City
Turneffe Is.
BELIZE
Dangriga

Acapulco
Ometepec
Oaxaca
Juchitán
Tehuantepec
3139
Comitán
GUATEMALA
Belmopan

Salina Cruz
Tonalá
Huixtla
4093
Cobán
GUATEMALA
Puerto Barrios
Tela
La Ceiba
HONDURAS

G. de Tehuantepec
Tapachula
Quezaltenango
6662
Escuintla
Sonsonate
Santa Ana
Comayagua
San Pedro Sula
Tegucigalp

PACIFIC OCEAN

Guatemala Trench
SAN SALVADOR
EL SALVADOR
San Vincente
San Miguel
La Unión
G. de Fonseca
Chinandega
León
Choluteca
NICA Mana

Pen. de Nicoya
Punta

JAMAICA 1:3 000 000
a

CARIBBEAN SEA

Montego Bay
Lucea
Falmouth
Runaway Bay
St. Ann's Bay
Galina Point
Port Maria

Negril
Cambridge
Wakefield
The Cockpit Country
Ocho Rios
Dry Harbour Mountains
Moneague
Annotto Bay
Port Antonio

South Negril Pt.
Savanna-la-Mar
Maggotty
Mount Denham 985▲
Linstead
The Blue Mountains
2256▲ Blue Mt. Pk.
John Crow Mts.
Morant Point

Black River
Don Figuero Mts.
Mandeville
Santa Cruz Mts.
May Pen
Spanish Town
Portmore
KINGSTON
Port Morant

Great Pedro Bluff
Alligator Pond
Portland Bight
Morant Bay
Port Morant

JAMAICA
Portland Point

GUADELOUPE AND MARTINIQUE 1:2 000 000
G

b
Pte. de la Grande Vigie
Port-Louis
Grande-Terre
Petit-Canal
Moule
La Désirade
Pointe Allègre
Ste-Rose
Pointe-à-Pitre
Ste-Anne
Pointe des Châteaux
Pointe-Noire
Gosier
Îles de la Petite Terre
Basse-Terre
Bouillante
GUADELOUPE (Fr.)
Soufrière 1467
Capesterre-Belle-Eau
St-Louis
Marie-Galante
Basse-Terre
Trois-Rivières
204▲ Capesterre
Îles des Saintes
Grand-Bourg
Pte. des Basses

Projection : Bonne

c
Cap St-Martin
Basse-Pointe
Le Prêcheur
1397
Montagne Pelée
Ste-Marie
Presqu'île de la Caravelle
St-Pierre
La Trinité
Le Robert
Schœlcher
St-Joseph
Le François
Fort-de-France
Le Lamentin
Rivière-Salée
Le St-Esprit
Le Marin
MARTINIQUE (Fr.)
Rivière-Pilote
Pte. d'Enfer

8 **43** **9**

PUERTO RICO **d**
1:3 000 000

ATLANTIC OCEAN

PUERTO RICO
(U.S.A.)

Pta. Agujereada
Isabela
Aguadilla
Arecibo
Barceloneta
Manati
Vega Baja
SAN JUAN
Bayamón
Rio Grande
Carolina
Mayagüez
San Sebastian
Adjuntas
Utuado
Caguas
Sierra de Luquillo
Fajardo
Pta. Puerca
Dewey
Culebra
Uroyan Mts.
Cordillera Central
1338
Cayey
Humacoa
Naguabo
Vieques
San German
Yauco
Coamo
Esperanza
Guanica
Ponce
Guayama
Yabucoa
Pta. Aguila
I. Caja de Muertos

VIRGIN IS. **e**
1:2 000 000

Rufling Pt.
The Settlement
Anegada
East Pt.

Virgin Islands
(U.K.)

Jost Van Dyke I.
Great Camanoe
Guana I.
Hans Lollik I.
Tortola 521
Beef
Virgin Gorda
Spanish Town

Virgin Is.
(U.S.A.)

Cruz Bay
Road Town
Peter I.
Charlotte Amalie – St. – St. John I.
Thomas I.

ST. LUCIA **f**
1:1 000 000

Cap Point
Pte. Hardy
Gros Islet
Esperance Bay
Castries
Marquis
Babonneau
L'Anse la Raye
Canaries
Millet
Dennery
Trou Gras Pt.
Soufrière
Mt. Gimie 950
750
Soufrière Bay
Petit Piton
Micoud
Gros Piton Pt.
795 Gros Piton
Vierge Pt.
Choiseul
ST. LUCIA
Laborie
Vieux Fort
C. Moule à Chique

BARBADOS

ATLANTIC OCEAN

Crabhill
North Point
Spring Hall
Fustic
Boscobelle
245
Belleplaine
Speightstown
Bathsheba
Hillcrest
BARBADOS
Westmoreland
440
Mt. Hillaby
Martin's Bay
Alleynes Bay
Massiah Street
Holetown
Jackson
Bridgefield
Ragged Pt.
Six Cross Roads
Black Rock
Ellerton
The Crane
Bridgetown
Carlisle Bay
Worthing
Oistins
St. Martins
Oistins Bay
Chancery Lane
South Point

BARBADOS **g**
1:1 000 000

CUBA, JAMAICA, HISPANIOLA region

Columbia
Wilmington
C. Fear
Long Bay
ATLANTA
Augusta
C. Romain
Macon
Charleston
Savannah
Jacksonville
Daytona Beach
Orlando
C. Canaveral
Melbourne
TAMPA
West Palm Beach
Grand Bahama I.
Petersburg
Sarasota
Freeport
L. Okeechobee
Fort Lauderdale
Great Abaco I.
MIAMI
C. Sable
Bimini Is.
Eleuthera I.
Key West
New Providence I.
Nassau
Cat I.
Straits of Florida
Andros I.
San Salvador I.
BAHAMAS
HAVANA
Matanzas
Córdenas
Sagua la Grande
Great Exuma I.
Long I.
G. de Batabanó
Guines
Santa Clara
Placetas
Crooked I.
Cienfuegos
Trinidad
Morón
Acklins
I. de la Juventud
Sancti-Spiritus
Ciego de Avila
Mayaguana I.
CUBA
Camagüey
Nuevitas
Great Inagua I.
Victoria de Las Tunas
Holguín
Turks & Caicos Is.
(U.K.)
Manzanillo
Bayamo
Banes
2005
Santiago de Cuba
Puerto Plata
Monte Christi
Santiago de los Cabelleros
Guantánamo
Cap-Haïtien
San Francisco de Macorís
Port-de-Paix
9200 *Puerto Rico Trench*
Grand Cayman (U.K.)
Gonaïves
3175
La Vega
Arecibo
Puerto Rico Passage
SAN JUAN
Montego Bay
St-Marc
DOMINICAN
La Romana
Virgin Is.
Anguilla (U.K.)
7680
Jérémie
REP.
La Romana
St-Martin (Fr. – Neth.)
Mandeville
Spanish Town
Les Cayes
San Juan
San Pedro de Macorís
Ponce
Caguas
ST. KITTS & NEVIS
JAMAICA
Kingston
Jacmel
Barahona
Bani
796
St. Croix (U.S.A.)
Basseterre
ANTIGUA & BARBUDA
PORT-AU-PRINCE
HAITI
SANTO DOMINGO
Mayagüez
PUERTO RICO (U.S.A.)
St. John's
Montserrat
GUADELOUPE (Fr.)
Hispaniola
Pointe-à-Pitre
Basse-Terre
Antilles
DOMINICA
Roseau
Leeward Islands
MARTINIQUE (Fr.)
Fort-de-France
Castries
Lesser
ST. LUCIA
L. de Caratasca
C. Gracias a Dios
Antilles
ST. VINCENT &
THE GRENADINES
Kingstown
BARBADOS
Puerto Cabezas
Bridgetown
I. de Providencia (Colombia)
Windward
Islands
GRENADA
St. George's
Rio Grande
La Blanquilla (Ven.)
Tobago
I. de San Andrés (Colombia)
I. de Margarita
Bluefields
Porlamar
Cumaná
Carúpano
Guiria
Port of Spain
TRINIDAD & TOBAGO
COSTA RICA
Irazú 3432
Coro
Puerto Cabello
G. de Paria
San Fernando
Santa Marta
Ríohacha
Punto Fijo
La Tortuga
Limón
Pen. de la Guajira
Aruba (Neth.)
Curacao
Willemstad
Bonaire
Barcelona
Cartago
Santa Marta
NETH.
Maiquetía
El Tigre
Tucupita
Volcán Barú 3475
Colón
Barranquilla
Sierra Nevada de Santa Marta 5800
San Felipe
Maracay
CARACAS
Puerto La Cruz
Maturín
David
Panama Canal
Cartagena
Soledad
Valledupar
Cabimas
ANTILLES
Ciudad Guayana
Puerto Armuelles
PANAMÁ
Calamar
MARACAIBO
VALENCIA
Ciudad Bolívar
Chitré
Mompós
L. de Maracaibo
Barquisimeto
Barcelona
Embalse de Guri
Santiago
Arch. de las Perlas
La Palma
El Real
Magdalena
Valera
Acarigua
San Fernando de Apure
Tumeremo
Pen. de Azuero
Jaque
Riosucio
Barrancabermeja
Mérida
Barinas
Caicara
Georgetown
I. de Coiba
G. de Panamá
Antioquia
Yarumal
3960
5007
Apure
Arauca
Orinoco
Mt. Roraima 2810
Bartica
New Amsterdam
Linden
Wismar
G. de Cupica
Bello
MEDELLÍN
Puerto Wilches
Cúcuta
GUYANA
Cuyuni
C. Corrientes
Quibdó
Sogamoso
Pamplona
VENEZUELA
Angel Falls
Caroní
Quibdó
Manizales
Bucaramanga
San Cristóbal
Puerto Carreño
Essequibo
SURINAME
Pereira
Tunja
Meta
Puerto Ayacucho
Sierra Pacaraima
Buenaventura
Tolima 5215
BOGOTÁ
Villavicencio
Vichada
Sierra Parima
Armenia
Ibagué
Girardot
Puerto Inírida
BRAZIL
Palmira
Huila 5750
Neiva
COLOMBIA
Guaviare
Ventuari
Boa Vista
CALI
Popayán
Volcán Puracé 4646
Guaviare
Casiquiare
Orinoco

CARIBBEAN SEA

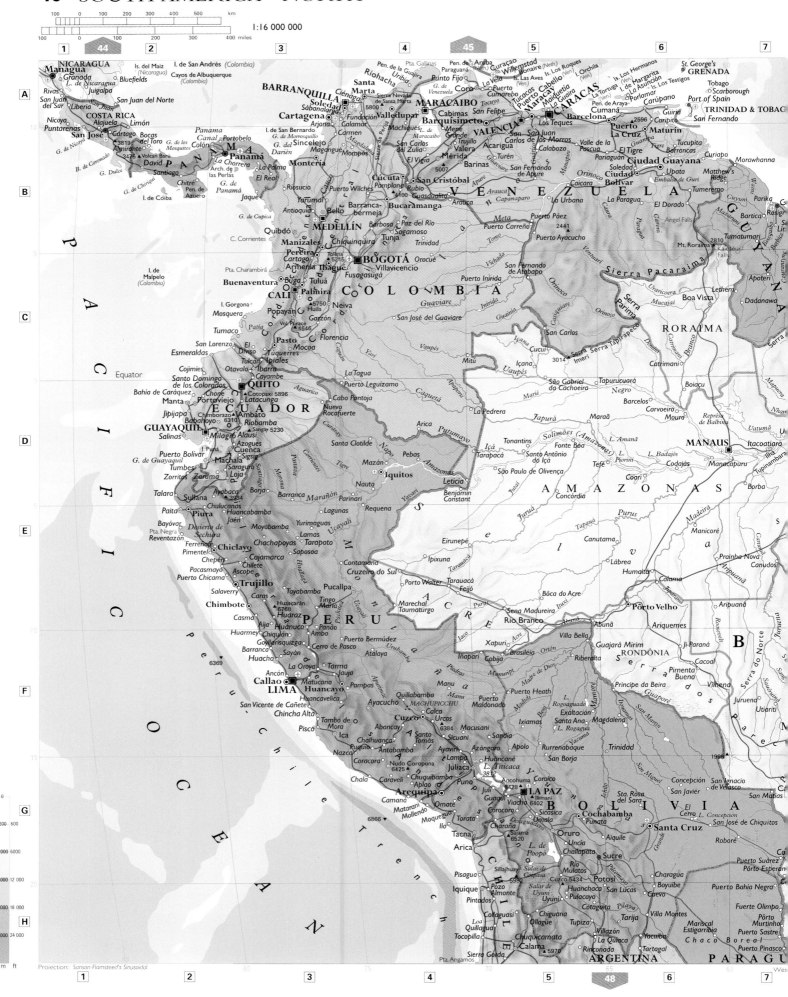

1:16 000 000

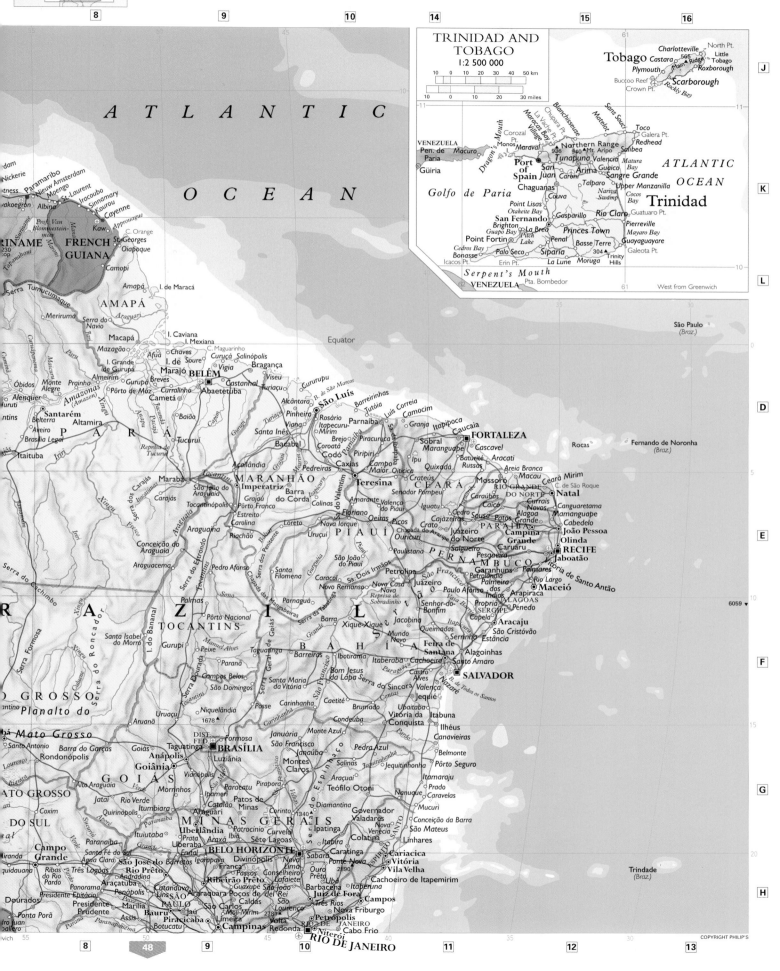

ATLANTIC OCEAN

TRINIDAD AND TOBAGO
1:2 500 000

10 0 10 20 30 40 50 km
10 0 10 20 30 miles

Tobago
Charlotteville   North Pt.
Castara   565   Little   Tobago
Plymouth   Main Ridge   Roxborough
Buccoo Reef   **Scarborough**
Crown Pt.   Rockly Bay

ATLANTIC OCEAN

VENEZUELA
Pen. de Paria
Macuro
Corozal Pt.
Monos   Maraval
Güiria

La Vache Pt.   Chupara Pt.   Blanchisseuse
Maracas Bay   Sans Souci
Northern Range   Matelot
940   Mt. Aripo
Tunapuna   Valencia
Port of Spain   San Juan   **Arima**   Guaico
Caroni   Talparo   Sangre Grande
Chaguanas   Couva   Upper Manzanilla
Golfo de Paria   Point Lisas   Nariva Swamp
Otaheite Bay   Gasparillo   Rio Claro
San Fernando   Princes Town
Brighton   La Brea   Penal   Basse Terre
Point Fortin   Pitch Lake   304   Trinity Hills
Cedros Bay   Palo Seco   Siparia   La Lune   Moruga
Icacos Pt.   Bonasse   Erin Pt.

Toco   Galera Pt.
Redhead
Salibea
Matura Bay
Matelot
Cocos Bay
Trinidad
Pierreville
Mayaro Bay
Guayaguayare
Galeota Pt.

Serpent's Mouth
VENEZUELA   Pta. Bombedor   West from Greenwich

BRAZIL

AMAPÁ, PARÁ, MARANHÃO, PIAUÍ, CEARÁ, RIO GRANDE DO NORTE, PARAÍBA, PERNAMBUCO, ALAGOAS, SERGIPE, BAHIA, TOCANTINS, GOIÁS, MINAS GERAIS, ESPÍRITO SANTO

BELÉM   **São Luís**   **FORTALEZA**   **Natal**   **RECIFE**   **Maceió**   **Aracaju**   **SALVADOR**   **BRASÍLIA**   **Goiânia**   **BELO HORIZONTE**   **Vitória**   **RIO DE JANEIRO**

COPYRIGHT PHILIP'S

1:16 000 000

km
100 0 100 200 300 400 500

100 0 100 200 300 400 miles

Projection: Sanson-Flamsteed's Sinusoidal

West from Greenwich

COPYRIGHT PHILIP'S

PARAGUAY

BRAZIL

PARANÁ

SANTA CATARINA

RIO GRANDE DO SUL

URUGUAY

ARGENTINA

CHILE

PATAGONIA

SOUTH ATLANTIC OCEAN

PACIFIC OCEAN

FALKLAND ISLANDS
(ISLAS MALVINAS) (U.K.)
West Falkland
East Falkland
Weddell I.
Port Darwin
Stanley
King George B.
C. Dolphin
C. Meredith
Falkland Sd.

South Georgia
(U.K.)

Tropic of Capricorn

RIO DE JANEIRO
NOVA IGUAÇU
SÃO PAULO
GUARULHOS
Ribeirão Prêto
Campinas
CURITIBA
PORTO ALEGRE
Florianópolis

Asunción
Resistencia
Corrientes
Posadas
Encarnación
Formosa

SANTIAGO
Valparaíso
Viña del Mar
Mendoza
CÓRDOBA
ROSARIO
BUENOS AIRES
La Plata
Avellaneda
MONTEVIDEO
Mar del Plata
Bahía Blanca

Concepción
Talcahuano
Temuco
Valdivia
Osorno
Puerto Montt
Coihaique
Comodoro Rivadavia
Punta Arenas
Ushuaia
Río Gallegos
Tierra del Fuego
Isla Grande de

Antofagasta
Calama
Salta
San Miguel de Tucumán
Santiago del Estero
Catamarca
La Rioja
San Juan
San Luis
La Serena
Coquimbo

Estrecho de Magallanes (Magellan's Str.)
C. Horn (C. de Hornos)

INDEX

The index contains the names of all the principal places and features shown on the maps. The alphabetical order of names composed of two or more words is governed primarily by the first word and then by the second. This is an example of the rule:

Physical features composed of a proper name (Erie) and a description (Lake) are positioned alphabetically by the proper name. The description is positioned after the proper name and is usually abbreviated:

Where a description forms part of a settlement name or administrative name, however, it is always written in full and put in its true alphabetical position:

The number in bold type which follows each name in the index refers to the number of the map page where that place or feature will be found. This is usually the largest scale at which the place or feature appears.

The letter and figure which are immediately after the page number give the grid square on the map page, within which the feature is situated. The letter represents the latitude and the figure the longitude. In some cases the feature itself may fall within the specified square, while the name is outside.

Rivers are indexed to their mouths or confluences and carry the symbol → after their names. A solid square ■ follows the name of a country, while an open square □ refers to a first order administrative area.

Black Forest

Cornwall □ 9 G3
Corny Pt. 32 B2
Coro 33 G5
Coromandel 33 G5
Coromandel Coast 25 D7
Corona, Calif., U.S.A. 39 K5
Corona, N. Mex., U.S.A. 39 J11
Coronation Gulf 36 B8
Corowa 32 C4
Corpus Christi 41 M6
Corpus Christi, L. 41 L6
Corraun Pen. 11 C2
Corrib, L. 11 C2
Corrientes 44 C4
Corrientes, C. 44 C3
Corrigan 41 K7
Corry 42 E6
Corse 12 F8
Corse, C. 12 E8
Corsica = Corse 12 F8
Corsicana 41 J6
Corte 12 E8
Cortez 39 H9
Cortland 42 D7
Corumbá 46 G7
Corunna = A Coruña 13 A1
Corvallis 38 D2
Corydon 40 E8
Cosenza 14 E7
Coshocton 42 E5
Costa Blanca 13 C5
Costa Brava 13 B7
Costa del Sol 13 D3
Costa Rica ■ 45 F8
Cotabato 23 C6
Côte-d'Azur 12 E7
Côte-d'Ivoire = Ivory Coast ■ 28 G4
Coteau des Prairies 40 C6
Coteau du Missouri 40 B4
Cotentin 12 B3
Cotonou 28 G6
Cotopaxi 46 D3
Cotswold Hills 9 F5
Cottage Grove 38 E2
Cottbus 16 C8
Cottonwood 39 J7
Cotulla 41 L5
Coudersport 42 E6
Couedic, C. du 32 B2
Coulee City 38 C4
Council 38 D5
Council Bluffs 40 E7
Council Grove 40 F6
Courantyne → 46 B7
Courtenay 36 D7
Courtrai = Kortrijk 16 C1
Coushatta 41 J8
Coutts Crossing 32 A5
Coventry 9 E6
Covington, Ga., U.S.A. 43 J4
Covington, Ky., U.S.A. 42 F3
Covington, Okla., U.S.A. 41 G6
Covington, Tenn., U.S.A. 41 H10
Covington, Va., U.S.A. 42 G6
Cowal, L. 32 B4
Cowangie 32 C3
Coward Springs 32 A2
Cowdenbeath 10 C5
Cowell 32 B2
Cowes 9 G6
Cowra 32 B4
Cozad 40 E5
Cozumel, Isla 44 C7
Crabhill 45 g
Cracow = Kraków 16 C9
Cracow 32 A5
Cradle Mt.-Lake St. Clair Nat. Park 32 D4
Cradock, Australia 32 B2
Cradock, S. Africa 29 L5
Craig 38 F10
Craigavon 11 B5
Craignure 10 C3
Craiova 15 B10
Cranbrook 36 C10
Crandon 40 C10
Crane, Oreg., U.S.A. 38 E4
Crane, Tex., U.S.A. 41 K3
Crater L. 38 E2
Crater Lake Nat. Park 38 E2
Crawford 40 D3
Crawfordsville 42 E2
Crawley 9 F7
Crazy Mts. 38 C8
Cree →, Canada 36 B9
Cree →, U.K. 10 G4
Creede 39 H10
Creighton 40 D6
Cremona 14 B4
Crescent City 38 F1
Creston 40 E7
Crestview 43 K2
Crete = Kríti 15 G11
Crete 40 E6
Creuse → 12 C4
Crewe 9 D5
Crewkerne 9 G5
Crieff 10 C5
Crimean Pen. = Krymskyy Pivostriv 17 B4
Crna Gora = Montenegro □ 15 C8
Croagh Patrick 11 C2
Croatia ■ 14 B7
Crockett 41 K7
Crohy Hd. 11 B3
Croker, C. 30 C5
Cromarty 10 D4
Cromer 9 E9
Cromwell 33 L2
Crook 38 D3
Crooked →, Canada 36 C8
Crooked →, U.S.A. 38 D3
Crooked I. 45 C10
Crookston, Minn., U.S.A. 40 B6
Crookston, Nebr., U.S.A. 40 D4
Crookwell 32 B4
Crosby, U.K. 8 D4
Crosbyton 41 J4
Cross City 43 L4
Cross Fell 8 C5
Cross Sound 36 C6
Crossett 41 J9
Crosshaven 11 E3
Crossville 43 G3
Crow Agency 38 D10
Crow Hd. 11 E1
Crowell 41 J5
Crowley 41 K8
Crown Point 42 E2
Crows Nest 32 A5
Crowsnest Pass 36 D8
Croydon 9 F7
Crozet, Is. 5 G12
Cruz Bay 45 e
Cruzeiro do Sul 46 E4
Crystal Brook 32 B2
Crystal City 41 L5
Crystal Falls 42 B1
Crystal River 43 L4
Crystal Springs 41 K9
Cuando → 29 H4
Cuango = Kwango → 28 E3
Cuanza → 26 F2
Cuauhtémoc 44 B3
Cuba ■ 45 C9
Cuba 39 J10
Cuckfield 9 F7
Cúcuta 46 B4
Cuenca, Ecuador 46 D3
Cuenca, Spain 13 B4
Cuernavaca 44 D5
Cuero 41 L6
Cuiabá 46 G7
Cuihangcun 21 F10
Cuillin Hills 10 D2
Cuillin Sd. 10 D2
Culbertson 38 B11

Culebra, Isla de 45 d
Culgoa → 32 A4
Culiacán 44 C3
Cullarin Ra. 32 B4
Cullen 10 D6
Cullman 43 H2
Culpeper 42 F7
Culverden 33 K4
Cumaná 46 A6
Cumberland 42 F6
Cumberland, L. 43 G3
Cumberland Pen. 37 B13
Cumberland Plateau 43 H3
Cumberland Sd. 37 B13
Cumbernauld 10 F5
Cumborah 32 A4
Cumbria □ 8 C5
Cumbrian Mts. 8 C5
Cummins 32 B2
Cumnock, Australia 32 B4
Cumnock, U.K. 10 F4
Cunene → 29 H2
Cúneo 14 D7
Cunnamulla 32 D7
Cupar 10 F6
Curaçao 45 E11
Currabubula 32 B5
Currant 38 G6
Current → 41 G9
Currie, Australia 32 C3
Currie, U.S.A. 38 F6
Curtis Group 32 C4
Cushing 41 H6
Custer 40 D3
Cut Bank 38 B7
Cuthbert 43 K3
Cuttaburra → 32 A3
Cuttack 25 C7
Cuvier I. 33 G5
Cuxhaven 16 B4
Cuyahoga Falls 42 E5
Cuzco 46 F4
Cwmbran 9 F4
Cyclades = Kikládhes 15 F11
Cynthiana 42 F3
Cyprus ■ 17 D4
Cyrenaica 27 C10
Częstochowa 16 C9

D

Da Hinggan Ling 21 B7
Da Lat 23 B2
Da Nang 23 B2
Da Qaidam 20 C4
Daba Shan 21 C5
Dacca = Dhaka 25 C8
Dade City 43 L4
Dagupan 23 B4
Dahlak Kebir 24 D3
Dahlonega 43 H4
Daingean 11 C4
Dajarra 30 E6
Dakar 28 F1
Dakhla 26 D2
Dakhla, El Wâhât el 27 C11
Dakota City 40 D6
Dalandzadgad 20 B5
Dalap-Uliga-Darrit 34 G9
Dalbeattie 10 G5
Dalby 32 A5
Dale City 42 F7
Dale Hollow L. 43 G3
Dalhart 41 G3
Dali 20 D5
Dalian 21 C7
Daliang Shan 20 D5
Dalkeith 10 F5
Dallas, Oreg., U.S.A. 38 D2
Dallas, Tex., U.S.A. 41 J6
Dalmacija 14 C7
Dalmatia = Dalmacija 14 C7
Dalmellington 10 F4
Daloa 28 G3
Dalry 10 F4
Dalton, Ga., U.S.A. 43 H3
Dalton, Nebr., U.S.A. 40 E3
Dalton-in-Furness 8 C4
Daly Waters 30 B5
Damanhûr 27 B12
Damaraland 29 H3
Damascus = Dimashq 24 B2
Damävand, Qolleh-ye 24 B4
Damietta = Dumyât 27 B12
Dammam = Ad Dammām 24 C4
Dammām 24 C4
Damoh 25 H11
Dampier 30 D2
Danbury 42 E9
Danby L. 39 J6
Dandeldhura 25 C7
Dandenong 32 C4
Dandong 21 B7
Danfeng 21 C5
Danger Is. = Pukapuka 35 J11
Daniel 38 E8
Dannemora 42 C9
Dannevirke 33 J6
Dansville 42 D7
Danube = Dunărea → 15 B13
Danville, Ill., U.S.A. 42 E2
Danville, Ky., U.S.A. 42 G3
Danville, Va., U.S.A. 43 G6
Danzig = Gdańsk 16 A9
Dar el Beida = Casablanca 26 B4
Dar es Salaam 28 F7
Darbhanga 25 C7
Dardanelles = Çanakkale Boğazı 15 D12
Dargaville 33 F4
Darhan 20 B5
Darién, G. del 46 B3
Darjeeling = Darjiling 25 C7
Darjiling 25 C7
Darling → 32 B3
Darling Downs 32 A5
Darling Ra. 30 G2
Darlington, U.K. 8 C6
Darlington, S.C., U.S.A. 43 H5
Darmstadt 16 D4
Darnah 27 B10
Darnley, C. 5 C6
Darnley B. 36 B7
Darrington 38 B3
Darwha 25 J10
Darwin 30 B5
Dashen, Ras 28 E7
Dasht → 24 C5
Dasht-i-Tahlab 24 C5
Datong 21 B6
Dauphin 36 C9
Dauphiné 12 D6
Davao 23 C7
Davao G. 23 C7
Davenport, Iowa, U.S.A. 40 E9
Davenport, Wash., U.S.A. 38 C4
Daventry 9 E6
David 45 F8
David City 40 E6
Davis Str. 37 B14
Dawei = Tavoy 23 B1
Dawlish 9 G4
Dawson, Canada 36 B6
Dawson, U.S.A. 43 K3
Dawson Creek 36 C7

Daxian 20 C5
Daxue Shan 20 C5
Dayr az Zawr 24 B3
Dayton, Ohio, U.S.A. 42 F3
Dayton, Tenn., U.S.A. 43 H3
Dayton, Wash., U.S.A. 38 C4
Daytona Beach 43 L5
De Aar 29 L4
De Funiak Springs 43 K2
De Land 43 L5
De Leon 41 J5
De Pere 42 C1
De Queen 41 H7
De Ridder 41 K8
De Soto 40 F9
De Tour Village 42 C4
De Witt 41 H9
Dead Sea 17 D5
Deadwood 40 D3
Deal 9 F9
Deal I. 32 F4
Dease, Forest of 36 C7
Dease Lake 36 C6
Death Valley 39 H5
Death Valley Junction 39 H5
Death Valley Nat. Park 39 H5
Debrecen 17 A2
Decatur, Ala., U.S.A. 43 H2
Decatur, Ga., U.S.A. 43 J3
Decatur, Ill., U.S.A. 40 F10
Decatur, Ind., U.S.A. 42 E3
Decatur, Tex., U.S.A. 41 J6
Deccan 25 D6
Deception Bay 32 A5
Decorah 40 D8
Dee →, Aberds., U.K. 10 D6
Dee →, Dumf. & Gall., U.K. 10 G4
Dee →, Wales, U.K. 8 D4
Deepwater 32 A5
Deer Lake 37 D14
Deer Lodge 38 C7
Deer Park 38 C5
Deer River 40 B8
Defiance 42 E3
Dehra Dun 25 B6
Del Norte 39 H10
Del Rio 41 L4
Delano 39 J4
Delano Peak 39 G7
Delavan 40 D10
Delaware 42 E4
Delaware □ 42 F8
Delaware → 42 F8
Delegate 32 C4
Delgado, C. 28 G8
Delhi, India 25 C6
Delhi, U.S.A. 41 J9
Delicias 44 B3
Déline 36 B7
Dell City 39 L11
Dell Rapids 40 D6
Deloraine 32 G4
Delphi 42 E2
Delphos 42 E3
Delray Beach 43 M5
Delta, Colo., U.S.A. 39 G9
Delta, Utah, U.S.A. 38 G7
Delta Junction 36 B5
Delungra 32 A5
Delvinë 15 E9
Demopolis 43 J2
Den Haag = 's-Gravenhage 16 B2
Den Helder 16 B2
Denbigh 8 D4
Denbighshire □ 8 D4
Denham, Mt. 45 a
Denial B. 32 B1
Denison, Iowa, U.S.A. 40 E7
Denison, Tex., U.S.A. 41 J6
Denizli 17 C3
Denmark ■ 7 F6
Denmark Str. 6 C6
Dennery 45 f
Denny 10 F5
Denpasar 22 F5
Denton, Mont., U.S.A. 38 C9
Denton, Tex., U.S.A. 41 J6
D'Entrecasteaux Is. 30 B9
Denver 40 F2
Denver City 41 J3
Dera Ismail Khan 24 B5
Derby, Australia 30 C3
Derby, U.K. 8 E6
Derby, U.S.A. 42 E9
Derbyshire □ 8 D6
Derg → 11 B4
Derg, L. 11 D3
Dermott 41 J9
Derry = Londonderry 11 A4
Derry □ 11 A4
Derryveagh Mts. 11 B3
Derwent →, Cumb., U.K. 8 C4
Derwent →, Derby, U.K. 8 E6
Derwent →, N. Yorks., U.K. 8 D7
Derwent Water 8 C4
Des Moines, Iowa, U.S.A. 40 E8
Des Moines, N. Mex., U.S.A. 41 G3
Des Moines → 40 E9
Deschutes → 38 D3
Desert Center 39 K6
Dessau 16 C7
Detour, Pt. 42 C2
Detroit 42 D4
Detroit Lakes 40 B7
Deutsche Bucht 16 A4
Deventer 16 B3
Deveron → 10 D6
Devils Lake 40 A5
Devils Tower Junction 40 C2
Devizes 9 F6
Devon □ 9 G4
Devon I. 4 B3
Devonport, Australia 32 G4
Devonport, N.Z. 33 G5
Dewey 45 d
Dewsbury 8 D6
Dexter, Maine, U.S.A. 43 C11
Dexter, N. Mex., U.S.A. 41 J2
Dezfūl 24 B3
Dezhneva, Mys 19 C19
Dhahran = Az Zahrān 24 C4
Dhaka 25 C8
Dhamar 24 E3
Dhanbad 25 C7
Dharwad 25 D6
Dhaulagiri 25 C7
Dhenkanal 25 C7
Dhodhekánisos 15 F12
Dhule 25 D6
Diamantina → 32 A2
Diamond Harbour 25 D7
Diamond Is. 30 B9
Diamond Springs 38 G3
Diaobu 21 G10
Dickinson 40 B3
Dickson 43 G2
Dickson City 42 E8
Didcot 9 F6
Diefenbaker, L. 36 C9
Diego Garcia 3 E13
Dieppe 12 B4
Digby 37 D13
Digne-les-Bains 12 D7
Dijlah, Nahr → 24 D3
Dijon 12 C6
Dili 23 F7
Dillingham 36 C4
Dillon, Mont., U.S.A. 38 D7
Dillon, S.C., U.S.A. 43 H6
Dimashq 24 B2
Dimitrovgrad 15 C11

E

Dimmitt 41 H3
Dinan 12 B2
Dinant 14 C7
Dinara Planina 14 C7
Dinaric Alps = Dinara Planina 14 C7
Dingle 11 D1
Dingle B. 11 D1
Dingwall 10 D4
Dinosaur Nat. Monument 38 F9
Dinuba 39 H4
Dipolog 23 C6
Dire Dawa 24 E3
Dirranbandi 32 A4
Disappointment, C. 38 C1
Disappointment, L. 30 E3
Disaster B. 32 C4
Discovery B., Australia 32 C3
Discovery B., China 21 G11
Diss 9 E9
Divide 38 D7
Dixon 40 E10
Dixon Entrance 36 C6
Diyarbakır 24 B3
Djakarta = Jakarta 22 D2
Djerid, Chott 26 B7
Djibouti 24 D3
Djibouti ■ 24 D3
Dnepr = Dnipro → 17 A4
Dneprodzerzhinsk = Dniprodzerzhynsk 17 A5
Dnepropetrovsk = Dnipropetrovsk 17 A5
Dnestr = Dnister → 17 A4
Dnieper = Dnipro → 17 A4
Dniester = Dnister → 17 A4
Dnipro → 17 A4
Dniprodzerzhynsk 17 A5
Dnipropetrovsk 17 A5
Dnister → 17 A4
Dnyapro = Dnipro → 17 A4
Doberai, Jazirah 23 D8
Dobrich 15 C12
Dodecanese = Dhodhekánisos 15 F12
Dodge City 41 G5
Dodgeville 40 D9
Dodoma 28 F7
Dodson 38 B9
Doha = Ad Dawḥah 24 C4
Dolbeau 37 D12
Dole 12 C6
Dolgellau 8 E4
Dolomites = Dolomiti 14 A4
Dolomiti 14 A4
Dolores 39 H9
Dolores → 39 G9
Dolphin and Union Str. 36 B8
Dominica ■ 45 D12
Dominican Rep. ■ 45 D10
Domville, Mt. 32 A5
Don →, Russia 17 A5
Don →, Aberds., U.K. 10 D6
Don →, S. Yorks., U.K. 8 D7
Don Figuero Mts. 44 a
Donaghadee 11 B6
Donald 32 C3
Donaldsonville 41 K9
Donalsonville 43 K3
Donau = Dunărea → 15 B13
Doncaster 8 D6
Dondra Head 25 E7
Donegal 11 B3
Donegal □ 11 B4
Donegal B. 11 B3
Donets → 17 A5
Donetsk 17 A5
Dongara 30 E1
Dongbei 21 B7
Dongchuan 20 D5
Dongding Hu 21 D6
Dongola 27 E12
Dongting Hu 21 D6
Donington 8 E7
Doniphan 41 G9
Donna 41 M5
Donnelly's Crossing 33 F4
Donostia-San Sebastián 13 A4
Doon → 10 F4
Dorchester 9 G5
Dorchester, C. 37 B12
Dordogne → 12 D3
Dordrecht 16 C2
Dori 28 F5
Dornoch 10 D4
Dornoch Firth 10 D4
Döröö Nuur 20 B4
Dorris 38 F2
Dorset □ 9 G5
Dortmund 16 C3
Dothan 43 K3
Douai 12 A5
Douala 28 H6
Double Island Pt. 32 A5
Double Mountain Fork → 41 J4
Doubtful Sd. 33 L1
Doubtless B. 33 F4
Douglas, U.K. 8 C3
Douglas, Ariz., U.S.A. 39 L9
Douglas, Ga., U.S.A. 43 K4
Douglas, Wyo., U.S.A. 40 D2
Dounreay 10 C5
Dourados 47 H8
Douro → 13 B1
Dove → 8 E6
Dove Creek 39 H9
Dover, Australia 32 G4
Dover, U.K. 9 F9
Dover, Del., U.S.A. 42 F8
Dover, N.H., U.S.A. 42 D10
Dover, Ohio, U.S.A. 42 E5
Dover, Str. of 9 G9
Dover-Foxcroft 43 C11
Dovey = Dyfi → 9 E4
Dowagiac 42 E2
Down □ 11 B5
Downey 38 E7
Downham Market 9 E8
Downieville 38 G3
Downpatrick 11 B6
Downpatrick Hd. 11 B2
Draguignan 12 E7
Drain 38 E2
Drake 40 B4
Drake Passage 5 B17
Drakensberg 29 L5
Drammen 7 F6
Drava → 14 B8
Dresden 16 C7
Dreux 12 B4
Driffield 8 C7
Driggs 38 E8
Drina → 15 B8
Drobeta-Turnu Severin 15 B10
Drogheda 11 C5
Droichead Nua 11 C5
Droitwich 9 E5
Dromedary, C. 32 C5
Dromore 11 B4
Dromore West 11 B3
Dronfield 8 D6
Drummond 38 C7
Drummond I. 42 C4
Drummond Pt. 32 B2
Drummondville 42 C12
Drumright 41 H6
Du Bois 42 E6
Du Quoin 40 G10
Dubai = Dubayy 24 C4
Dubawnt → 36 B9
Dubawnt, L. 36 B9
Dubayy 24 C4
Dubbo 32 B4
Dublin, Ireland 11 C5
Dublin, Ga., U.S.A. 43 J4
Dublin, Tex., U.S.A. 41 J5
Dublin □ 11 C5
Dubois 38 D7
Dubrovnik 15 C8
Dubuque 40 D9

Duchesne 38 F8
Ducie I. 35 K15
Duck → 43 H2
Dudinka 19 C9
Dudley 9 E5
Duero = Douro → 13 B1
Dufftown 10 D5
Duisburg 16 C3
Dulce → 44 C3
Duluth 40 B8
Dumaguete 23 C6
Dumaran 23 B5
Dumas, Ark., U.S.A. 41 J9
Dumas, Tex., U.S.A. 41 H4
Dumbarton 10 F4
Dumfries 10 F5
Dumfries & Galloway □ 10 F5
Dumyât 27 B12
Dun Laoghaire 11 C5
Duna = Dunărea → 15 B13
Dunaj = Dunărea → 15 B13
Dunărea → 15 B13
Dunav = Dunărea → 15 B13
Dunback 33 L3
Dunblane 10 E5
Duncan, Ariz., U.S.A. 39 K9
Duncan, Okla., U.S.A. 41 H6
Duncansby Head 10 C5
Dundalk, Ireland 11 B5
Dundalk Bay 11 C5
Dundee 10 E6
Dundrum 11 B6
Dundrum B. 11 B6
Dunedin, U.S.A. 43 L4
Dunedin, N.Z. 31 K13
Dunfermline 10 E5
Dungannon 11 B5
Dungarvan 11 D4
Dungarvan Harbour 11 D4
Dungeness 9 G8
Dunhuang 20 B4
Dunkeld, Australia 32 B4
Dunkeld, U.K. 10 E5
Dunkerque 12 A5
Dunkery Beacon 9 F4
Dunkirk = Dunkerque 12 A5
Dunkirk 42 D6
Dunleer 11 C5
Dunmanus B. 11 E2
Dunmanway 11 E2
Dunmore 42 E8
Dunmore Hd. 11 D1
Dunnellon 43 L4
Dunnet Hd. 10 C5
Dunning 40 E4
Dunolly 32 C3
Dunoon 10 F4
Duns 10 F6
Dunseith 40 A4
Dunsmuir 38 F2
Dunstable 9 F7
Dunstan Mts. 33 L2
Dupree 40 C4
Dupuyer 38 B7
Durance → 12 E6
Durango, Mexico 44 C4
Durango, U.S.A. 39 H10
Durant, Miss., U.S.A. 41 J10
Durant, Okla., U.S.A. 41 J6
Durban 29 K6
Düren 16 C3
Durham, U.K. 8 C6
Durham, N.C., U.S.A. 43 H6
Durham □ 8 C6
Durness 10 C4
Durrow 11 D4
D'Urville I. 33 J4
Dushanbe 18 F7
Dusky Sd. 33 L1
Düsseldorf 16 C3
Dutch Harbor 36 C3
Duyun 20 D5
Dvina, Severnaya → 18 C5
Dvinsk = Daugavpils 7 H12
Dwarka 25 C3
Dyce 10 D6
Dyer, C. 37 B13
Dyersburg 41 G10
Dyfi → 9 E4
Dzhambul = Taraz 18 E8
Dzhugdzur, Khrebet 19 D14
Dzungaria = Junggar Pendi 20 B3
Dzungarian Gates 20 B3
Dzuumod 20 B5

Eastland 41 J5
Eastleigh 9 G6
Eastmain 37 D12
Eastman 43 J4
Easton, Md., U.S.A. 42 F7
Easton, Pa., U.S.A. 42 E8
Eastport 43 C12
Eau Claire, L. à l' 37 C12
Ebbw Vale 9 F4
Ebro → 13 B6
Echo Bay 36 B8
Echuca 32 C3
Eclipse Sd. 37 A11
Ecuador ■ 46 D3
Eday 10 B6
Eddrachillis B. 10 C3
Eddystone Pt. 32 G4
Eden, N.C., U.S.A. 43 G6
Eden, Tex., U.S.A. 41 K5
Eden → 8 C4
Edenton 43 G7
Edgar 40 E6
Edgefield 43 J5
Edgeley 40 B5
Edgemont 40 D3
Edievale 33 L2
Edina 40 E8
Edinburg 41 M5
Edinburgh 10 F5
Edirne 15 C12
Edmonds 38 C2
Edmonton 36 C8
Edmundston 37 D13
Edson 36 C8
Edward → 32 C3
Edward, L. 28 E5
Edward VII Land 5 E17
Edwards Plateau 41 K4
Effate 33 L3
Egan Range 38 G6
Eger = Cheb 16 C6
Egmont, Mt. = Taranaki, Mt. 33 H5
Egypt ■ 27 C12
Eifel 16 C3
Eigg 10 E2
Eil, L. 10 E3
Eildon, L. 32 C4
Eindhoven 16 C2
Eire = Ireland ■ 11 C4
Eivissa 13 C6
Eketahuna 33 J5
El Aaiún 26 C3
El Asnam = Ech Chélif 26 A6
El Cajon 39 K5
El Campo 41 L6
El Centro 39 K6
El Djouf 28 D3
El Dorado, Ark., U.S.A. 41 J8
El Dorado, Kans., U.S.A. 41 G6
El Faiyûm 27 C12
El Fâsher 27 F11
El Fuerte 44 B3
El Gîza 27 C12
El Iskandarîya 27 B11
El Jadida 26 B4
El Khârga 27 C12
El Mahalla el Kubra 27 B12
El Mansûra 27 B12
El Minyâ 27 C12
El Obeid 27 F12
El Paso 39 L10
El Qâhira 27 B12
El Reno 41 H6
El Salvador ■ 44 E7
El Suweis 27 C12
Elâzığ 24 B3
Elba, Italy 14 C4
Elba, U.S.A. 43 K2
Elbasani 15 D9
Elbe → 16 B5
Elbert, Mt. 39 G10
Elbeuf 12 B4
Elbląg 16 A9
Elbrus 18 E5
Elburz Mts. = Alborz, Reshteh-ye Kūhhā-ye 24 B4
Elche 13 C5
Eldon 40 F8
Eldora 40 D8
Eldorado, Ill., U.S.A. 40 G10
Eldorado, Tex., U.S.A. 41 K4
Eldorado Springs 41 G8
Eldoret 28 D7
Electra 41 H5
Elephant Butte Reservoir 39 K10
Elephant I. 5 C18
Eleuthera 45 C9
Elgin, U.K. 10 D5
Elgin, Ill., U.S.A. 42 D1
Elgin, N. Dak., U.S.A. 40 B4
Elgin, Oreg., U.S.A. 38 D5
Elgin, Tex., U.S.A. 41 K6
Elgon, Mt. 28 D6
Elista 18 E5
Elizabeth, Australia 32 B2
Elizabeth, U.S.A. 42 E8
Elizabeth City 43 G7
Elizabethton 43 G4
Elizabethtown 42 G3
Elk → 42 F5
Elk City 41 H5
Elk River, Idaho, U.S.A. 38 C5
Elk River, Minn., U.S.A. 40 C8
Elkhart, Ind., U.S.A. 42 E3
Elkhart, Kans., U.S.A. 41 G4
Elkhorn → 40 E6
Elkins 42 F6
Elko 38 F6
Elkton 43 H2
Elland 8 D6
Ellef Ringnes I. 4 B2
Ellendale 40 B5
Ellensburg 38 C3
Ellenville 42 E8
Ellery, Mt. 32 C4
Ellesmere I. 4 B4
Ellesmere Port 8 D5
Ellice Is. = Tuvalu ■ 34 H9
Elliot Lake 42 B3
Elliston 32 B1
Ellon 10 D6
Ellsworth, Kans., U.S.A. 40 F5
Ellsworth, Maine, U.S.A. 43 C11
Ellsworth Land 5 D17
Ellwood City 42 E5
Elm Creek 40 E5
Elma 38 C2
Elmhurst 42 E2
Elmira 42 D7
Elmore 32 C3
Elmshorn 16 B5
Elmwood 42 E2
Elorza 46 B5
Eltham 33 H5
Eluru 25 D7
Elvas 13 C2
Elverum 7 F6
Ely, U.K. 9 E8
Ely, Minn., U.S.A. 40 B9
Ely, Nev., U.S.A. 38 G6
Elyria 42 E5
Emāmrūd 24 B4
Embarcación 44 A3
Emden 16 B3
Emerald 30 E8
Emmen 16 B3
Emmett 38 E5

Emmetsburg 40 D7
Emmonak 36 B3
Empalme 44 B2
Empangeni 29 K6
Emperor Seamount Chain 34 D9
Emporia, Kans., U.S.A. 40 F6
Emporia, Va., U.S.A. 43 G7
Emporium 42 E6
Empty Quarter = Rub' al Khali 24 D3
Ems → 16 B3
Enard B. 10 C3
Encampment 38 F10
Encinal 41 L5
Encino 39 J11
Encounter B. 32 C2
Enderby Land 5 C5
Enderlin 40 B6
Endicott 42 D7
Enewetak Atoll 34 F8
Enfer, Pte. d' 45 c
Engadin 12 C9
Engels 18 D5
Enggano 22 D2
England 41 H9
England □ 7 E6
Englewood 40 F2
English → 36 C10
English Channel 9 G6
Enid 41 G6
Ennadai 36 B9
Ennedi 27 E10
Ennis, Ireland 11 D3
Ennis, Mont., U.S.A. 38 D8
Ennis, Tex., U.S.A. 41 J6
Enniscorthy 11 D5
Enniskillen 11 B4
Ennistimon 11 D2
Enns → 16 D7
Enschede 16 B3
Ensenada 44 A1
Entebbe 28 D6
Enterprise, Ala., U.S.A. 43 K3
Enterprise, Oreg., U.S.A. 38 D5
Enugu 26 G7
Épernay 12 B5
Ephraim 38 G8
Ephrata 38 C4
Épinal 12 B7
Equatorial Guinea ■ 28 D1
Er Rachidia 26 B5
Erdenet 20 B5
Erebus, Mt. 5 E15
Erfurt 16 C6
Erg Chech 26 D4
Erie 42 D5
Erie, L. 42 D5
Erigavo 24 E4
Eriskay 10 D1
Eritrea ■ 24 D3
Erlangen 16 D5
Ermelo 29 K5
Erne →, Ireland 11 B3
Erne, Lower L. 11 B4
Erne, Upper L. 11 B4
Eromanga 32 A3
Errigal 11 A3
Erris Hd. 11 B1
Erzgebirge 16 C7
Erzincan 24 B3
Erzurum 24 B3
Es Sahrâ' Esh Sharqîya 27 C12
Esbjerg 7 F5
Escalante 39 H8
Escalante → 39 H8
Escanaba 42 C2
Esch-sur-Alzette 16 D2
Escondido 39 K5
Escuinapa 44 C3
Escuintla 44 E6
Eşfahān 24 B4
Esha Ness 10 A7
Esk →, Cumb., U.K. 8 C4
Esk →, N. Yorks., U.K. 8 C7
Eskilstuna 7 G7
Eskimo Pt. 36 B10
Eskişehir 17 C4
Esmeraldas 46 C3
Espanola 39 H10
Esperance 30 G3
Esperance B. 45 f
Esperanza 5 C18
Espinhaço, Serra do 47 G10
Espoo 7 F11
Essaouira 26 B4
Essen 16 C3
Essendon, Mt. 30 E3
Essequibo → 46 B7
Essex □ 9 F8
Estância 46 F6
Estcourt 29 K5
Estevan 36 D9
Estherville 40 D7
Eston 8 C6
Estonia ■ 7 G11
Estrela, Serra da 13 B2
Etawah 25 C6
Ethiopia ■ 24 F3
Ethiopian Highlands 3 D11
Etna 14 F6
Etosha Pan 29 H3
Ettrick Water → 10 F6
Euboea = Évvoia 15 E11
Eucla 30 F4
Euclid 42 E5
Eucumbene, L. 32 C4
Eudora 41 J9
Eufaula, Ala., U.S.A. 43 K3
Eufaula, Okla., U.S.A. 41 H7
Eugene 38 E2
Euphrates = Furāt, Nahr al → 24 D3
Eureka, Calif., U.S.A. 38 F1
Eureka, Kans., U.S.A. 41 G6
Eureka, Mont., U.S.A. 38 B6
Eureka, Nev., U.S.A. 38 G6
Eureka, S. Dak., U.S.A. 40 C5
Euroa 32 C4
Europa, Île 29 J8
Eustis 43 L5
Eva Downs 30 C5
Evans, L. 37 C12
Evans Head 32 A5
Evanston, Ill., U.S.A. 42 D2
Evanston, Wyo., U.S.A. 38 F8
Evansville 42 G2
Everard, L. 32 B1
Everest, Mt. 25 C7
Everett 38 C2
Everglades, The 43 N5
Everglades City 43 N5
Everglades Nat. Park 43 N5
Evergreen, Ala., U.S.A. 43 K2
Evergreen, Mont., U.S.A. 38 B6
Evesham 9 E6
Évora 13 C2
Évreux 12 B4
Évvoia 15 E11
Ewe, L. 10 D3
Ewing 40 D5
Exe → 9 G4
Exeter, U.K. 9 G4
Exmoor 9 F4
Exmouth 9 G4
Eyasi, L. 28 E6
Eye (North), U.K. 9 E9
Eye (South), U.K. 9 E8
Eyemouth 10 F6
Eyre (North), L. 32 A2
Eyre (South), L. 32 A2
Eyre Mts. 33 L2
Eyre Pen. 32 B2

F

F.Y.R.O.M. = Macedonia ■ 15 D9
Fabens 39 L10
Faeroe Is. = Føroyar 4 C4
Fair Haven 39 L10
Fair Isle 10 C7
Fairbanks 36 B5
Fairbury 40 E6
Fairfield, Ala., U.S.A. 43 J2
Fairfield, Calif., U.S.A. 38 G2
Fairfield, Idaho, U.S.A. 38 E6
Fairfield, Tex., U.S.A. 41 K7
Fairhope 43 K2
Fairlie 33 L3
Fairmont, Minn., U.S.A. 40 D7
Fairmont, W. Va., U.S.A. 42 F5
Fairplay 39 G11
Fairport 42 D7
Fairview, Mont., U.S.A. 40 B2
Fairview, Okla., U.S.A. 41 G5
Fairweather, Mt. 36 C6
Faisalabad 24 B5
Faith 40 C3
Fajardo 45 d
Fakenham 9 E8
Fakfak 23 D8
Falcon Reservoir 41 M5
Falfurrias 41 M5
Falkirk 10 F5
Falkland 10 E5
Falkland Is. □ 48 G5
Fall River 42 E10
Falls City 40 E7
Falmouth, Jamaica 44 a
Falmouth, U.K. 9 G2
Falun 7 F7
Fannich, L. 10 D4
Farāh 24 B5
Faranah 28 F2
Farasān, Jazā'ir 24 D3
Fareham 9 G6
Farewell, C. = Farvel, Kap 4 D5
Fargo 40 B6
Faribault 40 C8
Farmerville 41 J8
Farmington, Maine, U.S.A. 43 C10
Farmington, Mo., U.S.A. 41 G9
Farmington, N. Mex., U.S.A. 39 H9
Farmington, Utah, U.S.A. 38 F8
Farmville 42 G6
Farne Is. 8 B6
Faro 13 D2
Farrell 42 E5
Farson 38 E9
Fartak, Ra's 24 D4
Farvel, Kap = Nunap Isua 4 D5
Fataka 31 C12
Faulkton 40 C5
Fayette, Ala., U.S.A. 43 J2
Fayette, Mo., U.S.A. 40 F8
Fayetteville, Ark., U.S.A. 41 G7
Fayetteville, N.C., U.S.A. 43 H6
Fayetteville, Tenn., U.S.A. 43 H2
Fdérik 26 D3
Feale → 11 D2
Fear, C. 43 J7
Feather → 38 G3
Featherston 33 J5
Fécamp 12 B4
Feilding 33 J5
Feira de Santana 47 F11
Felipe Carrillo Puerto 44 D7
Felixstowe 9 F9
Felton 42 F7
Fenton 42 D4
Fenyang 21 C6
Fergana = Farghona 18 E8
Fergus Falls 40 B6
Fermanagh □ 11 B4
Fermoy 11 D3
Fernandina Beach 43 K5
Fernando Póo = Bioko 26 H6
Ferndale 38 B2
Fernie 36 D8
Fernley 38 G4
Ferrara 14 B4
Ferret, C. 12 D3
Ferriday 41 K9
Fertile 40 B6
Fès 26 B5
Feshi 28 E3
Fetlar 10 A8
Feuilles → 37 C12
Feyzābād 24 B5
Fezzan 27 C8
Fianarantsoa 29 J9
Fichtelgebirge 16 C6
Fiji ■ 31 D8
Filey 8 C7
Filey B. 8 C7
Filiatrá 15 F9
Findhorn → 10 D5
Findlay 42 E4
Finger Lakes 42 D7
Finisterre, C. = Fisterra, C. 13 A1
Finke → 32 A2
Finland ■ 7 E9
Finland, G. of 7 F9
Finlay → 36 C7
Finley, Australia 32 C3
Finley, U.S.A. 40 B6
Finn → 11 B4
Finningley 8 D7
Firat = Furāt, Nahr al → 24 D3
Firenze 14 C4
Fish → 29 K3
Fishguard 9 F3
Fisterra, C. 13 A1
Fitchburg 42 D10
Fitzgerald 43 K4
Fitzroy →, Queens., Australia 30 E9
Fitzroy →, W. Austral., Australia 30 C3
Flagler 40 F3
Flagstaff 39 J8
Flaming Gorge Reservoir 38 F9
Flamborough Hd. 8 C7
Flandre 16 C1
Flannan Is. 10 C1
Flateyri 6 B2
Flathead L. 38 C6
Flattery, C. 38 B1
Fleetwood 8 D4
Flensburg 16 A5
Flers 12 B3
Flin Flon 36 C9
Flinders → 30 B7
Flinders, B. 30 G2
Flinders I., S. Austral., Australia 32 B1
Flinders I., Tas., Australia 32 F4
Flinders Ranges 32 B2
Flint, U.K. 8 D4
Flint, U.S.A. 42 D4
Flint → 43 K3
Flint I. 35 J12
Flintshire □ 8 D4
Flodden 8 B5
Flora 42 F2
Florala 43 K2

Florence = Firenze 14 C4
Florence, Ala., U.S.A. 43 H2
Florence, Ariz., U.S.A. 39 K8
Florence, Colo., U.S.A. 40 F2
Florence, Oreg., U.S.A. 38 E1
Florence, S.C., U.S.A. 43 H6
Flores 23 D4
Flores Sea 23 D4
Floresville 41 L5
Florianópolis 48 B7
Florida 45 B9
Florida □ 43 L4
Florida, Straits of 45 C9
Florida Keys 43 N5
Floydada 41 J4
Fly → 30 A7
Foča 15 C8
Focşani 15 B12
Fóggia 14 D6
Foix 12 E4
Foley 43 K2
Folkston 43 K5
Fond-du-Lac, Canada 36 B9
Fond du Lac, U.S.A. 40 D10
Fontainebleau 12 B5
Fontenay-le-Comte 12 C3
Fontenelle Reservoir 38 E8
Foochow = Fuzhou 21 D6
Forbes 32 B4
Ford's Bridge 32 A4
Fordyce 41 J8
Forel, Mt. 4 C6
Forest 41 J10
Forest City, Iowa, U.S.A. 40 D8
Forest City, N.C., U.S.A. 43 H5
Forest Grove 38 D2
Forestier Pen. 32 G4
Forfar 10 E6
Forlì 14 B5
Forman 40 B6
Formby Pt. 8 D4
Formosa = Taiwan ■ 21 D7
Formosa 44 B5
Forres 10 D5
Forrest City 41 H9
Forsayth 30 B7
Forsyth 38 C10
Fort Albany 37 C11
Fort Augustus 10 D4
Fort Benton 38 C8
Fort Bragg 38 G2
Fort Bridger 38 F8
Fort Chipewyan 36 B8
Fort Collins 40 E2
Fort-de-France 45 c
Fort Defiance 39 J9
Fort Dodge 40 D7
Fort Garland 39 H11
Fort Good-Hope 36 B7
Fort Hancock 39 L11
Fort Kent 43 B11
Fort Klamath 38 E3
Fort Laramie 40 E2
Fort Lauderdale 43 M5
Fort Liard 36 B7
Fort Lupton 40 E2
Fort Mackay 36 B8
Fort Macleod 36 D8
Fort McMurray 36 B8
Fort McPherson 36 B6
Fort Madison 40 E9
Fort Morgan 40 E3
Fort Myers 43 M5
Fort Nelson 36 B7
Fort Nelson → 36 B7
Fort Payne 43 H3
Fort Peck 38 B10
Fort Peck Dam 38 C10
Fort Peck L. 38 C10
Fort Pierce 43 M5
Fort Pierre 40 C4
Fort Providence 36 B8
Fort Resolution 36 B8
Fort St. John 36 C7
Fort Scott 41 G7
Fort Simpson 36 B7
Fort Smith, Canada 36 B8
Fort Smith, U.S.A. 41 H7
Fort Stockton 41 K3
Fort Sumner 41 H2
Fort Thompson 40 C5
Fort Valley 43 J4
Fort Walton Beach 43 K2
Fort Wayne 42 E3
Fort William 10 E3
Fort Worth 41 J6
Fort Yates 40 B4
Fort Yukon 36 B5
Fortaleza 46 D6
Forth → 10 E5
Forth, Firth of 10 E6
Fortuna, Calif., U.S.A. 38 F1
Fortuna, N. Dak., U.S.A. 40 A3
Fortune B. 37 D14
Foshan 21 D6
Fossano 14 D7
Fostoria 42 E4
Fougères 12 B3
Foula 10 A6
Foulness I. 9 F8
Fouta Djalon 28 F2
Foveaux Str. 33 M2
Fowey 9 G3
Fowler 40 F3
Fowlers B. 30 G5
Foxe Basin 37 B12
Foxe Chan. 37 B11
Foxe Pen. 37 B12
Foyle, Lough 11 A4
Foynes 11 D2
Franca 46 H9
France ■ 12 C5
Franche-Comté 12 C6
Francis Case, L. 40 D5
Francistown 29 J5
François L. 36 C7
Frankford 42 E7
Frankfort, Ind., U.S.A. 42 E2
Frankfort, Ky., U.S.A. 42 F3
Frankfurt, Brandenburg, Germany 16 B7
Frankfurt, Hessen, Germany 16 C4
Franklin, Ky., U.S.A. 42 G3
Franklin, Nebr., U.S.A. 40 E5
Franklin, Ohio, U.S.A. 42 F3
Franklin, W. Va., U.S.A. 42 F6
Franklin, Pa., U.S.A. 42 E6
Franklin D. Roosevelt L. 38 B4
Franklin Mts. 36 B7
Franklin Str. 36 A10
Frankston 32 C4
Frantsa Iosifa, Zemlya 18 A7
Franz Josef Land = Frantsa Iosifa, Zemlya 18 A7
Fraser → 36 D7
Fraserburgh 10 D6
Frederick, Md., U.S.A. 42 F7
Frederick, Okla., U.S.A. 41 H5
Frederick, S. Dak., U.S.A. 40 C5
Fredericksburg, Tex., U.S.A. 41 K5

Fredericksburg, Va., U.S.A. 42 F7
Fredericktown 41 G9
Fredericton 37 D13
Frederikshavn 7 F6
Fredonia, Ariz., U.S.A. 39 H7
Fredonia, Kans., U.S.A. 41 G7
Fredonia, N.Y., U.S.A. 42 D6
Fredrikstad 7 G6
Free State □ 29 K5
Freeman 40 D6
Freeport, Bahamas 45 B9
Freeport, Ill., U.S.A. 40 D10
Freeport, N.Y., U.S.A. 42 E9
Freeport, Tex., U.S.A. 41 L7
Freetown 26 G3
Freiburg 16 E3
Freire 48 D2
Fremantle 30 G2
Fremont, Calif., U.S.A. 39 H2
Fremont, Mich., U.S.A. 42 D3
Fremont, Nebr., U.S.A. 40 E6
Fremont, Ohio, U.S.A. 42 E4
French Guiana ■ 46 C8
French Polynesia □ 35 K13
Frenchman Cr. →, N. Amer. 38 B10
Frenchman Cr. →, U.S.A. 40 E4
Fresnillo 44 C4
Fresno 39 H4
Fresno Reservoir 38 B9
Freycinet Pen. 32 G4
Fria, C. 29 H2
Frío → 41 L5
Friona 41 H3
Fritch 41 H4
Frobisher B. 37 B13
Frobisher L. 36 C9
Frome 9 F5
Frome, L. 32 B2
Front Royal 42 F6
Frostburg 42 F6
Frunze = Bishkek 18 E8
Frýdek-Místek 16 D9
Fuchū 19 G11
Fuengirola 13 D3
Fuentes de Oñoro 13 B2
Fuerte → 44 B3
Fuerteventura 26 C3
Fuhai 20 B3
Fuji 19 G11
Fuji-San 19 G11
Fujian □ 21 D6
Fukui 19 F11
Fukuoka 19 H5
Fukushima 19 F12
Fukuyama 19 G6
Fulda 16 C4
Fulda → 16 C4
Fullerton 40 E6
Fulton, Mo., U.S.A. 40 F9
Fulton, N.Y., U.S.A. 42 D7
Funabashi 19 G12
Funchal 26 B2
Fundy, B. of 37 D13
Furāt, Nahr al → 24 D3
Furneaux Group 32 G4
Fürth 16 D5
Fury and Hecla Str. 37 B11
Fushun 21 B7
Fustic 45 g
Futian 21 F10
Futuna 34 J9
Fuxin 21 B7
Fuyang 21 C6
Fuyu 21 B7
Fuzhou 21 D6
Fylde 8 D5
Fyn 7 F6
Fyne, L. 10 F3

G

Gabès, G. de 27 B8
Gabon ■ 28 E2
Gaborone 29 J5
Gabrovo 15 C11
Gadag 25 D6
Gadsden 43 H3
Gafsa 26 B7
Gagnoa 28 G3
Gagnon 37 C13
Gail 41 J4
Gaillimh = Galway 11 C2
Gainesville, Fla., U.S.A. 43 L4
Gainesville, Ga., U.S.A. 43 H4
Gainesville, Mo., U.S.A. 41 G8
Gainesville, Tex., U.S.A. 41 J6
Gainsborough 8 D7
Gairdner, L. 32 B2
Gairloch, L. 10 D3
Galápagos = Colón, Arch. de 35 H18
Galashiels 10 F6
Galax 43 G5
Galdhøpiggen 7 F5
Galena 36 B4
Galesburg 40 E9
Galicia □ 13 A2
Galle 25 E7
Gallinas, Pta. 46 A4
Gallipoli = Gelibolu 15 D12
Gällivare 7 C9
Galloway 10 G4
Galloway, Mull of 10 G4
Gallup 39 J9
Galty Mts. 11 D3
Galveston 41 L7
Galway 11 C2
Galway □ 11 C2
Galway B. 11 C2
Gambia ■ 28 F1
Gambia → 28 F1
Gan Jiang → 21 D6
Gäncä 18 F5
Gand = Gent 16 C1
Gandak → 25 C7
Ganga → 25 C8
Ganganagar 25 C5
Gangdisê Shan 25 C6
Ganges = Ganga → 25 C8
Gannett Peak 38 E9
Gansu □ 20 C5
Ganzhou 21 D6
Gap 12 D7
Gar 20 C2
Garabogazköl Aylagy 18 E6
Garberville 38 F2
Garda, L. di 14 B4
Garden City, Ga., U.S.A. 43 J5
Garden City, Kans., U.S.A. 41 G4
Garden City, Tex., U.S.A. 41 K4
Gardiner, Maine, U.S.A. 43 C11
Gardiner, Mont., U.S.A. 38 D8
Gardnerville 38 G4
Garfield 38 C5
Garforth 8 D6
Gargano, Mte. 14 D6
Garissa 28 E7
Garland, Tex., U.S.A. 41 J6
Garland, Utah, U.S.A. 38 F7
Garmo, Qullai = Kommunizma, Pik 18 F8
Garner 40 D8
Garoe 24 F4

Garonne

Garonne → 12 D3
Garrison, Mont., U.S.A. 38 C7
Garrison, N. Dak., U.S.A. 40 B4
Garron Pt. 11 A6
Garry → 10 E5
Garry, L. 36 B9
Garvie Mts. 33 L2
Gary 42 E2
Garzê 20 C5
Gascogne 12 E4
Gascogne, G. de 12 D2
Gascony = Gascogne 12 E4
Gaspé 37 D13
Gaspé, Pén. de 37 D13
Gasteiz = Vitoria-Gasteiz 13 A4
Gastonia 43 H5
Gatehouse of Fleet 10 G4
Gateshead 8 C6
Gatesville 41 K6
Gatton 32 A5
Gau 33 D8
Gävle 7 E7
Gawler 32 B2
Gaxun Nur 20 B5
Gaya 25 C7
Gaylord 42 C3
Gayndah 32 A5
Gaza 17 D4
Gaziantep 17 C5
Gcuwa 29 L5
Gdańsk 16 A9
Gdańska, Zatoka 16 A9
Gdynia 16 A9
Gebe 23 C4
Gedser 7 G6
Geelong 30 H7
Gejiu 20 D5
Gelibolu 15 D12
Gelsenkirchen 16 C3
General Santos 23 C4
Genesee 38 C5
Genesee → 42 D7
Geneseo, Ill., U.S.A. 40 E9
Geneseo, N.Y., U.S.A. 42 D7
Geneva = Genève 12 C7
Geneva, Ala., U.S.A. 43 K3
Geneva, N.Y., U.S.A. 42 D7
Geneva, Nebr., U.S.A. 40 E6
Geneva, Ohio, U.S.A. 42 E5
Geneva, L. = Léman, L. 12 C7
Geneva, L. 42 D1
Genève 12 C7
Gennargentu, Mti. del 14 D3
Genoa = Génova 12 D8
Genoa, Australia 32 C4
Genoa, U.S.A. 40 E6
Génova 12 D8
Gent 16 C1
George 29 L4
George → 37 C13
George, L., N.S.W., Australia 32 C4
George, L., S. Austral., Australia 32 C3
George, L., Fla., U.S.A. 43 L5
George, L., N.Y., U.S.A. 42 D9
George Sound 33 L1
George Town, Australia 32 D4
George Town, Malaysia 23 C2
George V Land 6 D14
George West 41 L5
Georgetown, Guyana 46 B7
Georgetown, Colo., U.S.A. 38 G11
Georgetown, Ky., U.S.A. 42 F3
Georgetown, Ohio, U.S.A. 42 F4
Georgetown, S.C., U.S.A. 43 J6
Georgetown, Tex., U.S.A. 41 K6
Georgia □ 43 K5
Georgian B. 37 D11
Gera 16 C6
Geraldine 38 C8
Geraldton 30 F1
Gereshk 24 B5
Gering 40 E3
Gerlach 38 F4
Germantown 41 M10
Germany ■ 16 C5
Germiston 29 K5
Gerona = Girona 13 B7
Getafe 13 B4
Gettysburg, Pa., U.S.A. 42 F7
Gettysburg, S. Dak., U.S.A. 40 C5
Geyser 38 C8
Ghana ■ 26 G5
Ghanzi 29 J4
Ghawdex = Gozo 14 F6
Ghazâl, Bahr el → 27 G12
Ghaznī 24 B5
Ghent = Gent 16 C1
Giants Causeway 11 A5
Gibbon 40 E5
Gibraltar ■ 13 D3
Gibraltar, Str. of 13 E3
Gibson Desert 30 E4
Giddings 41 K6
Gifu 22 F5
Gigha 10 F3
Gijón 13 A3
Gila → 39 K6
Gila Bend 39 K7
Gila Bend Mts. 39 K7
Gilbert Is. 34 G9
Gilgandra 32 B4
Gilgit 25 B6
Gillam 36 C10
Gilles, L. 32 B2
Gillette 40 C2
Gillingham 9 F8
Gilmer 41 J7
Gilroy 39 H3
Gimie, Mt 45 f
Gin Gin 32 A5
Girard 41 G7
Girdle Ness 10 D6
Girona 13 B7
Gironde → 12 D3
Girvan 10 F4
Gisborne 31 H14
Giuba → 24 E3
Giza = El Gîza 27 C12
Gizhiga 19 C17
Gjoa Haven 36 B10
Glace Bay 37 D14
Glacier Nat. Park 38 B7
Glacier Peak 38 B3
Gladewater 41 J7
Gladstone, Queens., Australia 30 E9
Gladstone, S. Austral., Australia 32 B2
Gladstone, U.S.A. 42 C2
Gladwin 42 D3
Glasco 40 F6
Glasgow, U.K. 10 F4
Glasgow, Ky., U.S.A. 42 G3
Glasgow, Mont., U.S.A. 38 B10
Glastonbury 9 F5
Glen Affric 10 D3
Glen Canyon 39 H8
Glen Canyon Dam 39 H8
Glen Canyon Nat. Recr. Area 39 H8
Glen Coe 10 E3
Glen Garry 10 D3
Glen Innes 32 A5
Glen Mor 10 D4
Glen Moriston 10 D4
Glen Spean 10 E4
Glen Ullin 40 B4
Glencoe 40 C7
Glendale, Ariz., U.S.A. 39 K7
Glendale, Calif., U.S.A. 39 J4
Glendive 40 B2
Glendo 40 D2
Glenelg → 32 C3
Glengarriff 11 E2
Glenmorgan 32 A4
Glennallen 36 B5
Glennamaddy 11 C3
Glenns Ferry 38 E6
Glenreagh 32 B5
Glenrock 38 E11
Glenrothes 10 E5
Glens Falls 42 D9
Glenties 11 B3
Glenville 42 F5
Glenwood, Ark., U.S.A. 41 H8
Glenwood, Iowa, U.S.A. 40 E7
Glenwood, Minn., U.S.A. 40 C7
Glenwood Springs 38 G10
Gliwice 16 C9
Globe 39 K8
Głogów 16 C8
Glomma → 7 F6
Glossop 8 D6
Gloucester, Australia 32 B5
Gloucester, U.K. 9 F5
Gloucester Point 42 G7
Gloucestershire □ 9 F5
Gniezno 16 B8
Goa □ 25 D6
Goalen Hd. 32 C5
Goat Fell 10 F3
Gobabis 29 J3
Gobi 21 B5
Godavari → 25 D7
Godhavn = Qeqertarsuaq 37 B14
Gods → 36 C10
Gods L. 36 C10
Godthåb = Nuuk 37 B14
Goeie Hoop, Kaap die = Good Hope, C. of 29 L3
Gogebic, L. 40 B10
Goiânia 47 G9
Goio-Erê 48 A6
Golconda 38 F5
Gold Beach 38 E1
Gold Coast, Australia 30 F9
Gold Coast, W. Afr. 26 H5
Gold Hill 38 E2
Golden B. 33 J4
Golden Gate 38 H2
Golden Vale 11 D3
Goldendale 38 D3
Goldfield 39 H5
Goldsboro 43 H7
Goldsmith 41 K3
Goldthwaite 41 K5
Goliad 41 L6
Golspie 10 D5
Gomel = Homyel 18 D4
Gómez Palacio 44 B4
Gonābād 24 B4
Gonaïves 45 D10
Gongbei 21 G10
Gonghe 20 C5
Gongming 21 F10
Gongolgon 32 B4
Gonzales, Calif., U.S.A. 39 H3
Gonzales, Tex., U.S.A. 41 L6
Good Hope, C. of 29 L3
Gooding 38 E6
Goodland 40 F4
Goodooga 32 A4
Goole 8 D7
Goolgowi 32 B4
Goomeri 32 A5
Goondiwindi 32 A5
Goose Creek 43 J5
Goose L. 38 F3
Gorakhpur 25 C7
Gordon 40 D3
Gordon → 32 D4
Gore 33 M2
Gorey 11 D5
Gorgān 24 B4
Gorki = Nizhniy Novgorod 18 D5
Gorkiy = Nizhniy Novgorod 18 D5
Görlitz 16 C7
Gorlovka = Horlivka 17 A5
Gorontalo 23 C4
Gort 11 C3
Gorzów Wielkopolski 16 B7
Gosford 32 B5
Goshen 42 E3
Gosier 44 b
Gosport 9 G6
Göta kanal 7 F7
Göteborg 7 F6
Gotha 16 C5
Gothenburg = Göteborg 7 F6
Gothenburg 40 E4
Gotland 7 F7
Göttingen 16 C4
Gottwaldov = Zlín 16 D8
Gouda 16 B2
Gough I. 4 G9
Gouin, Rés. 37 D12
Goulburn 30 G8
Gouverneur 42 C8
Governador Valadares 47 G10
Gowanda 42 D6
Gower 9 F3
Gowna, L. 11 C4
Goyder Lagoon 32 A2
Gozo 14 F6
Graaff-Reinet 29 L4
Gracias a Dios, C. 45 E8
Grady 41 H3
Grafham Water 9 E7
Grafton, Australia 30 F9
Grafton, N. Dak., U.S.A. 40 A6
Grafton, W. Va., U.S.A. 42 F5
Graham 41 J5
Graham, Mt. 39 K9
Graham Land 6 D3
Grahamstown 29 L5
Grain Coast 26 H3
Grampian Mts. 10 E5
Grampians, The 32 C3
Gran Canaria 26 C2
Gran Chaco 48 B4
Gran Sasso d'Itália 14 C5
Granada, Nic. 44 E7
Granada, Spain 13 D4
Granada, U.S.A. 41 F3
Granard 11 C4
Granbury 41 J6
Granby, Canada 37 D12
Granby, U.S.A. 38 F11
Grand →, Mo., U.S.A. 40 F8
Grand →, S. Dak., U.S.A. 40 C4
Grand Bahama 45 B9
Grand-Bourg 44 b
Grand Canyon 39 H7
Grand Canyon Nat. Park 39 H7
Grand Cayman 45 D8
Grand Centre 36 C8
Grand Coulee 38 C4
Grand Coulee Dam 38 C4
Grand Falls 37 D13
Grand Falls-Windsor 37 D14
Grand Forks 40 B6
Grand Haven 42 D2
Grand I. 42 B2
Grand Island 40 E5
Grand Isle 41 L9
Grand Junction 39 G9
Grand L. 41 L8
Grand Lake 38 F11
Grand Marais, Canada 40 B9
Grand Marais, U.S.A. 42 B3
Grand Portage 40 B10
Grand Prairie 41 J6
Grand Rapids, Canada 36 C10
Grand Rapids, Mich., U.S.A. 42 D2
Grand Rapids, Minn., U.S.A. 40 B8
Grand St-Bernard, Col du 12 D7
Grand Teton 38 E8
Grand Teton Nat. Park 38 D8
Grand Union Canal 9 E7
Grand-Vigie, Pte. de la 44 b
Grande, Rio → 41 N6
Grande Baleine, R. de la → 37 C12
Grande Prairie 36 C8
Grande-Terre, I. 44 b
Grandfalls 41 K3
Grandview 38 C4
Grangemouth 10 E5
Granger 38 F9
Grangeville 38 D5
Granite City 40 F9
Granite Falls 40 C7
Granite Pk. 38 D9
Granity 33 J3
Grant 40 E4
Grant, Mt. 38 G4
Grant City 40 E7
Grant Range 39 G6
Grantham 8 E7
Grantown-on-Spey 10 D5
Grants 39 J10
Grants Pass 38 E2
Grantsville 38 F7
Granville, N. Dak., U.S.A. 40 A4
Granville, N.Y., U.S.A. 42 D9
Grass Range 38 C9
Grass Valley, Calif., U.S.A. 38 G3
Grass Valley, Oreg., U.S.A. 38 D3
Grasse 12 E7
Grassy 32 D3
Graulhet 12 E4
's-Gravenhage 16 B2
Gravesend, Australia 32 A5
Gravesend, U.K. 9 F8
Grayling 42 C3
Grays Harbor 38 C1
Grays L. 38 E8
Graz 16 E7
Great Abaco I. 45 B9
Great Australian Bight 30 G5
Great Barrier I. 33 G5
Great Basin 38 G5
Great Basin Nat. Park 38 G6
Great Bear → 36 B7
Great Bear L. 36 B7
Great Bend 40 F5
Great Blasket I. 11 D1
Great Camanoe 45 e
Great Channel 25 E8
Great Driffield = Driffield 8 C7
Great Exuma I. 45 C9
Great Falls 38 C8
Great Inagua I. 45 C10
Great Karoo 29 L4
Great Lake 32 D4
Great Malvern 9 E5
Great Miami → 42 F3
Great Ormes Head 8 D4
Great Ouse → 8 E8
Great Pedro Bluff 44 a
Great Salt L. 38 F7
Great Salt Lake Desert 38 F7
Great Salt Plains L. 41 G5
Great Sandy Desert 30 E3
Great Skellig 11 E1
Great Slave L. 36 B8
Great Smoky Mts. Nat. Park 43 H4
Great Snow Mt. 36 C7
Great Stour = Stour → 9 F9
Great Victoria Desert 30 F4
Great Wall 21 C5
Great Whernside 8 C6
Great Yarmouth 9 E9
Greater Antilles 45 D10
Greater London □ 9 F7
Greater Manchester □ 8 D5
Greater Sunda Is. 23 D3
Greece ■ 15 E9
Greeley, Colo., U.S.A. 40 E2
Greeley, Nebr., U.S.A. 40 E5
Greem-Bell, Ostrov 18 A7
Green 38 E2
Green →, Ky., U.S.A. 42 G2
Green →, Utah, U.S.A. 39 G9
Green B. 42 C2
Green Bay 42 C2
Green C. 32 C5
Green Cove Springs 43 L5
Green River, Utah, U.S.A. 39 G8
Green River, Wyo., U.S.A. 38 F9
Green Valley 39 L8
Greenbush 40 A6
Greencastle 42 F2
Greenfield, Ind., U.S.A. 42 F3
Greenfield, Iowa, U.S.A. 40 E7
Greenfield, Mass., U.S.A. 42 D9
Greenfield, Mo., U.S.A. 41 G8
Greenland ■ 6 C4
Greenland Sea 6 B6
Greenock 10 F4
Greenore 11 B5
Greenore Pt. 11 D5
Greensboro, Ga., U.S.A. 43 J4
Greensboro, N.C., U.S.A. 43 G6
Greensburg, Ind., U.S.A. 42 F3
Greensburg, Kans., U.S.A. 41 G5
Greensburg, Pa., U.S.A. 42 E6
Greenstone Pt. 10 D3
Greenville, Ala., U.S.A. 43 K2
Greenville, Calif., U.S.A. 38 F3
Greenville, Maine, U.S.A. 43 C11
Greenville, Mich., U.S.A. 42 D3
Greenville, Miss., U.S.A. 41 J9
Greenville, Mo., U.S.A. 41 G9
Greenville, N.C., U.S.A. 43 H7
Greenville, Ohio, U.S.A. 42 E3
Greenville, Pa., U.S.A. 42 E5
Greenville, S.C., U.S.A. 43 H4
Greenville, Tenn., U.S.A. 43 G4
Greenville, Tex., U.S.A. 41 J6
Greenwich □ 9 F8
Greenwood, Ark., U.S.A. 41 H7
Greenwood, Ind., U.S.A. 42 F2
Greenwood, Miss., U.S.A. 41 J9
Greenwood, S.C., U.S.A. 43 H4
Gregory 40 D5
Gregory, L. 32 A2
Grenada 41 J10
Grenada ■ 45 E12
Grenfell 32 B4
Grenoble 12 D6
Gresham 38 D2
Gretna 10 F5
Grey → 33 K3
Grey Ra. 30 F7
Greybull 38 D9
Greymouth 31 J13
Greystones 11 C5
Greytown 33 J5
Gridley 38 G3
Griffin 43 J3
Griffith 30 G8
Grimsay 10 D1
Grimsby 8 D7
Grinnell 40 E8
Gris-Nez, C. 12 A4
Grodno = Hrodna 18 D3
Groesbeck 41 K6
Groningen 16 B3
Groom 41 H4
Groote Eylandt 30 C6
Gros Islet 45 f
Gros Piton 45 f
Gros Piton Pt. 45 f
Grossglockner 16 E6
Groton 40 C5
Grove Hill 43 K2
Groves 41 L8
Groveton 42 C10
Groznyy 17 B7
Grudziądz 16 B9
Gruinard B. 10 D3
Grundy Center 40 D8
Gruver 41 G4
Guadalajara, Mexico 44 C4
Guadalajara, Spain 13 B4
Guadalcanal 34 H8
Guadalete → 13 D2
Guadalquivir → 13 D2
Guadalupe 39 J3
Guadalupe → 41 L6
Guadalupe Mts. Nat. Park 41 K2
Guadalupe Peak 41 K2
Guadarrama, Sierra de 13 B4
Guadeloupe ■ 44 b
Guadiana → 13 D2
Guadix 13 D4
Guam ■ 34 F6
Guamúchil 44 B3
Guana I. 45 e
Guanajuato 44 C4
Guane 45 C8
Guangdong □ 21 D6
Guangxi Zhuangzu Zizhiqu □ 21 D5
Guangzhou 21 D6
Guanica 45 d
Guantánamo 45 C9
Guaporé → 46 F5
Guarapuava 48 B6
Guardafui, C. = Asir, Ras 24 D4
Guatemala 44 E6
Guatemala ■ 44 D6
Guaviare → 46 C5
Guayama 45 d
Guayaquil 46 D3
Guayaquil, G. de 46 D2
Guaymas 44 B2
Guéret 12 C4
Guernsey, U.K. 9 H5
Guernsey, U.S.A. 40 D2
Guildford 9 F7
Guilin 21 D6
Guinea ■ 26 F3
Guinea, Gulf of 5 D10
Guinea-Bissau ■ 26 F3
Güines 45 C8
Guingamp 12 B2
Guiyang 20 D5
Guizhou □ 20 D5
Gujarat □ 25 C6
Gulbarga 25 D6
Gulf, The 24 C4
Gulfport 41 K10
Gulgong 32 B4
Gunnbjørn Fjeld 6 C5
Gunnedah 32 B5
Gunnewin 32 A4
Gunningbar Cr. → 32 B4
Gunnison, Colo., U.S.A. 39 G10
Gunnison, Utah, U.S.A. 38 G8
Gunnison → 39 G9
Guntersville 43 H2
Guntur 25 D7
Gurdon 41 J8
Gurley 32 A4
Guryev = Atyraū 18 E6
Gusinoozersk 19 D11
Gustine 39 H3
Guthrie, Okla., U.S.A. 41 H6
Guthrie, Tex., U.S.A. 41 J4
Guttenberg 40 D9
Guyana ■ 46 C7
Guyenne 12 D4
Guymon 41 G4
Guyra 32 B5
Gwabegar 32 B4
Gwādar 24 C5
Gwalior 25 C6
Gweebarra B. 11 B3
Gweedore 11 A3
Gweru 29 H5
Gwinn 42 B2
Gwydir → 32 A4
Gwynedd □ 8 E3
Gyandzha = Gäncä 17 B7
Gyaring Hu 20 C4
Gympie 30 F9
Győr 16 E8
Gyumri 17 B6

H

Ha Tinh 23 B2
Ha'apai Group 31 D16
Haarlem 16 B2
Haast → 33 K2
Hachinohe 22 C7
Ḥadd, Ra's al 24 C4
Haḍramawt 24 D3
Hadrian's Wall 8 B5
Haeju 21 C7
Hagen 16 C3
Hagerman 41 J2
Hagerstown 42 F7
Hagondange 12 B7
Hags Hd. 11 D2
Hague, C. de la 12 B3
Hague, The = 's-Gravenhage 16 B2
Haguenau 12 B7
Haifa = Ḥefa 17 D5
Haikou 21 D6
Ḥā'il 24 C3
Hailar 21 B6
Hailey 38 E6
Hainan □ 21 E5
Haines 38 D5
Haines City 43 L5
Haines Junction 36 B6
Haiphong 20 D5
Haiti ■ 45 D10
Hakodate 22 C7
Ḥalab 24 B2
Halberstadt 16 C5
Halcombe 33 J5
Halden 7 F6
Halesowen 9 E5
Haleyville 43 H2
Halfmoon Bay 33 M2
Halifax, Canada 37 D13
Halifax, U.K. 8 D6
Halīl → 24 C4
Halkirk 10 C5
Hall Pen. 37 B13
Halle 16 C5
Hallett 32 B2
Hallettsville 41 L6
Hallock 40 A6
Halls Creek 30 D4
Halmahera 23 C4
Halmstad 7 F6
Halstead 9 F8
Halton □ 8 D5
Haltwhistle 8 C5
Hamadān 24 B3
Hamāh 24 B2
Hamamatsu 22 F5
Hamar 7 E6
Hamburg, Germany 16 B4
Hamburg, Ark., U.S.A. 41 J9
Hamburg, N.Y., U.S.A. 42 D6
Hämeenlinna 7 E8
Hameln 16 B4
Hamersley Ra. 30 E2
Hami 20 B4
Hamilton, Australia 32 C3
Hamilton, Canada 37 D12
Hamilton, N.Z. 31 H14
Hamilton, U.K. 10 F4
Hamilton, Ala., U.S.A. 43 H1
Hamilton, Mont., U.S.A. 38 C6
Hamilton, N.Y., U.S.A. 42 D8
Hamilton, Ohio, U.S.A. 42 F3
Hamilton, Tex., U.S.A. 41 K5
Hamlet 43 H6
Hamley Bridge 32 B2
Hamlin 41 J4
Hamm 16 C3
Hammerfest 7 C8
Hammond, Ind., U.S.A. 42 E2
Hammond, La., U.S.A. 41 K9
Hammonton 42 F8
Hampden 33 L3
Hampshire □ 9 F6
Hampshire Downs 9 F6
Hampton, Ark., U.S.A. 41 J8
Hampton, Iowa, U.S.A. 40 D8
Hampton, S.C., U.S.A. 43 J5
Hampton, Va., U.S.A. 42 G7
Hancock 40 B10
Handan 21 C6
Hanford 39 H4
Hangayn Nuruu 20 B4
Hangzhou 21 C7
Hangzhou Wan 21 C7
Hankinson 40 B6
Hanksville 39 G8
Hanmer Springs 33 K4
Hanna, Canada 36 C8
Hanna, U.S.A. 38 F10
Hannibal 40 F9
Hannover 16 B4
Hanoi 20 D5
Hanover = Hannover 16 B4
Hanover, N.H., U.S.A. 42 D9
Hanover, Pa., U.S.A. 42 F7
Hans Lollik I. 45 e
Hanson, L. 32 B2
Hanzhong 20 C5
Haparanda 7 D8
Happy 41 H4
Happy Camp 38 F2
Happy Valley-Goose Bay 37 C13
Har Hu 20 C4
Har Us Nuur 20 B4
Harare 29 H6
Harbin 21 B7
Harbor Beach 42 D4
Hardangerfjorden 7 E5
Hardin 38 D10
Hardy, Pte. 45 f
Harer 24 E3
Hargeisa 24 E3
Hari → 23 D2
Haridwar 25 C6
Harlan, Iowa, U.S.A. 40 E7
Harlan, Ky., U.S.A. 43 G4
Harlech 8 E3
Harlem 38 B9
Harlingen 41 M6
Harlow 9 F8
Harlowton 38 C9
Harney Basin 38 E4
Harney L. 38 E4
Harney Peak 40 D3
Härnösand 7 E7
Haroldswick 10 A8
Harricana → 37 C12
Harriman 43 H3
Harris 10 D2
Harris, Sd. of 10 D1
Harris L. 32 B2
Harrisburg, Ill., U.S.A. 41 G10
Harrisburg, Nebr., U.S.A. 40 E3
Harrisburg, Pa., U.S.A. 42 E7
Harrison, Ark., U.S.A. 41 G8
Harrison, Nebr., U.S.A. 40 D3
Harrison, C. 37 C14
Harrisonburg 42 F6
Harrisonville 40 F7
Harrisville 42 C4
Harrodsburg 42 G3
Harrogate 8 C6
Harrow □ 9 F7
Harry S. Truman Reservoir 40 F7
Hart 42 D2
Hart, L. 32 B2
Hartford, Conn., U.S.A. 42 E9
Hartford, Ky., U.S.A. 42 G2
Hartford, S. Dak., U.S.A. 40 D6
Hartford, Wis., U.S.A. 40 D10
Hartford City 42 E3
Hartland Pt. 9 F3
Hartlepool 8 C6
Hartselle 43 H2
Hartshorne 41 H7
Hartsville 43 H5
Hartwell 43 H4
Harvey, Ill., U.S.A. 42 E2
Harvey, N. Dak., U.S.A. 40 B5
Harwich 9 F9
Haryana □ 25 C6
Harz 16 C5
Hasa □ 24 C3
Haskell 41 J5
Haslemere 9 F7
Hastings, N.Z. 33 H6
Hastings, U.K. 9 G8
Hastings, Mich., U.S.A. 42 D3
Hastings, Minn., U.S.A. 40 C8
Hastings, Nebr., U.S.A. 40 E5
Hastings Ra. 32 B5
Hat Yai 23 C2
Hatay = Antalya 17 C4
Hatch 39 K10
Hatfield P.O. 32 B3
Hatgal 20 A5
Hattah 32 B3
Hatteras, C. 43 H8
Hattiesburg 41 K10
Haugesund 7 F5
Hauraki G. 33 G5
Haut Atlas 26 B4
Havana = La Habana 45 C8
Havana 40 E9
Havant 9 G7
Havasu, L. 39 J6
Havel → 16 B6
Havelock, N.Z. 33 J4
Havelock, U.S.A. 43 H7
Haverfordwest 9 F3
Haverhill 42 D10
Havre 38 B9
Havre-St.-Pierre 37 C13
Haw → 43 H6
Hawaiian Is. 35 E12
Hawaiian Ridge 35 E11
Hawarden 40 D6
Hawea, L. 33 L2
Hawera 33 H5
Hawick 10 F6
Hawke B. 33 H6
Hawker 32 B2
Hawkinsville 43 J4
Hawley 40 B6
Hawthorne 38 G4
Hay 32 B3
Hay →, Australia 30 G8
Hay →, Canada 36 B8
Hay-on-Wye 9 E4
Hay River 36 B8
Hay Springs 40 D3
Hayden 38 F10
Hayes 40 C4
Hayes → 36 C10
Hayle 9 G2
Hayling I. 9 G7
Hays 40 F5
Hayward, Calif., U.S.A. 39 G2
Hayward, Wis., U.S.A. 40 B9
Haywards Heath 9 G7
Hazard 42 G4
Hazelton 40 B4
Hazen 40 B4
Hazlehurst, Ga., U.S.A. 43 K4
Hazlehurst, Miss., U.S.A. 41 K9
Hazleton 42 E8
Healdsburg 38 G2
Healdton 41 H6
Healesville 32 C4
Heard I. 5 G13
Hearne 41 K6
Hearst 37 D11
Heart → 40 B4
Heavener 41 H7
Hebbronville 41 M5
Hebei □ 21 C6
Hebel 32 A4
Heber City 38 F8
Heber Springs 41 H9
Hebgen L. 38 D8
Hebrides, Sea of the 10 D2
Hebron, Canada 37 C13
Hebron, N. Dak., U.S.A. 40 B3
Hebron, Nebr., U.S.A. 40 E6
Hecate Str. 36 C6
Hechi 20 D5
Hechuan 20 C5
Hecla 40 C5
Heerlen 12 A6
Ḥefa 17 D5
Hefei 21 C6
Hegang 21 B8
Hei Ling Chau 21 G11
Heidelberg 16 D4
Heilbronn 16 D4
Heilongjiang □ 21 B7
Hejaz = Ḥijāz □ 24 C3
Hekou 20 D5
Helena, Ark., U.S.A. 41 H9
Helena, Mont., U.S.A. 38 C7
Helensburgh 10 E4
Helensville 33 G5
Helgoland 16 A3
Heligoland B. = Deutsche Bucht 16 A4
Hellespont = Çanakkale Boğazı 15 D12
Helmand → 24 B5
Helmsdale 10 C5
Helmsdale → 10 C5
Helper 38 G8
Helsingborg 7 F6
Helsingfors = Helsinki 7 E9
Helsinki 7 E9
Helston 9 G2
Helvellyn 8 C4
Hemel Hempstead 9 F7
Hemet 39 K5
Hemingford 40 D3
Hempstead 41 K6
Henan □ 21 C6
Henderson, Ky., U.S.A. 42 G2
Henderson, N.C., U.S.A. 43 G6
Henderson, Nev., U.S.A. 39 H6
Henderson, Tenn., U.S.A. 43 H1
Henderson, Tex., U.S.A. 41 J7
Hendersonville, N.C., U.S.A. 43 H4
Hendersonville, Tenn., U.S.A. 43 G2
Henggang 21 F11
Hengmen 21 F10
Hengqin Dao 21 G10
Hengyang 21 D6
Henlopen, C. 42 F8
Hennessey 41 G6
Henrietta 41 J5
Henrietta Maria, C. 37 C11
Henry 40 E10
Henryetta 41 H7
Hentiyn Nuruu 21 B5
Henty 32 C4
Heppner 38 D4
Herāt 24 B5
Hereford, U.K. 9 E5
Hereford, U.S.A. 41 H3
Herefordshire □ 9 E5
Herford 16 B4
Herington 40 F6
Herkimer 42 D8
Herm 9 H5
Hermann 40 F9
Hermidale 32 B4
Hermiston 38 D4
Hermosillo 44 B2
Hernando 41 H10
Herne Bay 9 F9
Heroica Nogales = Nogales 44 A2
Herreid 40 C4
Herrin 41 G10
Hertford 9 F7
Hertfordshire □ 9 F7
's-Hertogenbosch 16 C2
Hesperia 39 J5
Hessen □ 16 C4
Hettinger 40 C3
Hewitt 41 K6
Hexham 8 C5
Heysham 8 C5
Heywood 32 C3
Hialeah 43 N5
Hiawatha 40 F7
Hibbing 40 B8
Hibbs B. 32 D4
Hickman 41 G10
Hickory 43 H5
Hicks, Pt. 32 C4
Hidalgo del Parral 44 B3
Higashiōsaka 22 F4
Higgins 41 G4
High Island Res. 21 G11
High Level 36 C8
High Point 43 H6
High Prairie 36 C8
High River 36 C8
High Wycombe 9 F7
Highland □ 10 D4
Highland Park 42 D2
Highmore 40 C5
Ḥijāz □ 24 C3
Hiko 39 H6
Hikurangi, Gisborne, N.Z. 33 H6
Hikurangi, Northland, N.Z. 33 F5
Hildesheim 16 B4
Hill City, Idaho, U.S.A. 38 E6
Hill City, Kans., U.S.A. 40 F5
Hill City, S. Dak., U.S.A. 40 D3
Hillaby, Mt. 45 g
Hillcrest 45 g
Hillsboro, Kans., U.S.A. 40 F6
Hillsboro, N. Dak., U.S.A. 40 B6
Hillsboro, N.H., U.S.A. 42 D10
Hillsboro, Ohio, U.S.A. 42 F4
Hillsboro, Tex., U.S.A. 41 J6
Hillsdale 42 E3
Hillston 32 B4
Hilton Head Island 43 J5
Hilversum 16 B2
Himachal Pradesh □ 25 B6
Himalaya 25 C7
Himeji 22 F4
Ḥimş 24 B2
Hinckley, U.K. 9 E6
Hinckley, U.S.A. 40 B8
Hindmarsh, L. 32 C3
Hindu Kush 25 B6
Hinesville 43 K5
Hingham 38 B8
Hinton 42 G5
Hirosaki 22 C7
Hiroshima 22 F3
Hispaniola 45 D10
Hitachi 22 E7
Hitchin 9 F7
Hjälmaren 7 F7
Ho Chi Minh City = Thanh Pho Ho Chi Minh 23 B2
Hoare B. 37 B13
Hobart, Australia 30 J8
Hobart, U.S.A. 41 H5
Hobbs 41 J3
Hobe Sound 43 M5
Hodgson 36 C10
Hōfu 22 F2
Hogan Group 32 C4
Hoggar = Ahaggar 26 D7
Hohenwald 43 H2
Hohhot 21 B6
Hoisington 40 F5
Hokianga Harbour 33 F4
Hokitika 33 K3
Hokkaidō □ 22 B8
Holbrook, Australia 32 C4
Holbrook, U.S.A. 39 J8
Holden 38 G7
Holdenville 41 H6
Holdrege 40 E5
Holetown 45 g
Holguín 45 C9
Holland 42 D2
Hollandale 41 J9
Hollidaysburg 42 E6
Hollis 41 H5
Hollister, Calif., U.S.A. 39 H3
Hollister, Idaho, U.S.A. 38 E6
Holly Hill 43 L5
Holly Springs 41 H10
Hollywood 43 N5
Holman 36 A8
Holmen 40 D9
Holsworthy 9 G3
Holton 40 F7
Holtville 39 K6
Holy I., Angl., U.K. 8 D3
Holy I., Northumberland, U.K. 8 B6
Holyhead 8 D3
Holyoke, Colo., U.S.A. 40 E3
Holyoke, Mass., U.S.A. 42 D9
Home B. 37 B13
Homedale 38 E5
Homer, Alaska, U.S.A. 36 C4
Homer, La., U.S.A. 41 J8
Homestead 43 N5
Homs = Ḥimş 24 B2
Homyel 18 D4
Hondo 41 L5
Honduras ■ 44 E7
Honduras, G. de 44 D7
Honey L. 38 F3
Hong → 20 D5
Hong Kong □ 21 G11
Hong Kong I. 21 G11
Hongjiang 21 D5
Hongshui He → 21 D5
Hongze Hu 21 C6
Honiara 34 H7
Honiton 9 G4
Honolulu 35 E12
Honshū 22 F6
Hood, Mt. 38 D3
Hood River 38 D3
Hoodsport 38 C2
Hook Hd. 11 D5
Hooker 41 G4
Hooper Bay 36 B3
Hoopeston 42 E2
Hoorn 16 B2
Hoover 43 J2
Hoover Dam 39 J6
Hope 41 J8
Hope, L. 32 A2
Hopedale 37 C13
Hopetoun 32 C3
Hopetown 29 K4
Hopewell 42 G7
Hopkinsville 43 G2
Hopland 38 G2
Hoquiam 38 C2
Horlivka 17 A5
Hormuz, Str. of 24 C4
Horn, Cape = Hornos, C. de 48 H3
Horn, Is. 31 C15
Horn Head 11 A3
Hornavan 7 D7
Hornbeck 41 K8
Hornbrook 38 F2
Horncastle 8 D7
Hornell 42 D7
Hornos, C. de 48 H3
Hornsea 8 D7
Horqin Youyi Qianqi 21 B7
Horse Creek 40 E3
Horsham, Australia 30 H7
Horsham, U.K. 9 F7
Horton 40 F7
Horton → 36 B7
Hot Creek Range 38 G6
Hot Springs, Ark., U.S.A. 41 H8
Hot Springs, S. Dak., U.S.A. 40 D3
Hotan 20 C2
Hotchkiss 39 G10
Hou Hai 21 F10
Houghton 40 B10
Houghton L. 42 C3
Houhora Heads 33 F4
Houlton 43 B12
Houma 41 L9
Houston, Mo., U.S.A. 41 G9
Houston, Tex., U.S.A. 41 L7
Hovd 20 B4
Hove 9 G7
Hövsgöl Nuur 20 A5
Howard, Australia 32 A5
Howard, U.S.A. 40 C6
Howe 38 E7
Howe, C. 30 H9
Howell 42 D4
Howitt, L. 32 A2
Howland I. 34 G10
Howth Hd. 11 C5
Hoy 10 C5
Høyanger 7 E5
Hoylake 8 D4
Hradec Králové 16 C7
Hrodna 18 D3
Hron → 16 E9
Hsinchu 21 D7
Huai He → 21 C6
Huainan 21 C6
Huaiyin 21 C6
Hualapai Peak 39 J7
Huambo 29 G3
Huancayo 46 F3
Huang He → 21 C6
Huangshan 21 D6
Huangshi 21 C6
Huánuco 46 E3
Huascarán 46 E3
Huatabampo 44 B3
Hubbard 41 K6
Hubei □ 21 C6
Hucknall 8 D6
Huddersfield 8 D6
Hudiksvall 7 E7
Hudson, N.Y., U.S.A. 42 D9
Hudson, Wis., U.S.A. 40 C8
Hudson, Wyo., U.S.A. 38 E9
Hudson → 42 E8
Hudson Bay, Nunavut, Canada 37 C11
Hudson Bay, Sask., Canada 36 C9
Hudson Falls 42 D9
Hudson Str. 37 B13
Hue 23 B2
Huelva 13 D2
Huesca 13 A5
Hughenden 30 E7
Hugo, Colo., U.S.A. 40 F3
Hugo, Okla., U.S.A. 41 H7
Hugoton 41 G4
Huize 20 D5
Hull = Kingston upon Hull 8 D7
Hull 37 D12
Hull → 8 D7
Hulun Nur 21 B6
Humacao 45 d
Humber → 8 D7
Humboldt, Canada 36 C9
Humboldt, Iowa, U.S.A. 40 D7
Humboldt, Tenn., U.S.A. 41 H10
Humboldt → 38 F4
Hume, L. 32 C4
Humen 21 F10
Humphreys Peak 39 J8
Hunan □ 21 D6
Hungary ■ 16 E9
Hungerford 32 A3
Hŭngnam 21 C7
Hunsrück 16 D3
Hunstanton 8 E8
Hunter I. 32 D3
Hunter Ra. 32 B5
Hunterville 33 H5
Huntingburg 42 F2
Huntingdon, U.K. 9 E7
Huntingdon, U.S.A. 42 E7
Huntington, Ind., U.S.A. 42 E3
Huntington, Oreg., U.S.A. 38 D5
Huntington, Utah, U.S.A. 38 G8
Huntington, W. Va., U.S.A. 42 F4
Huntington Beach 39 K5
Huntly, N.Z. 33 G5
Huntly, U.K. 10 D6
Huntsville, Canada 37 D12
Huntsville, Ala., U.S.A. 43 H2
Huntsville, Tex., U.S.A. 41 K7
Huonville 32 D4
Hurley, N. Mex., U.S.A. 39 K9
Hurley, Wis., U.S.A. 40 B9
Huron 40 C5
Huron, L. 42 C4
Hurricane 39 H7
Hurunui → 33 K4
Hutchinson, Kans., U.S.A. 41 F6
Hutchinson, Minn., U.S.A. 40 C7
Hutton, Mt. 32 A4
Huzhou 21 C7
Hwang Ho = Huang He → 21 C6
Hyannis, Mass., U.S.A. 42 E10
Hyannis, Nebr., U.S.A. 40 E4
Hyargas Nuur 20 B4
Hyderabad, India 25 D6
Hyderabad, Pakistan 24 C5
Hyères 12 E7
Hyères, Îs. d' 12 E7
Hyndman Peak 38 E6
Hyrum 38 F8
Hysham 38 C10
Hythe 9 F9

I

Ialomiţa → 15 B12
Iaşi 17 A3
Ibadan 26 G6
Ibagué 46 C3
Iberian Peninsula 2 B9
Ibiza = Eivissa 13 C6
Ica 46 F3
Içel = Mersin 17 C4
Iceland ■ 7 B2
Ichihara 22 F7
Ichinomiya 22 F5
Ida Grove 40 D7
Idabel 41 J7
Idaho □ 38 D7
Idaho City 38 E6
Idaho Falls 38 E7
Idar-Oberstein 16 D3
Ife 26 G6
Igarka 18 C9
Iglésias 14 E3
Igloolik 37 B11
Igluligaarjuk 37 B10
Iguaçu, Cat. del 48 B6
Iguala 44 D5
Iisalmi 7 E9
IJsselmeer 16 B2
Ikaluktutiak 36 B9
Ikeda 22 F3
Ilagan 23 B4
Ile → 18 E8
Île-de-France □ 12 B5
Ilesha 26 G6
Ilfracombe 9 F3
Ilhéus 47 F11
Iliamna L. 36 C4
Iligan 23 C4
Ilkeston 8 E6
Ilkley 8 D6
Illampu = Ancohuma, Nevada 46 G5
Iller → 16 D4
Illinois □ 40 E10
Illinois → 40 F9
Iloilo 23 B4
Ilorin 26 G6
Imabari 22 F3
Imbil 32 A5
Imlay 38 F4
Immingham 8 D7
Immokalee 43 M5
Imperatriz 47 E9
Imperial 40 E4
Imperial Dam 39 K6
Imphal 25 C8
Inangahua 33 J3
Inari 7 D9
Inarijärvi 7 D9
Inch'ŏn 21 C7
Incline Village 38 G4
Incomáti → 29 K6
Indalsälven → 7 E7
Independence, Calif., U.S.A. 39 H4
Independence, Iowa, U.S.A. 40 D9
Independence, Kans., U.S.A. 41 G7
Independence, Ky., U.S.A. 42 F3
Independence, Mo., U.S.A. 40 F7
Independence Mts. 38 F5
India ■ 25 C6
Indian → 43 M5
Indian Ocean 5 E13
Indian Springs 39 G6
Indiana 42 E6
Indiana □ 42 F3
Indianapolis 42 F2
Indianola, Iowa, U.S.A. 40 E8
Indianola, Miss., U.S.A. 41 J9
Indigirka → 19 B15
Indio 39 K5
Indonesia ■ 23 D3
Indore 25 C6
Indravati → 25 D7
Indre → 12 C4
Indulkana 32 A1
Indus → 24 C5
Indus, Mouths of the 24 C5
Ingleborough 8 C5
Inglewood, Queens., Australia 32 A5
Inglewood, Vic., Australia 32 C3
Inglewood, N.Z. 33 H5
Inglewood, U.S.A. 39 K4
Ingolstadt 16 D5
Ingomar 38 C10
Inishbofin 11 C1
Inisheer 11 C2
Inishfree B. 11 A3
Inishkea North 11 B1
Inishkea South 11 B1
Inishmaan 11 C2
Inishmore 11 C2
Inishowen Pen. 11 A4
Inishshark 11 C1
Inishturk 11 C1
Inishvickillane 11 D1
Injune 32 A4
Inland Kaikoura Ra. 33 J4
Inn → 16 D6
Innamincka 32 A3
Inner Hebrides 10 E2
Inner Mongolia = Nei Monggol Zizhiqu □ 21 B6
Inner Sound 10 D3
Innsbruck 16 E5
Inny → 11 C4
Inowrocław 16 B9
Insein 25 D8
Interlaken 12 C7
International Falls 40 A8
Inukjuak 37 C12
Inuvik 36 B6
Inveraray 10 E3
Inverbervie 10 E6
Invercargill 31 K12
Inverclyde □ 10 F4
Inverell 32 A5
Invergordon 10 D4
Inverloch 32 C4
Inverness, U.K. 10 D4
Inverness, U.S.A. 43 L4
Inverurie 10 D6
Investigator Group 32 B1
Investigator Str. 32 C2
Inyo Mts. 39 H5
Inyokern 39 J5
Iola 41 G7
Iona 10 E2
Ione 38 G3
Ionia 42 D3
Ionian Is. = Iónioi Nísoi 15 E9
Ionian Sea 15 E7
Iónioi Nísoi 15 E9
Iowa □ 40 D8
Iowa → 40 E9
Iowa City 40 E9
Iowa Falls 40 D8
Iowa Park 41 J5
Ipatinga 47 G10
Ipin = Yibin 20 D5
Ipoh 23 C2
Ipswich, Australia 30 F9
Ipswich, U.K. 9 E9
Ipswich, U.S.A. 40 C5
Iqaluit 37 B13
Iquique 46 H4
Iquitos 46 D4
Iráklion 15 G11
Iran ■ 24 B4
Irapuato 44 C4
Iraq ■ 24 B3
Ireland ■ 11 C4
Irian Jaya = Papua □ 23 D5
Iringa 28 F7
Irish Republic ■ 11 C3
Irish Sea 8 D3
Irkutsk 19 D11
Iron Baron 32 B2
Iron Gate = Portile de Fier 15 B10
Iron Knob 32 B2
Iron Mountain 42 C1
Iron River 40 B10
Ironton, Mo., U.S.A. 41 G9
Ironton, Ohio, U.S.A. 42 F4
Ironwood 40 B9
Irrara Cr. → 32 A4
Irrawaddy → 25 D8
Irtysh → 18 C7
Irunea = Pamplona 13 A5
Irvine, U.K. 10 F4
Irvine, U.S.A. 42 G4
Irvinestown 11 B4
Irving 41 J6
Irymple 32 B3
Isabel 40 C4
Isabela 45 d
Isar → 16 D6
Isère → 12 D6
Isfahan = Eşfahān 24 B4
Ishim → 18 D8
Ishinomaki 22 D7
Ishpeming 42 B2
İskenderun 17 C5
Isla → 10 E5
Islamabad 25 B6
Island L. 36 C10
Island Lagoon 32 B2
Island Pond 42 C10
Islands, B. of 33 F5
Islay 10 F2
Isle of Wight □ 9 G6
Isle Royale Nat. Park 40 B10
Ismâ'ilîya 27 B12
Israel ■ 17 D4
Issoire 12 D5
İstanbul 15 D13
İstanbul Boğazı 15 D13
Istokpoga, L. 43 M5
Istra 14 B6
Istres 12 E6
Istria = Istra 14 B6
Itabuna 47 F11
Itaipú, Reprêsa de 48 B6
Italy ■ 14 C5
Itapipoca 47 D11
Itchen → 9 G6
Ithaca 42 D7
Ivanhoe, Australia 32 B3
Ivanhoe, U.S.A. 40 C6
Ivano-Frankivsk 18 E3
Ivanovo 18 D5
Ivory Coast ■ 26 G4
Ivujivik 37 B12
Ivybridge 9 G4
Iwaki 22 E7
Iwakuni 22 F3
Iwo 26 G6
Izhevsk 18 D6
İzmir 15 E12
İzmit = Kocaeli 17 B3

J

Jabalpur 25 C6
Jaboatão 47 E11
Jackman 43 C10
Jacksboro 41 J5
Jackson, Barbados 45 g
Jackson, Ala., U.S.A. 43 K2
Jackson, Calif., U.S.A. 38 G3
Jackson, Ky., U.S.A. 42 G4
Jackson, Mich., U.S.A. 42 D3
Jackson, Minn., U.S.A. 40 D7
Jackson, Miss., U.S.A. 41 J9
Jackson, Mo., U.S.A. 41 G10
Jackson, Ohio, U.S.A. 42 F4
Jackson, Tenn., U.S.A. 43 H1
Jackson, Wyo., U.S.A. 38 E8
Jackson B. 33 K2
Jackson L. 38 E8
Jacksons 33 K3
Jacksonville, Ala., U.S.A. 43 J3
Jacksonville, Ark., U.S.A. 41 H8
Jacksonville, Fla., U.S.A. 43 K5
Jacksonville, Ill., U.S.A. 40 F9
Jacksonville, N.C., U.S.A. 43 H7
Jacksonville, Tex., U.S.A. 41 K7
Jacksonville Beach 43 K5
Jacmel 45 D10
Jacob Lake 39 H7
Jaén 13 D4
Jaffa = Tel Aviv-Yafo 17 D4
Jaffa, C. 32 C2
Jaffna 25 E7
Jagdalpur 25 D7
Jahrom 24 C4
Jaipur 25 C6
Jakarta 23 D2
Jal 41 J3
Jalapa Enríquez = Xalapa 44 D5
Jalna 25 D6
Jaluit I. 34 G8
Jamaica ■ 44 a
Jambi 23 D2
James →, S. Dak., U.S.A. 40 D6
James →, Va., U.S.A. 42 G7
James B. 37 C11
Jamestown, Australia 32 B2
Jamestown, N. Dak., U.S.A. 40 B5
Jamestown, N.Y., U.S.A. 42 D6
Jammu 25 B6
Jammu & Kashmir □ 25 B6
Jamnagar 25 C6
Jamshedpur 25 C7
Jan Mayen 6 B6
Jandowae 32 A5
Janesville 40 D10
Japan ■ 22 F5
Japan, Sea of 22 D4
Japan Trench 34 D6
Japurá → 46 D5
Jarvis I. 35 H12
Jāsk 24 C4
Jasper, Canada 36 C8
Jasper, Ala., U.S.A. 43 J2
Jasper, Fla., U.S.A. 43 K4
Jasper, Ind., U.S.A. 42 F2
Jasper, Tex., U.S.A. 41 K8
Jaunpur 25 C7
Java = Jawa 23 D3
Java Sea 23 D2
Java Trench 23 D2
Jawa 23 D3
Jaya, Puncak 23 D5
Jayton 41 J4
Jean 39 J6
Jeanerette 41 L9
Jebel, Bahr el → 27 G12
Jedburgh 10 F6
Jedda = Jiddah 24 C2
Jefferson, Iowa, U.S.A. 40 D7
Jefferson, Tex., U.S.A. 41 J7
Jefferson, Mt., Nev., U.S.A. 38 G5
Jefferson, Mt., Oreg., U.S.A. 38 D3
Jefferson City, Mo., U.S.A. 40 F8
Jefferson City, Tenn., U.S.A. 43 G4
Jeffersontown 42 F3
Jeffersonville 42 F3
Jeffrey City 38 E10
Jekyll I. 43 K5
Jelenia Góra 16 C7
Jena, Germany 16 C5
Jena, U.S.A. 41 K8
Jenkins 42 G4
Jennings 41 K8
Jeparit 32 C3
Jequié 47 F10
Jérémie 45 D10
Jerez de la Frontera 13 D2
Jerid, Chott el = Djerid, Chott 26 B7
Jerilderie 32 C4
Jerome 38 E6
Jersey 9 H5
Jersey City 42 E8
Jersey Shore 42 E7
Jerseyville 40 F9
Jerusalem 17 D5
Jervis B. 32 C5
Jesup 43 K5
Jetmore 41 F5
Jhansi 25 C6
Jharkhand □ 25 C7
Jhelum → 25 B6
Jiamusi 21 B8
Ji'an 21 D6
Jiangcheng 20 D5
Jiangmen 21 D6
Jiangsu □ 21 C7
Jiangxi □ 21 D6
Jiaxing 21 C7
Jiddah 24 C2
Jihlava → 16 D8
Jilin 21 B7
Jilin □ 21 B7
Jiménez 44 B4
Jinan 21 C6
Jinchang 20 C5
Jindabyne 32 C4
Jinding 21 G10
Jingdezhen 21 D6
Jinggu 20 D5
Jinhua 21 D6
Jining, Nei Monggol Zizhiqu, China 21 B6
Jining, Shandong, China 21 C6
Jinja 28 D6
Jinsha Jiang → 20 D5
Jinzhou 21 B7
Jiujiang 21 D6
Jixi 21 B8
João Pessoa 47 E12
Jodhpur 25 C6
Johannesburg 29 K5
John Crow Mts. 44 a
John Day 38 D4
John Day → 38 D3
John H. Kerr Reservoir 43 G6
John o' Groats 10 C5
Johnson 41 G4
Johnson City, Tenn., U.S.A. 43 G4
Johnson City, Tex., U.S.A. 41 K5
Johnston I. 35 F11
Johnstown, N.Y., U.S.A. 42 D8
Johnstown, Pa., U.S.A. 42 E6
Johor Baharu 23 C2
Joinville 48 B7
Joliet 42 E1
Joliette 37 D12
Jolo 23 C4
Jonesboro, Ark., U.S.A. 41 H9
Jonesboro, La., U.S.A. 41 J8
Jönköping 7 F6
Jonquière 37 D12
Joplin 41 G7
Jordan 38 C10
Jordan ■ 24 B2
Jordan → 17 D5
Jordan Valley 38 E5
Jos 26 G7
Joseph Bonaparte G. 30 C4
Joshua Tree Nat. Park 39 K5
Jost Van Dyke 45 e
Jotunheimen 7 E5
Jourdanton 41 L5
Juan de Fuca Str. 38 B1
Juan Fernández, Arch. de 35 L20
Juàzeiro do Norte 47 E11
Juchitán 44 D5
Judith → 38 C9
Judith Gap 38 C9
Juiz de Fora 47 H10
Julesburg 40 E3
Juliaca 46 G4
Julian 39 K5
Julianehåb = Qaqortoq 37 B6
Jullundur 25 B6
Junagadh 25 C6
Junction, Tex., U.S.A. 41 K5
Junction, Utah, U.S.A. 39 G7
Junction City, Kans., U.S.A. 40 F6
Junction City, Oreg., U.S.A. 38 D2
Jundiaí 48 A7
Juneau 36 C6
Junee 32 B4
Junggar Pendi 20 B3
Juntura 38 E4
Jura 10 F3
Jura, Mts. du 12 C7
Jura, Sd. of 10 F3
Juruá → 46 D5
Jutland = Jylland 7 F5
Juventud, I. de la 45 C8
Jylland 7 F5
Jyväskylä 7 E9

Mapleton

K

Kabaena 23 D4
Kabetogama 40 A8
Kābul 25 B5
Kābul □ 25 B5
Kabwe 29 G5
Kachchh, Gulf of 25 C5
Kachin □ 25 C8
Kadavu 31 E14
Kadina 32 B2
Kadoka 40 D4
Kaduna 26 F7
Kaesŏng 21 C7
Kagoshima 22 H2
Kahoka 40 E9
Kahramanmaraş 17 C5
Kai, Kepulauan 23 D5
Kaiapoi 33 K4
Kaifeng 21 C6
Kaikohe 33 F4
Kaikoura 33 K4
Kaimanawa Mts. 33 H5
Kaipara Harbour 33 G5
Kaiserslautern 16 D3
Kaitaia 31 H13
Kaitangata 33 M2
Kajaani 7 E9
Kajabbi 30 E7
Kakanui Mts. 33 L3
Kakinada 25 D7
Kalaallit Nunaat = Greenland ■ 6 C4
Kalahari 29 J4
Kalama 38 D2
Kalamazoo 42 D3
Kalamazoo → 42 D2
Kalemie 28 F5
Kalgoorlie-Boulder 30 G3
Kalimantan □ 23 D3
Kalinin = Tver 18 D4
Kaliningrad 16 A10
Kalispell 38 B6
Kalisz 16 C9
Kalkaska 42 C3
Kalmar 7 F7
Kaluga 18 D4
Kama → 18 D6
Kamchatka, Poluostrov 19 D16
Kamchatka Pen. = Kamchatka, Poluostrov 19 D16
Kamensk Uralskiy 18 D7
Kamiah 38 C5
Kamina 28 F5
Kamloops 36 C7
Kampala 28 D6
Kampong Saom 23 B2
Kamyanets-Podilskyy 17 A3
Kamyshin 18 D5
Kanaaupscow → 37 C12
Kanab 39 H7
Kanab → 39 H7
Kananga 28 F4
Kanawha → 42 F4
Kanazawa 22 E5
Kandahar = Qandahār 24 B5
Kandanghaur 23 D2
Kandos 32 B4
Kandy 25 E7
Kane 42 E6
Kane Basin 6 B3
Kangaroo I. 30 H6
Kangean, Kepulauan 23 D3
Kangiqsualujjuaq 37 C13
Kangiqsujuaq 37 B12
Kangirsuk 37 B13
Kaniapiskau = Caniapiscau → 37 C13
Kanin, Poluostrov 18 C5
Kanin Pen. = Kanin, Poluostrov 18 C5
Kaniva 32 C3
Kankakee 42 E2
Kankakee → 42 E1
Kankan 26 F4
Kannapolis 43 H5
Kano 26 F7
Kanpur 25 C7
Kansas □ 40 F6
Kansas → 40 F7
Kansas City, *Kans., U.S.A.* 40 F7
Kansas City, *Mo., U.S.A.* 40 F7
Kansk 19 D10
Kanturk 11 D3
Kanye 29 J5
Kaohsiung 21 D7
Kaolack 26 F2
Kapiti I. 33 J5
Kaplan 41 K8
Kaposvár 16 E8
Kapuas → 23 D2
Kapuas Hulu, Pegunungan 23 C3
Kapunda 32 B2
Kapuni 33 H5
Kaputar 32 B5
Kara Kalpak Republic = Qoraqalpoghistan □ 18 E6
Kara Kum 18 F6
Kara Sea 18 B7
Karachi 24 C5
Karaganda = Qaraghandy 18 E8
Karaklis = Vanadzor 17 B6
Karakoram Ra. 25 B6
Karamay 20 B3
Karamea Bight 33 J3
Karasburg 29 K3
Karawang 23 D2
Karbalā' 24 B3
Karimata, Kepulauan 23 D2
Karimata, Selat 23 D2
Karimunjawa, Kepulauan 23 D3
Karl-Marx-Stadt = Chemnitz 16 C6
Karlskrona 7 F7
Karlsruhe 16 D4
Karlstad, *Sweden* 7 F6
Karlstad, *U.S.A.* 40 A6
Karnataka □ 25 D6
Karnes City 41 L6
Karnische Alpen 14 A5
Kärnten □ 16 E6
Karoonda 32 C2
Karsakpay 18 E7
Karshi = Qarshi 18 F7
Kasai → 28 E3
Kasba L. 36 B9
Kāshān 24 B4
Kashgar = Kashi 20 C2
Kashi 20 C2
Kaskaskia → 40 G10
Kassalâ 27 E13
Kassel 16 C4
Kasson 40 C8
Katahdin, Mt. 43 C11
Katanga □ 28 F4
Katha 25 C8
Katherine → 30 C5
Kathmandu = Katmandu 25 C7
Katmandu 25 C7
Katoomba 32 B5
Katowice 16 C9
Katrine, L. 10 E4
Katsina 26 F7
Kattegat 7 F6
Kaufman 41 J6
Kaukauna 42 C1
Kaunas 18 D3
Kavála 15 D11
Kavieng 30 A9
Kavīr, Dasht-e 24 B4
Kawagoe 22 F6
Kawaguchi 22 F6
Kawasaki 22 F6
Kawerau 33 H6
Kawhia Harbour 33 H5
Kayan → 23 C3
Kaycee 38 E10
Kayenta 39 H8
Kayes 26 F3
Kayseri 17 C5
Kaysville 38 F8
Kazakhstan ■ 18 E7
Kazan 18 D5
Kazan-Rettō 34 E6
Kāzerūn 24 C4
Keady 11 B5
Kearney 40 E5
Kearny 39 K8
Kebnekaise 7 D7
Kebri Dehar 24 E3
Kebumen 23 D2
Kecskemét 16 E9
Kediri 23 D3
Keeling Is. = Cocos Is. 23 E1
Keene 42 D9
Keeper Hill 11 D3
Keetmanshoop 29 K3
Kefallinía 15 E9
Keighley 8 D6
Keith, *Australia* 32 C3
Keith, *U.K.* 10 D6
Keizer 38 D2
Kelang 23 C2
Kellogg 38 C5
Kelowna 36 D8
Kelso, *N.Z.* 33 L2
Kelso, *U.K.* 10 F6
Kelso, *U.S.A.* 38 C2
Keluang 23 C2
Kemerovo 18 D9
Kemi 7 D8
Kemijoki → 7 D8
Kemmerer 38 F8
Kemp, L. 41 J5
Kemp Land 6 D9
Kempsey 32 B5
Kempton 32 D4
Kenai 36 B4
Kendal 8 C5
Kendall, *Australia* 32 B5
Kendall, *U.S.A.* 43 N5
Kendallville 42 E3
Kendari 23 D4
Kenedy 41 L6
Kenitra 26 B4
Kenmare, *Ireland* 11 E2
Kenmare, *U.S.A.* 40 A3
Kenmare River 11 E2
Kennebec 40 D5
Kennebec → 43 D11
Kenner 41 L9
Kennet → 9 F7
Kennett 41 G9
Kennewick 38 C4
Kenogami → 37 C11
Kenora 36 D10
Kenosha 42 D2
Kent 41 K2
Kent □ 9 F8
Kent Group 32 C4
Kent Pen. 36 B9
Kentland 42 E2
Kenton 42 E4
Kentucky □ 42 G3
Kentucky → 42 F3
Kentucky L. 43 G2
Kentville 37 D13
Kentwood 41 K9
Kenya ■ 28 D7
Kenya, Mt. 28 E7
Keokuk 40 E9
Kerala □ 25 D6
Kerang 32 C3
Kerch 17 A5
Kerguelen 5 G13
Kerinci 23 D2
Kérkira 15 E8
Kermadec Is. 34 L10
Kermadec Trench 34 L10
Kermān 24 B4
Kermānshāh = Bākhtarān 24 B3
Kermit 41 K3
Kern → 39 J4
Kerrera 10 E3
Kerrobert 36 C9
Kerrville 41 K5
Kerry □ 11 D2
Kerry Hd. 11 D2
Kerulen → 21 B6
Keswick 8 C4
Ketchikan 36 C6
Ketchum 38 E6
Kettering, *U.K.* 9 E7
Kettering, *U.S.A.* 42 F3
Kettle Falls 38 B4
Kewanee 40 E10
Kewaunee 42 C2
Keweenaw B. 42 B1
Keweenaw Pen. 42 B2
Keweenaw Pt. 42 B2
Key Largo 43 N5
Keynsham 9 F5
Keyser 42 F6
Khabarovsk 19 E14
Khambhat, G. of 25 C6
Khaniá 15 G11
Kharagpur 25 C7
Kharkiv 18 E4
Kharkov = Kharkiv 18 E4
Khartoum = El Khartûm 27 E12
Khaskovo 15 D11
Khatanga 19 B11
Kherson 17 A4
Khíos 15 E12
Khodzent = Khŭjand 18 E7
Khon Kaen 23 B2
Khorrāmshahr 24 B3
Khouribga 26 B4
Khudzhand = Khŭjand 18 E7
Khŭjand 18 E7
Khulna 25 C7
Khurīyā Murīyā, Jazā'ir 24 D4
Khyber Pass 25 B6
Kiama 32 B5
Kicking Horse Pass 36 C8
Kidderminster 9 E5
Kidnappers, C. 33 H6
Kidsgrove 8 D5
Kiel 16 A5
Kiel Canal = Nord-Ostsee-Kanal 16 A4
Kielce 16 C10
Kielder Water 8 B5
Kiev = Kyyiv 18 D4
Kigali 28 E6
Kigoma-Ujiji 28 E5
Kikládhes 15 F11
Kikwit 28 E3
Kilbrannan Sd. 10 F3
Kilcoy 32 A5
Kildare 11 C5
Kildare □ 11 C5
Kilfinnane 11 D3
Kilgore 41 J7
Kilimanjaro 28 E7
Kilkee 11 D2
Kilkeel 11 B5
Kilkenny 11 D4
Kilkenny □ 11 D4
Kilkieran B. 11 C2
Killala 11 B2
Killala B. 11 B2
Killaloe 11 D3
Killarney, *Australia* 32 A5
Killarney, *Ireland* 11 D2
Killary Harbour 11 C2
Killdeer 40 B3
Killeen 41 K6
Killin 10 E4
Killorglin 11 D2
Killybegs 11 B3
Kilmarnock 10 F4
Kilmore 32 C3
Kilrush 11 D2
Kilwinning 10 F4
Kim 41 G3
Kimba 32 B2
Kimball, *Nebr., U.S.A.* 40 E3
Kimball, *S. Dak., U.S.A.* 40 D5
Kimberley, *Australia* 30 D4
Kimberley, *S. Africa* 29 K4
Kimberly 38 E6
Kimmirut 37 B13
Kinabalu, Gunong 23 C3
Kinder Scout 8 D6
Kindersley 36 C9
Kindu 28 E5
King City 39 H3
King George I. 6 D4
King George Is. 37 C11
King I. 30 H7
King William I. 36 B10
Kingaroy 32 A5
Kingfisher 41 H6
Kingman, *Ariz., U.S.A.* 39 J6
Kingman, *Kans., U.S.A.* 41 G5
Kingoonya 32 B2
Kings → 39 H4
Kings Canyon Nat. Park 39 H4
King's Lynn 8 E8
Kings Mountain 43 H5
King's Peak 38 F8
Kingsbridge 9 G4
Kingsburg 39 H4
Kingscote 32 C2
Kingscourt 11 C5
Kingsford 42 C1
Kingsland 43 K5
Kingsley 40 D7
Kingsport 43 G4
Kingston, *Canada* 37 D12
Kingston, *Jamaica* 44 a
Kingston, *N.Z.* 33 L2
Kingston, *N.Y., U.S.A.* 42 E9
Kingston, *Pa., U.S.A.* 42 E8
Kingston South East 32 C2
Kingston upon Hull 8 D7
Kingston-upon-Thames □ 9 F7
Kingstown 45 E12
Kingstree 43 J6
Kingsville 41 M6
Kingussie 10 D4
Kingwood 41 K7
Kinleith 33 H5
Kinnairds Hd. 10 D6
Kinross 10 E5
Kinsale 11 E3
Kinsale, Old Hd. of 11 E3
Kinshasa 28 E3
Kinsley 41 G5
Kinston 43 H7
Kintyre 10 F3
Kintyre, Mull of 10 F3
Kiowa, *Kans., U.S.A.* 41 G5
Kiowa, *Okla., U.S.A.* 41 H7
Kippure 11 C5
Kirensk 19 D11
Kirghizia = Kyrgyzstan ■ 18 E8
Kiribati ■ 34 H10
Kırıkkale 17 C4
Kirinyaga = Kenya, Mt. 28 E7
Kiritimati 35 G12
Kirkby 8 D5
Kirkby Lonsdale 8 C5
Kirkcaldy 10 E5
Kirkcudbright 10 G4
Kirkland Lake 37 D11
Kirksville 40 E8
Kirkūk 24 B3
Kirkwall 10 C6
Kirov 18 D5
Kirovabad = Gäncä 17 B7
Kirovakan = Vanadzor 17 B6
Kirovograd = Kirovohrad 17 A4
Kirovohrad 17 A4
Kirriemuir 10 E5
Kirtland 39 H9
Kiruna 7 D8
Kiryū 22 E6
Kisangani 28 D5
Kishinev = Chişinău 17 A3
Kislovodsk 17 B6
Kissimmee 43 L5
Kissimmee → 43 M5
Kisumu 28 E6
Kit Carson 40 F3
Kitakyūshū 22 G2
Kitami 22 B8
Kitchener 37 D11
Kíthira 15 F10
Kitimat 36 C7
Kittakittaooloo, L. 32 A2
Kittanning 42 E6
Kittery 43 D10
Kitwe 29 G5
Kivu, L. 28 E5
Kiyev = Kyyiv 18 D4
Kızıl Irmak → 17 B5
Kladno 16 C7
Klagenfurt 16 E7
Klaipėda 18 D3
Klamath → 38 F1
Klamath Falls 38 E3
Klamath Mts. 38 F2
Klarälven → 7 F6
Klerksdorp 29 K5
Klickitat 38 D3
Kluane L. 36 B6
Klyuchevskaya, Gora 19 D17
Knaresborough 8 C6
Knighton 9 E4
Knock 11 C3
Knockmealdown Mts. 11 D4
Knossós 15 G11
Knox 42 E2
Knoxville, *Iowa, U.S.A.* 40 E8
Knoxville, *Tenn., U.S.A.* 43 H4
Kōbe 22 F4
København 7 F6
Koblenz 16 C3
Kocaeli 17 B3
Kōchi 22 G3
Kodiak 36 C4
Kodiak I. 36 C4
Koforidua 26 G5
Kōfu 22 F6
Kokand = Qŭqon 18 E8
Kokkola 7 E8
Kokomo 42 E2
Kökshetaū 18 D7
Koksoak → 37 C13
Kokstad 29 L5
Kola Pen. = Kolskiy Poluostrov 7 D11
Kolar 25 D6
Kolhapur 25 D6
Kolkata 25 C7
Köln 16 C3
Kolomna 18 D4
Kolskiy Poluostrov 7 D11
Kolwezi 28 G5
Kolyma → 19 C17
Kolymskoye Nagorye 19 C16
Komandorskiye Ostrova 19 D17
Komatsu 22 E5
Kommunarsk = Alchevsk 17 A5
Kommunizma, Pik 18 F8
Kompong Cham 23 B2
Komsomolets, Ostrov 19 A10
Komsomolsk 19 D14
Kong Frederik VI Kyst 37 B15
Königsberg = Kaliningrad 16 A10
Konin 16 B9
Konya 17 C4
Koocanusa, L. 38 B6
Koonibba 32 B1
Koorawatha 32 B4
Kooskia 38 C6
Kootenay L. 36 D8
Kopet Dagh 24 B4
Kopi 32 B2
Koppeh Dāgh = Kopet Dagh 24 B4
Korçë 15 D9
Korea, North ■ 21 C7
Korea, South ■ 21 C7
Korea Bay 21 C7
Korea Strait 21 C7
Korinthiakós Kólpos 15 E10
Kōriyama 22 E7
Korla 20 B3
Koro 33 C8
Koro Sea 33 C9
Koror 34 G5
Körös → 16 E10
Kortrijk 16 C1
Kos 15 F12
Kosciusko 41 J10
Kosciuszko, Mt. 30 H8
Kosovo □ 15 C9
Kôstî 27 F12
Kostroma 18 D5
Koszalin 16 A8
Kota 25 C6
Kota Baharu 23 C2
Kota Kinabalu 23 C3
Kotabumi 23 D2
Kotka 7 E9
Kotuy → 19 B11
Kotzebue 36 B3
Kounradskiy 18 E8
Kountze 41 K7
Kowloon 21 G11
Kozhikode = Calicut 25 D6
Kra, Isthmus of = Kra, Kho Khot 23 B1
Kra, Kho Khot 23 B1
Kragujevac 15 B9
Krajina 14 B7
Kraków 16 C9
Kramatorsk 17 A5
Krasnodar 17 A5
Krasnoyarsk 19 D10
Krasnýy Luch 17 A5
Krefeld 16 C3
Kremenchuk 17 A4
Kremmling 38 F10
Krishna → 25 D7
Kristiansand 7 F5
Kristiansund 7 E5
Kríti 15 G11
Krivoy Rog = Kryvyy Rih 17 A4
Kroonstad 29 K5
Krung Thep = Bangkok 23 B2
Kruševac 15 C9
Krymskiy Poluostrov = Krymskyy Pivostriv 17 B4
Krymskyy Pivostriv 17 B4
Kryvyy Rih 17 A4
Kuala Belait 23 C3
Kuala Lumpur 23 C2
Kuala Terengganu 23 C2
Kualakapuas 23 D3
Kuantan 23 C2
Kuban → 17 A5
Kuching 23 C3
Kudat 23 C3
Kugluktuk 36 B8
Kuichong 21 F11
Kulwin 32 C3
Kumagaya 22 E6
Kumamoto 22 G2
Kumanovo 15 C9
Kumara 33 K3
Kumasi 26 G5
Kumayri = Gyumri 17 B6
Kumbakonam 25 D6
Kumbarilla 32 A5
Kumbia 32 A5
Kunlun Shan 20 C3
Kunming 20 D5
Kuopio 7 E9
Kupang 23 E4
Kuqa 20 B3
Kür → 17 C7
Kura = Kür → 17 C7
Kurdistan 24 B3
Kure 22 F3
Kurgan 18 D7
Kuril Is. = Kurilskiye Ostrova 19 E15
Kuril Trench 34 C7
Kurilskiye Ostrova 19 E15
Kurnool 25 D6
Kurow 33 L3
Kurri Kurri 32 B5
Kursk 18 D4
Kuruktag 20 B3
Kuruman 29 K4
Kurume 22 G2
Kushiro 22 B9
Kuskokwim B. 36 C3
Kustanay = Qostanay 18 D7
Kütahya 17 C4
Kutaisi 17 B6
Kuujjuaq 37 C13
Kuujjuarapik 37 C12
Kuwait = Al Kuwayt 24 C3
Kuwait ■ 24 C3
Kuybyshev = Samara 18 D6
KwaMashu 29 K6
Kwangju 21 C7
Kwango → 28 E3
Kwangtung = Guangdong □ 21 D6
Kwun Tong 21 G11
Kyabra Cr. → 32 A3
Kyabram 32 C4
Kyancutta 32 B2
Kyangin 25 D8
Kyaukse 25 C8
Kyle of Lochalsh 10 D3
Kyneton 32 C3
Kyogle 32 A5
Kyōto 22 F4
Kyrgyzstan ■ 18 E8
Kyūshū 22 G2
Kyyiv 18 D4
Kyzyl Kum 18 E7
Kzyl-Orda = Qyzylorda 18 E7

L

La Barge 38 E8
La Belle 43 M5
La Ceiba 44 D7
La Coruña = A Coruña 13 A1
La Crescent 40 D9
La Crosse, *Kans., U.S.A.* 40 F5
La Crosse, *Wis., U.S.A.* 40 D9
La Désirade 44 b
La Fayette 43 H3
La Follette 43 G3
La Grande 38 D4
La Grande → 37 C12
La Grange, *Ga., U.S.A.* 43 J3
La Grange, *Ky., U.S.A.* 42 F3
La Grange, *Tex., U.S.A.* 41 L6
La Habana 45 C8
La Junta 41 F3
La Loche 36 C9
La Mancha 13 C4
La Mesa 39 K5
La Moure 40 B5
La Paz, *Bolivia* 46 G5
La Paz, *Mexico* 44 C2
La Perouse Str. 21 B9
La Pine 38 E3
La Plata 48 D5
La Porte, *Ind., U.S.A.* 42 E2
La Porte, *Tex., U.S.A.* 41 L7
La Push 38 C1
La Rioja □ 13 A4
La Roche-sur-Yon 12 C3
La Rochelle 12 C3
La Romana 45 D11
La Ronge 36 C9
La Salle 40 E10
La Spézia 12 D8
La Trinité 44 c
La Tuque 37 D12
La Vega 45 D10
Labasa 33 C8
Labe = Elbe → 16 B4
Labé 26 F3
Laborie 45 f
Labrador 37 C13
Labrador City 37 C13
Labrador Sea 37 C14
Labyrinth, L. 32 B2
Lac La Biche 36 C8
Laccadive Is. = Lakshadweep Is. 25 E6
Lacepede B. 32 C2
Lachlan → 32 B3
Lacombe 36 C8
Laconia 42 D10
Ladoga, L. = Ladozhskoye Ozero 7 E10
Ladozhskoye Ozero 7 E10
Ladysmith, *S. Africa* 29 K5
Ladysmith, *U.S.A.* 40 C9
Lae 34 H6
Lafayette, *Colo., U.S.A.* 40 F2
Lafayette, *Ind., U.S.A.* 42 E2
Lafayette, *La., U.S.A.* 41 K9
Lafayette, *Tenn., U.S.A.* 43 G2
Lagan → 11 B6
Lagos, *Nigeria* 26 G6
Lagos, *Portugal* 13 D1
Laguna 39 J10
Lahat 23 D2
Lahn → 16 C3
Lahore 25 B6
Lahti 7 E9
Lairg 10 C4
Laizhou 21 C6
Lake Andes 40 D5
Lake Arthur 41 K8
Lake Cargelligo 32 B4
Lake Charles 41 K8
Lake City, *Colo., U.S.A.* 39 G10
Lake City, *Fla., U.S.A.* 43 K4
Lake City, *Mich., U.S.A.* 42 C3
Lake City, *Minn., U.S.A.* 40 C8
Lake City, *S.C., U.S.A.* 43 J6
Lake District 8 C4
Lake Havasu City 39 J6
Lake Jackson 41 L7
Lake Junction 38 D8
Lake Mead Nat. Recr. Area 39 J6
Lake Mills 40 D8
Lake Providence 41 J9
Lake Village 41 J9
Lake Wales 43 M5
Lake Worth 43 M5
Lakeba 33 D9
Lakeland 43 M5
Lakeport 38 G2
Lakes Entrance 32 C4
Lakeside, *Ariz., U.S.A.* 39 J9
Lakeside, *Nebr., U.S.A.* 40 D3
Lakeview 38 E3
Lakeville 40 C8
Lakewood, *Colo., U.S.A.* 40 F2
Lakewood, *Ohio, U.S.A.* 42 E5
Lakin 41 G4
Lakota 40 A5
Lakshadweep Is. 25 E6
Lamar, *Colo., U.S.A.* 40 F3
Lamar, *Mo., U.S.A.* 41 G7
Lambay I. 11 C5
Lame Deer 38 D10
Lameroo 32 C3
Lamesa 41 J4
Lamma I. 21 G11
Lammermuir Hills 10 F6
Lamon B. 23 B4
Lamont 38 E10
Lampasas 41 K5
Lampeter 9 E3
Lamy 39 J11
Lanark 10 F5
Lancang Jiang → 20 D5
Lancashire □ 8 D5
Lancaster, *U.K.* 8 C5
Lancaster, *Calif., U.S.A.* 39 J4
Lancaster, *Ky., U.S.A.* 42 G3
Lancaster, *N.H., U.S.A.* 42 C10
Lancaster, *Ohio, U.S.A.* 42 F4
Lancaster, *Pa., U.S.A.* 42 E7
Lancaster, *S.C., U.S.A.* 43 H5
Lancaster, *Wis., U.S.A.* 40 D9
Lancaster Sd. 37 A11
Lander 38 E9
Landes 12 D3
Land's End 9 G2
Lanett 43 J3
Langdon 40 A5
Langholm 10 F5
Langres 12 C6
Langres, Plateau de 12 C6
Langsa 23 C1
Langtry 41 L4
Languedoc 12 E5
Langwang 21 F9
Lannion 12 B2
Lansdowne 32 B5
L'Anse 42 B1
L'Anse la Raye 45 f
Lansing 42 D3
Lantau I. 21 G10
Lanzhou 20 C5
Laoag 23 B4
Laois □ 11 D4
Laon 12 B5
Laona 42 C1
Laos ■ 23 B2
Lapeer 42 D4
Lappland 7 D8
Laptev Sea 19 B13
Laramie 40 E2
Laramie → 38 F11
Laramie Mts. 40 E2
Laredo 41 M5
Largo 43 M4
Largs 10 F4
Larimore 40 B6
Lárisa 15 E10
Larne 11 B6
Larned 40 F5
Larose 41 L9
Larrimah 30 D5
Larvik 7 F6
Las Animas 40 F3
Las Cruces 39 K10
Las Palmas 26 C2
Las Vegas, *N. Mex., U.S.A.* 39 J11
Las Vegas, *Nev., U.S.A.* 39 H6
Lashio 25 C8
Lassen Pk. 38 F3
Lassen Volcanic Nat. Park 38 F3
Latakia = Al Lādhiqīyah 24 B2
Latina 14 D5
Latrobe 32 D4
Lau Fau Shan 21 G10
Lau Group 31 D15
Laughlin 39 J6
Launceston, *Australia* 30 J8
Launceston, *U.K.* 9 G3
Laune → 11 D2
Laurel, *Miss., U.S.A.* 41 K10
Laurel, *Mont., U.S.A.* 38 D9
Laurencekirk 10 E6
Laurens 43 H4
Laurinburg 43 H6
Laurium 42 B1
Lausanne 12 C7
Laut 23 C2
Laut, Pulau 23 D3
Laut Kecil, Kepulauan 23 D3
Lautoka 33 C7
Lavagh More 11 B3
Laval 12 B3
Lawrence, *N.Z.* 33 L2
Lawrence, *Kans., U.S.A.* 40 F7
Lawrence, *Mass., U.S.A.* 42 D10
Lawrenceburg, *Ind., U.S.A.* 42 F3
Lawrenceburg, *Tenn., U.S.A.* 43 H2
Lawrenceville 43 J4
Lawton 41 H5
Laxford, L. 10 C3
Layla 24 C3
Layton 38 F7
Laytonville 38 G2
Lazio □ 14 C5
Le Creusot 12 C6
Le François 44 c
Le Havre 12 B4
Le Lamentin 44 c
Le Mans 12 C4
Le Marin 44 c
Le Mars 40 D6
Le Prêcheur 44 c
Le Puy-en-Velay 12 D5
Le Robert 44 c
Le St-Esprit 44 c
Le Sueur 40 C8
Lea → 9 F8
Lead 40 C3
Leadville 39 G10
Leaf → 41 K10
Leamington 38 G7
Leamington Spa = Royal Leamington Spa 9 E6
Leane, L. 11 D2
Leatherhead 9 F7
Leavenworth, *Kans., U.S.A.* 40 F7
Leavenworth, *Wash., U.S.A.* 38 C3
Lebanon, *Ind., U.S.A.* 42 E2
Lebanon, *Kans., U.S.A.* 40 F5
Lebanon, *Ky., U.S.A.* 42 G3
Lebanon, *Mo., U.S.A.* 41 G8
Lebanon, *N.H., U.S.A.* 42 D9
Lebanon, *Oreg., U.S.A.* 38 D2
Lebanon, *Pa., U.S.A.* 42 E7
Lebanon, *Tenn., U.S.A.* 43 G2
Lebanon ■ 17 D5
Lebec 39 J4
Lecce 15 D8
Lee → 11 E3
Leech L. 40 B7
Leeds, *U.K.* 8 D6
Leeds, *U.S.A.* 43 J2
Leek 8 D5
Leesburg 43 L5
Leesville 41 K8
Leeton 32 B4
Leeuwarden 16 B2
Leeuwin, C. 30 G2
Leeward Is. 45 D12
Leganés 13 B4
Legazpi 23 B4
Legnica 16 C8
Leh 25 B6
Lehigh Acres 43 M5
Leicester 9 E6
Leicestershire □ 9 E6
Leiden 16 B2
Leine → 16 B4
Leinster □ 11 C4
Leinster, Mt. 11 D5
Leipzig 16 C6
Leith 10 F5
Leith Hill 9 F7
Leitrim 11 B3
Leitrim □ 11 B4
Leizhou Bandao 21 D6
Leland, *Mich., U.S.A.* 42 C3
Leland, *Miss., U.S.A.* 41 J9
Léman, L. 12 C7
Lemhi Ra. 38 D7
Lemmon 40 C3
Lemoore 39 H4
Lena → 19 B13
Leninabad = Khŭjand 18 E7
Leninakan = Gyumri 17 B6
Leningrad = Sankt-Peterburg 18 D4
Leninogorsk 18 D9
Leninsk-Kuznetskiy 18 D9
Lennox 40 D6
Lenoir 43 H5
Lenoir City 43 H3
Lens 12 A5
Leodhas = Lewis 10 C2
Leola 40 C5
Leominster, *U.K.* 9 E5
Leominster, *U.S.A.* 42 D10
León, *Mexico* 44 C4
León, *Nic.* 44 E7
León, *Spain* 13 A3
Leon, *U.S.A.* 40 E8
Leon → 41 K6
Leonardtown 42 F7
Leongatha 32 C4
Leonora 30 F3
Leoti 40 F4
Lérida = Lleida 13 B6
Lerwick 10 A7
Les Cayes 45 D10
Les Sables-d'Olonne 12 C3
Lesbos = Lésvos 15 E12
Leshan 20 D5
Leskovac 15 C9
Lesotho ■ 29 K5
Lesser Antilles 45 E12
Lesser Slave L. 36 C8
Lesser Sunda Is. 23 D4
Lésvos 15 E12
Leszno 16 C8
Letchworth 9 F7
Lethbridge 36 D8
Leti, Kepulauan 23 D4
Letterkenny 11 B4
Leuven 16 C2
Levelland 41 J3
Leven 10 E6
Leven, L. 10 E5
Levin 33 J5
Lévis 37 D12
Levittown 42 E9
Levkás 15 E9
Levkôsia = Nicosia 17 C4
Lewes, *U.K.* 9 G8
Lewes, *U.S.A.* 42 F8
Lewis 10 C2
Lewis, Butt of 10 C2
Lewis Range 38 C7
Lewisburg, *Tenn., U.S.A.* 43 H2
Lewisburg, *W. Va., U.S.A.* 42 G5
Lewisporte 37 D14
Lewiston, *Idaho, U.S.A.* 38 C5
Lewiston, *Maine, U.S.A.* 43 C11
Lewistown, *Mont., U.S.A.* 38 C9
Lewistown, *Pa., U.S.A.* 42 E7
Lexington, *Ill., U.S.A.* 40 E10
Lexington, *Ky., U.S.A.* 42 F3
Lexington, *Mo., U.S.A.* 40 F8
Lexington, *N.C., U.S.A.* 43 H5
Lexington, *Nebr., U.S.A.* 40 E5
Lexington, *Tenn., U.S.A.* 43 H1
Lexington, *Va., U.S.A.* 42 G6
Lexington Park 42 F7
Leyburn 8 C6
Leyland 8 D5
Leyte □ 23 B4
Lhasa 20 D4
Lhazê 20 D3
L'Hospitalet de Llobregat 13 B7
Lianyungang 21 C6
Liaoning □ 21 B7
Liaoyang 21 B7
Liaoyuan 21 B7
Liard → 36 B7
Libau = Liepāja 18 D3
Libby 38 B6
Liberal 41 G4
Liberec 16 C7
Liberia ■ 26 G4
Liberty, *Mo., U.S.A.* 40 F7
Liberty, *N.Y., U.S.A.* 42 E8
Liberty, *Tex., U.S.A.* 41 K7
Lîbîya, Sahrâ' 27 C10
Libourne 12 D3
Libreville 28 D1
Libya ■ 27 C9
Libyan Desert = Lîbîya, Sahrâ' 27 C10
Lichfield 9 E6
Lichinga 29 G7
Licking → 42 F3
Liechtenstein ■ 12 C8
Liège 16 C2
Liepāja 18 D3
Liffey → 11 C5
Lifford 11 B4
Lightning Ridge 32 A4
Liguria □ 12 D8
Ligurian Sea 14 C3
Lijiang 20 D5
Likasi 28 G5
Lille 12 A5
Lillehammer 7 E6
Lilongwe 29 G6
Lima, *Peru* 46 F3
Lima, *Mont., U.S.A.* 38 D7
Lima, *Ohio, U.S.A.* 42 E3
Limavady 11 A5
Limbe 28 D1
Limeira 47 H9
Limerick 11 D3
Limerick □ 11 D3
Limfjorden 7 F5
Límnos 15 E11
Limoges 12 D4
Limón, *Costa Rica* 45 F8
Limon, *U.S.A.* 40 F3
Limousin 12 D4
Limoux 12 E5
Limpopo → 29 K6
Linares, *Mexico* 44 C5
Linares, *Spain* 13 C4
Lincoln, *N.Z.* 33 K4
Lincoln, *U.K.* 8 D7
Lincoln, *Ill., U.S.A.* 40 E10
Lincoln, *Kans., U.S.A.* 40 F5
Lincoln, *Maine, U.S.A.* 43 C11
Lincoln, *N. Mex., U.S.A.* 39 K11
Lincoln, *Nebr., U.S.A.* 40 E6
Lincoln City 38 D1
Lincoln Sea 6 A4
Lincolnshire □ 8 D7
Lincolnshire Wolds 8 D7
Lincolnton 43 H5
Lind 38 C4
Linden, *Ala., U.S.A.* 43 J2
Linden, *Tex., U.S.A.* 41 J7
Lindesnes 7 F5
Lindsay, *Calif., U.S.A.* 39 H4
Lindsay, *Okla., U.S.A.* 41 H6
Lindsborg 40 F6
Lingding Yang 21 G10
Lingga, Kepulauan 23 D2
Lingle 40 D2
Linhai 21 D7
Linhares 47 G10
Linköping 7 F7
Linnhe, L. 10 E3
Linstead 44 a
Linton, *Ind., U.S.A.* 42 F2
Linton, *N. Dak., U.S.A.* 40 B4
Linxia 20 C5
Linz 16 D7
Lion, G. du 12 E6
Lipa 23 B4
Lipetsk 18 D4
Lippe → 16 C3
Lipscomb 41 G4
Liptrap C. 32 C4
Liquillo, Sierra de 45 d
Lisboa 13 C1
Lisbon = Lisboa 13 C1
Lisbon 40 B6
Lisbon Falls 43 D10
Lisburn 11 B5
Liscannor B. 11 D2
Lisianski I. 34 E10
Lisichansk = Lysychansk 17 A5
Lisieux 12 B4
Lismore, *Australia* 30 F9
Lismore, *Ireland* 11 D4
Liston 32 A5
Listowel 11 D2
Litchfield, *Ill., U.S.A.* 40 F10
Litchfield, *Minn., U.S.A.* 40 C7
Lithgow 32 B5
Little Andaman I. 25 D8
Little Barrier I. 33 G5
Little Belt Mts. 38 C8
Little Blue → 40 F6
Little Colorado → 39 H8
Little Falls, *Minn., U.S.A.* 40 C7
Little Falls, *N.Y., U.S.A.* 42 D8
Little Fork → 40 A8
Little Humboldt → 38 F5
Little Minch 10 D2
Little Missouri → 40 B3
Little Ouse → 9 E9
Little Red → 41 H9
Little River 33 K4
Little Rock 41 H8
Little Sable Pt. 42 D2
Little Sioux → 40 E6
Little Snake → 38 F9
Little Wabash → 42 G1
Little White → 40 D4
Littlefield 41 J3
Littlehampton 9 G7
Littleton 42 C10
Liuzhou 21 D5
Live Oak 43 K4
Livermore, Mt. 41 K2
Livermore Falls 43 C11
Liverpool, *Canada* 37 D13
Liverpool, *U.K.* 8 D4
Liverpool Bay 8 D4
Liverpool Plains 32 B5
Liverpool Ra. 32 B5
Livingston, *U.K.* 10 F5
Livingston, *Ala., U.S.A.* 43 J1
Livingston, *Mont., U.S.A.* 38 D8
Livingston, *S.C., U.S.A.* 43 J5
Livingston, *Tenn., U.S.A.* 43 G3
Livingston, *Tex., U.S.A.* 41 K7
Livingston, L. 41 K7
Livingstone 29 H5
Livonia 42 D4
Livorno 14 C4
Lizard Pt. 9 H2
Ljubljana 14 A6
Llandeilo 9 F4
Llandovery 9 F4
Llandrindod Wells 9 E4
Llandudno 8 D4
Llanelli 9 F3
Llangollen 8 E4
Llanidloes 9 E4
Llano 41 K5
Llano → 41 K5
Llano Estacado 41 J3
Llanos 46 C4
Llanwrtyd Wells 9 E4
Lleida 13 B6
Lleyn Peninsula 8 E3
Lloret de Mar 13 B7
Lloydminster 36 C9
Loa 39 G8
Lobatse 29 K5
Lobito 29 G2
Lochaber 10 E3
Locharbriggs 10 F5
Lochboisdale 10 D1
Loches 12 C4
Lochgilphead 10 E3
Lochinver 10 C3
Lochmaddy 10 D1
Lochnagar 10 E5
Lochy, L. 10 E4
Lock 32 B2
Lock Haven 42 E7
Lockerbie 10 F5
Lockhart 41 L6
Lockney 41 H4
Lockport 42 D6
Lodge Grass 38 D10
Lodgepole Cr. → 40 E2
Lodi 38 G3
Łódź 16 C9
Lofoten 7 D6
Logan, *Iowa, U.S.A.* 40 E7
Logan, *Ohio, U.S.A.* 42 F4
Logan, *Utah, U.S.A.* 38 F8
Logan, *W. Va., U.S.A.* 42 G5
Logan, Mt. 36 B5
Logansport, *Ind., U.S.A.* 42 E2
Logansport, *La., U.S.A.* 41 K8
Logroño 13 A4
Loir → 12 C3
Loire → 12 C2
Lolo 38 C6
Loma 38 C8
Lombárdia □ 12 D8
Lombardy = Lombárdia □ 12 D8
Lomblen 23 D4
Lombok 23 D3
Lomé 26 G6
Lomond, L. 10 E4
Lompoc 39 J3
London, *Canada* 37 D11
London, *U.K.* 9 F7
London, *Ky., U.S.A.* 42 G3
London, *Ohio, U.S.A.* 42 F4
London, Greater □ 9 F7
Londonderry 11 B4
Londonderry □ 11 B4
Londonderry, C. 30 C4
Londrina 48 A6
Lone Pine 39 H4
Long B. 43 J6
Long Beach, *Calif., U.S.A.* 39 K4
Long Beach, *Wash., U.S.A.* 38 C1
Long Branch 42 E9
Long Creek 38 D4
Long Eaton 8 E6
Long I., *Bahamas* 45 C9
Long I., *Ireland* 11 E2
Long I., *U.S.A.* 42 E9
Long Island Sd. 42 E9
Long Lake 42 D8
Long Prairie → 40 C7
Long Xuyen 23 B2
Longbenton 8 B6
Longboat Key 43 M4
Longford, *Australia* 32 D4
Longford, *Ireland* 11 C4
Longford □ 11 C4
Longhua 21 F11
Longmont 40 E2
Longreach 30 E7
Longview, *Tex., U.S.A.* 41 J7
Longview, *Wash., U.S.A.* 38 C2
Longxue Dao 21 F10
Lonoke 41 H9
Lons-le-Saunier 12 C6
Looe 9 G3
Lookout, C. 43 H7
Loop Hd. 11 D2
Lop Nur 20 B4
Lopez, C. 28 E1
Lora Cr. → 32 A2
Lorain 42 E4
Lorca 13 D5
Lord Howe I. 34 L7
Lord Howe Ridge 34 L8
Lordsburg 39 K9
Lorient 12 C2
Lorn 10 E3
Lorn, Firth of 10 E3
Lorne 32 C3
Lorraine □ 12 B7
Los Alamos 39 J10
Los Angeles, *Chile* 48 D2
Los Angeles, *U.S.A.* 39 K4
Los Angeles Aqueduct 39 J5
Los Banos 39 H3
Los Lunas 39 J10
Los Mochis 44 B3
Lossiemouth 10 D5
Lostwithiel 9 G3
Lot → 12 D4
Loughborough 8 E6
Loughrea 11 C3
Loughros More B. 11 B3
Louis Trichardt 29 J5
Louis XIV, Pte. 37 C12
Louisa 42 F4
Louisiade Arch. 34 J7
Louisiana 40 F9
Louisiana □ 41 K9
Louisville, *Ky., U.S.A.* 42 F3
Louisville, *Miss., U.S.A.* 41 J10
Loup City 40 E5
Lourdes 12 E3
Louth, *Australia* 32 B4
Louth, *Ireland* 11 C5
Louth, *U.K.* 8 D7
Louth □ 11 C5
Louvain = Leuven 16 C2
Loveland 40 E2
Lovell 38 D9
Lovelock 38 F4
Loving 41 J2
Lovington 41 J3
Lowell 42 D10
Lower Alkali L. 38 F3
Lower California = Baja California 44 A1
Lower Hutt 33 J5
Lower Red L. 40 B7
Lower Saxony = Niedersachsen □ 16 B4
Lowestoft 9 E9
Lowville 42 D8
Loxton 32 B3
Loyauté, Îs. 34 K8
Lu Wo 21 F11
Lualaba → 28 D5
Luanda 28 F2
Luang Prabang 23 B2
Luanshya 29 G5
Luapula → 28 F5
Lubbock 41 J4
Lübeck 16 B5
Lublin 7 G8
Lubumbashi 29 G5
Lucania, Mt. 36 B5
Luce Bay 10 G4
Lucea 44 a
Lucedale 43 K1
Lucena 23 B4
Lucerne = Luzern 12 C8
Lucknow 25 C7
Lüda = Dalian 21 C7
Lüderitz 29 K3
Ludhiana 25 B6
Ludington 42 D2
Ludlow, *U.K.* 9 E5
Ludlow, *U.S.A.* 39 J5
Ludwigshafen 16 D4
Lufkin 41 K7
Lugano 12 C8
Lugansk = Luhansk 17 A5
Lugnaquillia 11 D5
Lugo 13 A2
Luhansk 17 A5
Luimneach = Limerick 11 D3
Luing 10 E3
Lule älv → 7 D8
Luleå 7 D8
Luling 41 L6
Lumberton 43 H6
Lumsden 33 L2
Lundy 9 F3
Lune → 8 C5
Lüneburger Heide 16 B5
Lunéville 12 B7
Luni → 25 C6
Luning 38 G4
Luoyang 21 C6
Lupanshui 20 D5
Luray 42 F6
Lurgan 11 B5
Lusaka 29 H5
Lusk 40 D2
Lūt, Dasht-e 24 B4
Luton 9 F7
Lutselke 36 B8
Lutsk 18 D3
Luverne, *Ala., U.S.A.* 43 K2
Luverne, *Minn., U.S.A.* 40 D6
Luxembourg 12 B7
Luxembourg ■ 12 B7
Luxi 20 D4
Luzern 12 C8
Luzhou 20 D5
Luzon 23 B4
Lviv 18 E3
Lvov = Lviv 18 E3
Lyakhovskiye, Ostrova 19 B15
Lybster 10 C5
Lydenburg 29 K6
Lyell 33 J4
Lyman 38 F8
Lyme B. 9 G4
Lyme Regis 9 G5
Lymington 9 G6
Lynchburg 42 G6
Lynd Ra. 32 A4
Lynden 38 B2
Lyndhurst 32 B2
Lyndonville 42 C9
Lynn 42 D10
Lynn Lake 36 C9
Lynton 9 F4
Lyon 12 D6
Lyonnais 12 D6
Lyons, *Ga., U.S.A.* 43 J4
Lyons, *Kans., U.S.A.* 40 F5
Lysychansk 17 A5
Lytham St. Anne's 8 D4
Lyttelton 33 K4

M

Ma'ān 24 B2
Ma'anshan 21 C6
Maas → 16 C2
Maastricht 12 A6
Mablethorpe 8 D8
McAlester 41 H7
McAllen 41 M5
MacAlpine L. 36 B9
Macapá 47 C8
Macau 21 G10
McCall 38 D5
McCamey 41 K3
McCammon 38 E7
Macclenny 43 K4
Macclesfield 8 D5
M'Clintock Chan. 36 A9
McCloud 38 F2
M'Clure Str. 6 B1
McClusky 40 B4
McComb 41 K9
McConaughy, L. 40 E4
McCook 40 E4
McDermitt 38 F5
McDonald Is. 5 G13
MacDonnell Ranges 30 E5
Macduff 10 D6
Macedonia = Makedhonía □ 15 D10
Macedonia ■ 15 D9
Maceió 47 E11
Macfarlane, L. 32 B2
McGehee 41 J9
McGill 38 G6
Macgillycuddy's Reeks 11 E2
McGregor 40 D9
McGregor Ra. 32 A3
Machakos 28 E7
Machala 46 D3
Machias 43 C12
Machynlleth 9 E4
McIntosh 40 C4
Macintyre → 32 A5
Mackay, *Australia* 30 E8
Mackay, *U.S.A.* 38 E7
Mackay, L. 30 E4
McKeesport 42 E6
Mackenzie 36 C7
McKenzie 43 G1
Mackenzie → 36 B6
McKenzie → 38 D2
Mackenzie Mts. 36 B6
Mackinaw City 42 C3
McKinley, Mt. 36 B4
McKinley Sea 6 A6
McKinney 41 J6
Macksville 32 B5
McLaughlin 40 C4
Maclean 32 A5
McLean 41 H4
McLeansboro 40 F10
Maclear 29 L5
Macleay → 32 B5
McLoughlin, Mt. 38 E2
McMinnville, *Oreg., U.S.A.* 38 D2
McMinnville, *Tenn., U.S.A.* 43 H3
McMurdo Sd. 6 E15
Macomb 40 E9
Mâcon, *France* 12 C6
Macon, *Ga., U.S.A.* 43 J4
Macon, *Miss., U.S.A.* 43 J1
Macon, *Mo., U.S.A.* 40 F8
McPherson 40 F6
McPherson Ra. 32 A5
Macquarie → 32 B4
Macquarie Harbour 32 D4
Macquarie Is. 34 N7
Macroom 11 E3
Madadeni 29 K6
Madagascar ■ 29 J9
Madang 30 B8
Madeira 26 B2
Madeira → 46 D7
Madeleine, Îs. de la 37 D13
Madera 39 H3
Madhya Pradesh □ 25 C6
Madill 41 H6
Madīnat ash Sha'b 24 D3
Madison, *Fla., U.S.A.* 43 K4
Madison, *Ind., U.S.A.* 42 F3
Madison, *Nebr., U.S.A.* 40 E6
Madison, *S. Dak., U.S.A.* 40 D6
Madison, *Wis., U.S.A.* 40 D10
Madison → 38 D8
Madison Heights 42 G6
Madisonville, *Ky., U.S.A.* 42 G2
Madisonville, *Tex., U.S.A.* 41 K7
Madiun 23 D3
Madrakah, Ra's al 24 D4
Madras = Chennai 25 D7
Madras 38 D3
Madre, Laguna 41 M6
Madre de Dios → 46 F5
Madre de Dios, I. 48 G1
Madre Occidental, Sierra 44 B3
Madre Oriental, Sierra 44 C5
Madrid 13 B4
Madura 23 D3
Madurai 25 E6
Maebashi 22 E6
Maesteg 9 F4
Mafeteng 29 K5
Maffra 32 C4
Magadan 19 D16
Magallanes, Estrecho de 48 G2
Magdalena 39 J10
Magdalena → 46 A4
Magdeburg 16 B5
Magee 41 K10
Magelang 23 D3
Magellan's Str. = Magallanes, Estrecho de 48 G2
Maggiore, Lago 12 D8
Maggotty 44 a
Magherafelt 11 B5
Magnitogorsk 18 D6
Magnolia, *Ark., U.S.A.* 41 J8
Magnolia, *Miss., U.S.A.* 41 K9
Mahakam → 23 D3
Mahalapye 29 J5
Mahanadi → 25 C7
Maharashtra □ 25 C6
Maheno 33 L3
Mahia Pen. 33 H6
Mahilyow 18 D4
Mahnomen 40 B7
Maidenhead 9 F7
Maidstone 9 F8
Maiduguri 27 F8
Main →, *Germany* 16 D4
Main →, *U.K.* 11 B5
Maine 12 C3
Maine □ 43 C11
Maine → 11 D2
Mainland, *Orkney, U.K.* 10 C5
Mainland, *Shet., U.K.* 10 A7
Mainz 16 C4
Maitland, *N.S.W., Australia* 32 B5
Maitland, *S. Austral., Australia* 32 B2
Majorca = Mallorca 13 C7
Makale 23 D3
Makasar = Ujung Pandang 23 D3
Makasar, Selat 23 D3
Makedhonía □ 15 D10
Makeyevka = Makiyivka 17 A5
Makgadikgadi Salt Pans 29 J5
Makhachkala 17 B7
Makiyivka 17 A5
Makkah 24 C2
Mal B. 11 D2
Malabar Coast 25 D6
Malabo = Rey Malabo 28 D1
Malacca, Str. of 23 C2
Malad City 38 E7
Málaga 13 D3
Malahide 11 C5
Malaita 31 B11
Malakula 31 D12
Malang 23 D3
Malanje 28 F3
Mälaren 7 F7
Malatya 17 C5
Malawi ■ 29 G6
Malawi, L. = Nyasa, L. 29 G6
Malaysia ■ 23 C3
Malbooma 32 B1
Malden 41 G10
Malden I. 35 H12
Maldives ■ 25 E6
Maleny 32 A5
Malheur → 38 D5
Malheur L. 38 E4
Mali ■ 26 E5
Malin Hd. 11 A4
Malin Pen. 11 A4
Malines = Mechelen 16 C2
Mallacoota Inlet 32 C4
Mallaig 10 D3
Mallorca 13 C7
Mallow 11 D3
Malmö 7 F6
Malone 42 C8
Malpelo, I. de 35 G19
Malta, *Idaho, U.S.A.* 38 E7
Malta, *Mont., U.S.A.* 38 B10
Malta ■ 14 G6
Malton 8 C7
Maluku 23 D4
Malvern 41 H8
Malvern Hills 9 E5
Malvinas, Is. = Falkland Is. □ 48 G5
Mammoth 39 K8
Mammoth Cave Nat. Park 42 G3
Mamoré → 46 F5
Man, I. of 8 C3
Manado 23 C4
Managua 44 E7
Manapouri 33 L1
Manapouri, L. 33 L1
Manas 20 B3
Manassa 39 H11
Manatí 45 d
Manaus 46 D7
Manchester, *U.K.* 8 D5
Manchester, *Ga., U.S.A.* 43 J3
Manchester, *Iowa, U.S.A.* 40 D9
Manchester, *Ky., U.S.A.* 42 G4
Manchester, *N.H., U.S.A.* 42 D10
Manchester, *Tenn., U.S.A.* 43 H2
Manchuria = Dongbei 21 B7
Mandal 7 F5
Mandalay 25 C8
Mandan 40 B4
Mandeville 44 a
Mandsaur 25 C6
Mangalore 25 D6
Mangaweka 33 H5
Mangnai 20 C4
Mangole 23 D4
Mangonui 33 F4
Mangum 41 H5
Manhattan 40 F6
Manicouagan → 37 D13
Manicouagan, Rés. 37 C13
Manihiki 35 J11
Manila, *Phil.* 23 B4
Manila, *U.S.A.* 38 F9
Manila B. 23 B4
Manilla 32 B5
Manipur □ 25 C8
Manistee 42 C2
Manistee → 42 C2
Manistique 42 C2
Manitoba □ 36 C10
Manitoba, L. 36 C10
Manitou Is. 42 C3
Manitou Springs 40 F2
Manitoulin I. 37 D11
Manitowoc 42 C2
Manizales 46 B3
Mankato, *Kans., U.S.A.* 40 F5
Mankato, *Minn., U.S.A.* 40 C8
Mannahill 32 B3
Mannar 25 E6
Mannar, G. of 25 E6
Mannheim 16 D4
Manning, *Canada* 36 C8
Manning, *U.S.A.* 43 J5
Mannum 32 B2
Manokwari 23 D5
Manosque 12 E6
Mansel I. 37 B11
Mansfield, *Australia* 32 C4
Mansfield, *U.K.* 8 D6
Mansfield, *La., U.S.A.* 41 J8
Mansfield, *Ohio, U.S.A.* 42 E4
Mantalingajan, Mt. 23 C3
Manteca 39 H3
Manteo 43 H8
Mantes-la-Jolie 12 B4
Manti 38 G8
Manton 42 C3
Mántova 14 B4
Mantua = Mántova 14 B4
Manu'a Is. 33 B14
Manukau 33 G5
Many 41 K8
Manzanillo, *Cuba* 45 C9
Manzanillo, *Mexico* 44 D4
Manzano Mts. 39 J10
Manzhouli 21 B6
Maoming 21 D6
Mapam Yumco 20 C3
Mapia, Kepulauan 23 C5
Mapleton 38 D2

Maputo

Maputo 29 K6
Maquan He 20 D3
Maquoketa 40 D9
Mar Chiquita, L. 48 C4
Mar del Plata 48 D5
Marabá 47 E9
Maracaibo 46 A4
Maracaibo, L. de 46 B4
Maracay 46 A5
Marajó, I. de 47 D9
Marana 39 K8
Maranhão = São Luís 47 D10
Maranoa → 32 A4
Marañón → 46 D4
Maraş = Kahramanmaraş 17 C5
Marathon 41 K3
Marbella 13 D3
Marble Falls 41 K5
March 9 E8
Marche 12 C4
Marco 43 N5
Marcus I. = Minami-Tori-Shima 34 E7
Marcus Necker Ridge 34 F9
Maree, L. 10 D3
Marengo 40 E8
Marfa 41 K2
Margarita, I. de 46 A6
Margate 9 F9
Mārgow, Dasht-e 24 B5
Maria I. 32 D4
Maria van Diemen, C. 33 F4
Mariana Trench 34 F6
Marianna, *Ark., U.S.A.* 41 H9
Marianna, *Fla., U.S.A.* 43 K3
Marias → 38 C8
Maribor 14 A6
Maricopa, *Ariz., U.S.A.* 39 K7
Maricopa, *Calif., U.S.A.* 39 J4
Marie Byrd Land 6 E18
Marie-Galante 44 b
Mariental 29 J3
Marietta, *Ga., U.S.A.* 43 J3
Marietta, *Ohio, U.S.A.* 42 F5
Marília 47 H9
Marinette 42 C2
Maringá 48 A6
Marion, *Ala., U.S.A.* 43 J2
Marion, *Ill., U.S.A.* 41 G10
Marion, *Ind., U.S.A.* 42 E3
Marion, *Iowa, U.S.A.* 40 D9
Marion, *Kans., U.S.A.* 40 F6
Marion, *N.C., U.S.A.* 43 H5
Marion, *Ohio, U.S.A.* 42 E4
Marion, *S.C., U.S.A.* 43 H6
Marion, *Va., U.S.A.* 43 G5
Marion, L. 43 J5
Mariposa 39 H4
Maritimes, Alpes 12 D7
Mariupol 17 A5
Marked Tree 41 H9
Market Drayton 8 E5
Market Harborough 9 E7
Market Rasen 8 D7
Markham, Mt. 6 F15
Marksville 41 K8
Marla 32 A1
Marlborough 9 F6
Marlborough Downs 9 F6
Marlin 41 K6
Marlow 41 H6
Marmara Denizi 15 D13
Marne → 12 B5
Maroochydore 32 A5
Maroona 32 C3
Marquesas Is. = Marquises, Is. 35 H14
Marquette 42 B2
Marquis 45 f
Marquises, Is. 35 H14
Marrakech 26 B4
Marrawah 32 D3
Marree 30 F6
Marrero 41 L9
Marrowie Cr. → 32 B4
Mars Hill 43 B12
Marsden 32 B4
Marseille 12 E6
Marsh I. 41 L9
Marshall, *Ark., U.S.A.* 41 H8
Marshall, *Mich., U.S.A.* 42 D3
Marshall, *Minn., U.S.A.* 40 C7
Marshall, *Mo., U.S.A.* 40 F8
Marshall, *Tex., U.S.A.* 41 J7
Marshall Is. ■ 34 G9
Marshalltown 40 D8
Marshfield, *Mo., U.S.A.* 41 G8
Marshfield, *Wis., U.S.A.* 40 C9
Mart 41 K6
Martaban, G. of 25 D8
Martapura 23 D3
Martha's Vineyard 42 E10
Martigues 12 E6
Martin, *S. Dak., U.S.A.* 40 D4
Martin, *Tenn., U.S.A.* 41 G10
Martin, L. 43 J3
Martinborough 33 J5
Martinez 43 J4
Martinique ■ 44 c
Martin's Bay 45 g
Martins Ferry 42 E5
Martinsburg 42 F7
Martinsville, *Ind., U.S.A.* 42 F2
Martinsville, *Va., U.S.A.* 43 G6
Marton 33 J5
Maryborough, *Queens., Australia* 30 F9
Maryborough, *Vic., Australia* 32 C3
Maryland □ 42 F7
Maryport 8 C4
Marystown 37 D14
Marysville, *Calif., U.S.A.* 38 G3
Marysville, *Kans., U.S.A.* 40 F6
Marysville, *Ohio, U.S.A.* 42 E4
Maryville, *Mo., U.S.A.* 40 E7
Maryville, *Tenn., U.S.A.* 43 H4
Masan 21 C7
Masaya 44 E7
Masbate 23 B4
Maseru 29 K5
Mashhad 24 B4
Maşīrah 24 C4
Mask, L. 11 C2
Mason 41 K5
Mason City 40 D8
Masqat 24 C4
Massachusetts □ 42 D10
Massawa = Mitsiwa 24 D2
Massena 42 C8
Massiah Street 45 g
Massif Central 12 D5
Massillon 42 E5
Masterton 33 J5
Masvingo 29 J6
Mata Utu 31 C15
Matadi 28 F2
Matagalpa 44 E7
Matagami 37 D12
Matagami, L. 37 D12
Matagorda B. 41 L6
Matagorda I. 41 L6
Matamoros, *Coahuila, Mexico* 44 B5
Matamoros, *Tamaulipas, Mexico* 44 B5
Matane 37 D13
Matanzas 45 C8
Matapan, C. = Tainaron, Ákra 15 F10
Mataram 23 D3
Mataró 13 B7
Mataura 33 M2
Matehuala 44 C4
Matera 14 D7
Mathis 41 L6
Mathura 25 C6
Mati 23 C4
Matiri Ra. 33 J4
Matlock 8 D6
Mato Grosso □ 47 F8
Mato Grosso, Planalto do 47 G8
Matsue 22 F3
Matsumoto 22 E6
Matsusaka 22 F5
Matsuyama 22 G3
Mattagami → 37 C11
Mattancheri 25 E6
Matterhorn 12 D7
Matthew, I. 31 E13
Mattoon 42 F1
Maturín 46 B6
Maubeuge 12 A6
Maubin 25 D8
Maude 32 B3
Maudin Sun 25 D8
Maughold Hd. 8 C3
Maumee 42 E4
Maumee → 42 E4
Maumere 23 D4
Maun 29 H4
Maupin 38 D3
Maurepas, L. 41 K9
Mauritania ■ 26 E3
Mauritius ■ 5 F12
Mauston 40 D9
Max 40 B4
May, C. 42 F8
May Pen 44 a
Mayaguana 45 C10
Mayagüez 45 d
Maybell 38 F9
Maybole 10 F4
Maydena 32 D4
Mayer 39 J7
Mayfield 43 G1
Mayhill 39 K11
Maykop 17 B6
Maynooth 11 C5
Mayo 36 B6
Mayo □ 11 C2
Mayor I. 33 G6
Maysville 42 F4
Mayville 40 B6
Mazār-e Sharīf 24 B5
Mazatlán 44 C3
Mazurian Lakes = Mazurski, Pojezierze 16 B10
Mazurski, Pojezierze 16 B10
Mbabane 29 K6
Mbandaka 28 D3
Mbanza Ngungu 28 F2
Mbeya 28 F6
Mbini = Río Muni □ 28 D2
Mbuji-Mayi 28 F4
Mead, L. 39 H6
Meade 41 G4
Meadow Lake 36 C9
Meadow Valley Wash → 39 H6
Meadville 42 E5
Meares, C. 38 D2
Meath □ 11 C5
Meaux 12 B5
Mecca = Makkah 24 C2
Mechelen 16 C2
Mecklenburg 16 B5
Medan 23 C1
Médéa 26 A6
Medellín 46 B3
Medford, *Oreg., U.S.A.* 38 E2
Medford, *Wis., U.S.A.* 40 C9
Medicine Bow 38 F10
Medicine Bow Pk. 38 F10
Medicine Bow Ra. 38 F10
Medicine Hat 36 D8
Medicine Lake 40 A2
Medicine Lodge 41 G5
Medina = Al Madīnah 24 C2
Medina, *N. Dak., U.S.A.* 40 B5
Medina, *N.Y., U.S.A.* 42 D6
Medina, *Ohio, U.S.A.* 42 E5
Medina → 41 L5
Medina L. 41 L5
Mediterranean Sea 5 C10
Médoc 12 D3
Medway □ 9 F8
Medway → 9 F8
Meekatharra 30 F2
Meeker 38 F10
Meerut 25 C6
Meeteetse 38 D9
Meghalaya □ 25 C8
Mehlville 40 F9
Meizhou 21 D6
Mekele 24 D2
Meknès 26 B4
Mekong → 23 C2
Mekvari = Kür → 17 C7
Melaka 23 C2
Melanesia 34 H7
Melbourne, *Australia* 30 H8
Melbourne, *U.S.A.* 43 L5
Mélèzes → 37 C12
Melfort 36 C9
Melitopol 17 A5
Mellen 40 B9
Mellette 40 C5
Melrose, *Australia* 32 B4
Melrose, *U.K.* 10 F6
Melrose, *Minn., U.S.A.* 40 C7
Melrose, *N. Mex., U.S.A.* 41 H3
Melstone 38 C10
Melton Mowbray 8 E7
Melun 12 B5
Melville 36 C9
Melville I., *Australia* 30 C5
Melville I., *Canada* 6 B1
Melville Pen. 37 B11
Memel = Klaipėda 18 D3
Memphis, *Tenn., U.S.A.* 41 H10
Memphis, *Tex., U.S.A.* 41 H4
Mena 41 H7
Menai Strait 8 D3
Menard 41 K5
Mende 12 D5
Mendip Hills 9 F5
Mendocino 38 G2
Mendocino, C. 38 F1
Mendota, *Calif., U.S.A.* 39 H3
Mendota, *Ill., U.S.A.* 40 E10
Mendoza 48 C3
Mengzi 20 D5
Menindee 32 B3
Menindee L. 32 B3
Meningie 32 C2
Menominee 42 C2
Menominee → 42 C2
Menomonie 40 C9
Menorca 13 C8
Mentawai, Kepulauan 23 D1
Mentor 42 E5
Merbein 32 B3
Merced 39 H3
Mercedes 41 M6
Mercer 33 G5
Mercy C. 37 B13
Mere 9 F5
Meredith, L. 41 H4
Mergui 25 D8
Mergui Arch. = Myeik Kyunzu 25 D8
Mérida, *Mexico* 44 C7
Mérida, *Spain* 13 C2
Mérida, *Venezuela* 46 B4
Mérida, Cord. de 46 B4
Meriden, *U.K.* 9 E6
Meriden, *U.S.A.* 42 E9
Meridian, *Idaho, U.S.A.* 38 E5
Meridian, *Miss., U.S.A.* 43 J1
Merkel 41 J5
Merrick 10 F4
Merrill, *Oreg., U.S.A.* 38 E3
Merrill, *Wis., U.S.A.* 40 C10
Merriman 40 D4
Merritt 36 C7
Merritt Island 43 L5
Merriwa 32 B5
Merryville 41 K8
Mersea I. 9 F8
Mersey → 8 D4
Merseyside □ 8 D4
Mersin 17 C4
Merthyr Tydfil 9 F4
Mertzon 41 K4
Mesa 39 K8
Mesa Verde Nat. Park 39 H9
Mesilla 39 K10
Mesopotamia = Al Jazirah 24 B3
Mesquite 39 H6
Messina 14 E6
Messina, Str. di 14 F6
Meta → 46 B5
Meta Incognita Peninsula 37 B13
Metairie 41 L9
Metaline Falls 38 B5
Methven 33 K3
Metlakatla 36 C6
Metropolis 41 G10
Metz 12 B7
Meuse → 12 A6
Mexia 41 K6
Mexicali 44 A1
Mexican Water 39 H9
México, *Mexico* 44 D5
Mexico, *U.S.A.* 40 F9
Mexico ■ 44 C4
Mexico, G. of 44 C7
Meymaneh 24 B5
Mezen → 18 C5
Miami, *Fla., U.S.A.* 43 N5
Miami, *Okla., U.S.A.* 41 G7
Miami, *Tex., U.S.A.* 41 H4
Miami Beach 43 N5
Mianwali 25 B6
Miass 18 D7
Michigan □ 42 C3
Michigan, L. 42 D2
Michigan City 42 E2
Michurinsk 18 D5
Micoud 45 f
Micronesia 34 G7
Micronesia, Federated States of ■ 34 G7
Middelburg 29 L5
Middle Alkali L. 38 F3
Middle Loup → 40 E5
Middleburg 43 K5
Middlebury 42 C9
Middleport 42 F4
Middlesboro 43 G4
Middlesbrough 8 C6
Middletown, *U.K.* 11 B5
Middletown, *N.Y., U.S.A.* 42 E8
Middletown, *Ohio, U.S.A.* 42 F3
Midhurst 9 G7
Midi, Canal du → 12 E4
Midland, *Mich., U.S.A.* 42 D3
Midland, *Tex., U.S.A.* 41 K3
Midleton 11 E3
Midlothian 41 J6
Midlothian □ 10 F5
Midway Is. 34 E10
Midwest 38 E10
Midwest City 41 H6
Mieres 13 A3
Milaca 40 C8
Milan = Milano 12 D8
Milan, *Mo., U.S.A.* 40 E8
Milan, *Tenn., U.S.A.* 43 H1
Milano 12 D8
Milbank 40 C6
Mildenhall 9 E8
Mildura 30 G7
Miles 32 A5
Miles City 40 B2
Milford, *Del., U.S.A.* 42 F8
Milford, *Utah, U.S.A.* 39 G7
Milford Haven 9 F2
Milford Sd. 33 L1
Milford Sound 33 L1
Milk → 38 B10
Millau 12 D5
Mille Lacs L. 40 B8
Milledgeville 43 J4
Millen 43 J5
Millennium I. = Caroline I. 35 H12
Miller 40 C5
Millet 45 f
Millicent 32 C3
Millington 41 H10
Millinocket 43 C11
Millmerran 32 A5
Millom 8 C4
Milltown Malbay 11 D2
Millville 42 F8
Millwood L. 41 J8
Milo 43 C11
Milparinka 32 A3
Milton, *N.Z.* 33 M2
Milton, *Fla., U.S.A.* 43 K2
Milton, *Pa., U.S.A.* 42 E7
Milton-Freewater 38 D4
Milton Keynes 9 E7
Milwaukee 42 D2
Milwaukie 38 D2
Min Jiang →, *Fujian, China* 21 D6
Min Jiang →, *Sichuan, China* 20 D5
Minami-Tori-Shima 34 E7
Minas Gerais □ 47 G9
Minatitlán 44 D6
Minbu 25 C8
Mindanao 23 C4
Mindanao Sea = Bohol Sea 23 C4
Mindanao Trench 23 B4
Minden, *La., U.S.A.* 41 J8
Minden, *Nev., U.S.A.* 38 G4
Mindoro 23 B4
Mindoro Str. 23 B4
Minehead 9 F4
Mineola 41 J7
Mineral Wells 41 J5
Minidoka 38 E7
Minneapolis, *Kans., U.S.A.* 40 F6
Minneapolis, *Minn., U.S.A.* 40 C8
Minnesota □ 40 B8
Minnesota → 40 C8
Minnewaukan 40 A5
Minnipa 32 B2
Minorca = Menorca 13 C8
Minot 40 A4
Minsk 18 D3
Mintabie 32 A1
Minto, L. 37 C12
Minturn 38 G10
Minzhong 21 F10
Miramichi 37 D13
Mirbāţ 24 D4
Miri 23 C3
Mīrjāveh 24 C5
Mirzapur 25 C7
Mishan 21 B8
Mishawaka 42 E2
Misool 23 D5
Mişrātah 27 B9
Missinaibi → 37 C11
Mission, *S. Dak., U.S.A.* 40 D4
Mission, *Tex., U.S.A.* 41 M5
Mission Viejo 39 K5
Mississippi □ 41 J10
Mississippi → 41 L10
Mississippi River Delta 41 L9
Mississippi Sd. 41 K10
Missoula 38 C7
Missouri □ 40 F8
Missouri → 40 F9
Missouri City 41 L7
Missouri Valley 40 E7
Mistassini, L. 37 C12
Misurata = Mişrātah 27 B9
Mitchell, *Australia* 32 A4
Mitchell, *Nebr., U.S.A.* 40 E3
Mitchell, *Oreg., U.S.A.* 38 D3
Mitchell, *S. Dak., U.S.A.* 40 D6
Mitchell → 30 D7
Mitchell, Mt. 43 H4
Mitchelstown 11 D3
Mito 22 E7
Mitsiwa 24 D2
Mittagong 32 B5
Mitumba, Mts. 28 F5
Miyakonojō 22 H2
Miyazaki 22 H2
Mizen Hd., *Cork, Ireland* 11 E2
Mizen Hd., *Wicklow, Ireland* 11 D5
Mizoram □ 25 C8
Mjøsa 7 E6
Mmabatho 29 K5
Mo i Rana 7 D6
Moab 39 G9
Moala 33 D8
Moama 32 C3
Moate 11 C4
Moberly 40 F8
Mobile 43 K1
Mobile B. 43 K2
Mobridge 40 C4
Mochudi 29 J5
Moclips 38 C1
Módena, *Italy* 14 B4
Modena, *U.S.A.* 39 H7
Modesto 39 H3
Modimolle 29 J5
Moe 32 C4
Moffat 10 F5
Mogadishu = Muqdisho 24 E3
Mogi das Cruzes 48 A7
Mogilev = Mahilyow 18 D4
Mogollon Rim 39 J8
Mohall 40 A4
Mohave, L. 39 J6
Moidart, L. 10 E3
Moisie → 37 C13
Mojave 39 J4
Mojave Desert 39 J5
Mokai 33 H5
Mokau 33 H5
Mokopane 29 J5
Mold 8 D4
Moldavia = Moldova ■ 17 A3
Molde 7 E5
Moldova ■ 17 A3
Mole → 9 F7
Mole Creek 32 D4
Molepolole 29 J5
Moline 40 E9
Mollendo 46 G4
Molong 32 B4
Molopo → 29 K4
Molotov = Perm 18 D6
Molucca Sea 23 D4
Moluccas = Maluku 23 D4
Mombasa 28 E7
Mona, Canal de la 45 D11
Mona Passage = Mona, Canal de la 45 D11
Monaco ■ 12 E7
Monadhliath Mts. 10 D4
Monaghan 11 B5
Monaghan □ 11 B5
Monahans 41 K3
Monar, L. 10 D3
Monasterevin 11 C4
Monastir = Bitola 15 D9
Mönchengladbach 16 C3
Moncks Corner 43 J5
Monclova 44 B4
Moncton 37 D13
Moneague 44 a
Monessen 42 E6
Monett 41 G8
Moneymore 11 B5
Mongolia ■ 19 E10
Mongu 29 H4
Monifieth 10 E6
Monmouth, *U.K.* 9 F5
Monmouth, *Ill., U.S.A.* 40 E9
Monmouth, *Oreg., U.S.A.* 38 D2
Monmouthshire □ 9 F5
Mono L. 39 H4
Monroe, *Ga., U.S.A.* 43 J4
Monroe, *La., U.S.A.* 41 J8
Monroe, *Mich., U.S.A.* 42 E4
Monroe, *N.C., U.S.A.* 43 H5
Monroe, *Utah, U.S.A.* 39 G7
Monroe, *Wis., U.S.A.* 40 D10
Monroe City 40 F9
Monroeville 43 K2
Monrovia 26 G3
Mons 16 C1
Mont-de-Marsan 12 E3
Mont-Laurier 37 D12
Montana □ 38 C9
Montargis 12 C5
Montauban 12 D4
Montauk Pt. 42 E10
Montbéliard 12 C7
Montceau-les-Mines 12 C6
Monte-Carlo 12 E7
Monte Cristi 45 D10
Monte Vista 39 H10
Montego Bay 44 a
Montélimar 12 D6
Montello 40 D10
Montemorelos 44 B5
Montenegro □ 15 C8
Monterey 39 H3
Montería 46 B3
Monterrey 44 B4
Montes Claros 47 G10
Montesano 38 C2
Montevideo, *Uruguay* 48 C5
Montevideo, *U.S.A.* 40 C7
Montezuma 40 E8
Montgomery, *U.K.* 9 E4
Montgomery, *Ala., U.S.A.* 43 J2
Montgomery, *W. Va., U.S.A.* 42 F5
Montgomery City 40 F9
Monticello, *Ark., U.S.A.* 41 J9
Monticello, *Fla., U.S.A.* 43 K4
Monticello, *Ind., U.S.A.* 42 E2
Monticello, *Iowa, U.S.A.* 40 D9
Monticello, *Ky., U.S.A.* 43 G3
Monticello, *Minn., U.S.A.* 40 C8
Monticello, *Miss., U.S.A.* 41 K9
Monticello, *Utah, U.S.A.* 39 H9
Montluçon 12 C5
Montpelier, *Idaho, U.S.A.* 38 E8
Montpelier, *Vt., U.S.A.* 42 C9
Montpellier 12 E5
Montréal 37 D12
Montreux 12 C7
Montrose, *U.K.* 10 E6
Montrose, *U.S.A.* 39 G10
Montserrat ■ 45 D12
Monza 12 D8
Moonie 32 A5
Moonie → 32 A4
Moonta 32 B2
Moorcroft 40 C2
Moorefield 42 F6
Moorfoot Hills 10 F5
Moorhead 40 B6
Moose Jaw 36 C9
Moose Lake 40 B8
Moosehead L. 43 C11
Mooselookmeguntic L. 43 C10
Moosomin 36 C9
Moosonee 37 C11
Mopti 26 F5
Mora, *Sweden* 7 E6
Mora, *Minn., U.S.A.* 40 C8
Mora, *N. Mex., U.S.A.* 39 J11
Mora → 41 H2
Moradabad 25 C6
Moran, *Kans., U.S.A.* 41 G7
Moran, *Wyo., U.S.A.* 38 E8
Morant Bay 44 a
Morant Pt. 44 a
Morar, L. 10 E3
Morava →, *Serbia & M.* 15 B9
Morava →, *Slovak Rep.* 16 D8
Moravian Hts. = Českomoravská Vrchovina 16 D7
Moray □ 10 D5
Moray Firth 10 D5
Morden 36 D10
Moreau → 40 C4
Morecambe 8 C5
Morecambe B. 8 C5
Moree 30 F9
Morehead 42 F4
Morehead City 43 H7
Morelia 44 D4
Morena, Sierra 13 C3
Moresby I. 36 C6
Moreton I. 32 A5
Morgan 38 F8
Morgan City 41 L9
Morganfield 42 G2
Morganton 43 H5
Morgantown 42 F6
Moriarty 39 J10
Morioka 22 D7
Morlaix 12 B2
Mornington 32 C4
Moro G. 23 C4
Morocco ■ 26 B4
Morogoro 28 F7
Morón 45 C9
Moroni 38 G8
Morotai 23 C4
Morpeth 8 B6
Morrilton 41 H8
Morrinsville 33 G5
Morris, *Ill., U.S.A.* 40 E10
Morris, *Minn., U.S.A.* 40 C7
Morristown, *Ariz., U.S.A.* 39 K7
Morristown, *Tenn., U.S.A.* 43 G4
Morro Bay 39 J3
Mortlake 32 C3
Morton, *Tex., U.S.A.* 41 J3
Morton, *Wash., U.S.A.* 38 C2
Morundah 32 B4
Moruya 32 C5
Morven 32 A4
Morvern 10 E3
Morwell 32 C4
Moscow = Moskva 18 D4
Moscow 38 C5
Mosel → 12 A7
Moselle = Mosel → 12 A7
Moses Lake 38 C4
Mosgiel 33 L3
Moshi 28 E7
Moskva 18 D4
Mosquero 41 H3
Moss Vale 32 B5
Mossburn 33 L2
Mosselbaai 29 L4
Mossgiel 32 B3
Mossoró 47 E11
Most 16 C6
Mostaganem 26 A6
Mostar 15 C7
Mosul = Al Mawşil 24 B3
Motherwell 10 F5
Mott 40 B3
Motueka 33 J4
Motueka → 33 J4
Moulamein 32 C3
Moule 44 b
Moule à Chique, C. 45 f
Moulins 12 C5
Moulmein 25 D8
Moultrie 43 K4
Moultrie, L. 43 J5
Mound City, *Mo., U.S.A.* 40 E7
Mound City, *S. Dak., U.S.A.* 40 C4
Moundsville 42 F5
Mount Airy 43 G5
Mount Barker 32 C2
Mount Burr 32 C3
Mount Carmel 42 F2
Mount Desert I. 43 C11
Mount Dora 43 L5
Mount Gambier 30 H7
Mount Hagen 30 B7
Mount Hope, *N.S.W., Australia* 32 B4
Mount Hope, *S. Austral., Australia* 32 B2
Mount Isa 30 E6
Mount Lofty Ra. 32 B2
Mount Magnet 30 F2
Mount Maunganui 33 G6
Mount Perry 32 A5
Mount Pleasant, *Iowa, U.S.A.* 40 E9
Mount Pleasant, *Mich., U.S.A.* 42 D3
Mount Pleasant, *S.C., U.S.A.* 43 J6
Mount Pleasant, *Tenn., U.S.A.* 43 H2
Mount Pleasant, *Tex., U.S.A.* 41 J7
Mount Pleasant, *Utah, U.S.A.* 38 G8
Mount Rainier Nat. Park 38 C3
Mount Shasta 38 F2
Mount Sterling, *Ill., U.S.A.* 40 F9
Mount Sterling, *Ky., U.S.A.* 42 F4
Mount Vernon, *Ill., U.S.A.* 42 F1
Mount Vernon, *Ind., U.S.A.* 40 F10
Mount Vernon, *Ohio, U.S.A.* 42 E4
Mount Vernon, *Wash., U.S.A.* 38 B2
Mountain Ash 9 F4
Mountain City, *Nev., U.S.A.* 38 F6
Mountain City, *Tenn., U.S.A.* 43 G5
Mountain Grove 41 G8
Mountain Home, *Ark., U.S.A.* 41 G8
Mountain Home, *Idaho, U.S.A.* 38 E6
Mountain Iron 40 B8
Mountain View 41 H8
Mountainair 39 J10
Mountmellick 11 C4
Mountrath 11 D4
Mourne → 11 B4
Mourne Mts. 11 B5
Moville 11 A4
Moy → 11 B2
Moyen Atlas 26 B4
Mozambique ■ 29 H7
Mozambique Chan. 5 F11
Mu Us Shamo 21 C5
Muar 23 C2
Muck 10 E2
Muckadilla 32 A4
Mudanjiang 21 B7
Muddy Cr. → 39 H8
Mudgee 32 B4
Mufulira 29 G5
Mui Wo 21 G10
Muine Bheag 11 D5
Mulde → 16 C6
Mule Creek Junction 40 D2
Muleshoe 41 H3
Mulhacén 13 D4
Mülheim 21 C6
Mulhouse 12 C7
Mull 10 E3
Mull, Sound of 10 E3
Mullen 40 D4
Mullens 42 G5
Muller, Pegunungan 23 C3
Mullet Pen. 11 B1
Mullingar 11 C4
Mullins 43 H6
Mullumbimby 32 A5
Mulroy B. 11 A4
Multan 25 B6
Mulvane 41 G6
Mumbai 25 D6
Muna 23 D4
München 16 D5
Muncie 42 E3
Mundabbera 32 A5
Munday 41 J5
Mungallala 32 A4
Mungallala Cr. → 32 A4
Munich = München 16 D5
Munising 42 B2
Münster 16 C3
Munster □ 11 D3
Muqdisho 24 E3
Murchison → 30 F1
Murcia 13 D5
Murdo 40 D4
Mureş → 17 A2
Murfreesboro, *N.C., U.S.A.* 43 G7
Murfreesboro, *Tenn., U.S.A.* 43 H2
Murgon 32 A5
Müritz 16 B6
Murmansk 7 D10
Murom 18 D5
Murphy 38 E5
Murray, *Ky., U.S.A.* 43 G1
Murray, *Utah, U.S.A.* 38 F8
Murray → 30 H6
Murray, L. 43 H5
Murray Bridge 32 C2
Murrumbidgee → 32 B3
Murrumburrah 32 B4
Murrurundi 32 B5
Murtoa 32 C3
Mururoa 35 K14
Murwillumbah 32 A5
Mûsa, Gebel 27 C12
Muscat = Masqat 24 C4
Muscatine 40 E9
Musgrave Ranges 30 F5
Musi → 23 D2
Musina 29 J6
Muskegon 42 D2
Muskegon → 42 D2
Muskegon Heights 42 D2
Muskogee 41 H7
Musselburgh 10 F5
Musselshell → 38 C10
Muswellbrook 32 B5
Mutare 29 H6
Mutton I. 11 D2
Mwanza 28 E6
Mweelrea 11 C2
Mweru, L. 28 F5
My Tho 23 B2
Myanmar = Burma ■ 25 C8
Myeik Kyunzu 25 D8
Myingyan 25 C8
Myitkyina 25 C8
Mykolayiv 17 A4
Mynydd Du 9 F4
Myrtle Beach 43 J6
Myrtle Creek 38 E2
Myrtle Point 38 E1
Mysore 25 D6

N

Na Hearadh = Harris 10 D2
Naab → 16 D6
Naas 11 C5
Naberezhnyye Chelny 18 D6
Naches 38 C3
Nacimiento L. 39 J3
Nacogdoches 41 K7
Nacozari 44 A3
Nadi 33 C7
Nafud Desert = An Nafūd 24 C3
Naga 23 B4
Nagaland □ 25 C8
Nagano 22 E6
Nagaoka 22 E6
Nagasaki 22 G1
Nagercoil 25 E6
Nagoya 22 F5
Nagpur 25 C6
Naguabo 45 d
Naha 21 D7
Nain 37 C13
Nairn 10 D5
Nairobi 28 E7
Najd 24 C3
Nakhodka 19 E14
Nakhon Ratchasima 23 B2
Nakhon Sawan 23 B2
Nakhon Si Thammarat 23 C2
Nakina 37 C11
Nakuru 28 E7
Nalchik 17 B6
Nam Co 20 C4
Nam Dinh 23 A2
Namaland 29 K3
Namangan 18 E8
Nambour 32 A5
Nambucca Heads 32 B5
Namcha Barwa 20 D4
Namib Desert 29 J3
Namibe 29 H2
Namibia ■ 29 J3
Namlea 23 D4
Namoi → 32 B4
Nampa 38 E5
Namp'o 21 C7
Nampula 29 H7
Namumea 31 B14
Namur 16 C2
Nanaimo 36 D7
Nanango 32 A5
Nanchang 21 D6
Nanchong 20 C5
Nancy 12 B7
Nanded 25 D6
Nandewar Ra. 32 B5
Nanjing 21 C6
Nanking = Nanjing 21 C6
Nanlang 21 G10
Nanning 20 D5
Nanping 21 D6
Nansha 21 F10
Nantes 12 C3
Nanticoke 42 E7
Nantong 21 C7
Nantou 21 F10
Nantucket I. 42 E10
Nantwich 8 D5
Nanusa, Kepulauan 23 C4
Nanyang 21 C6
Napa 38 G2
Napier 31 H14
Naples = Nápoli 14 D6
Naples 43 M5
Napo → 46 D4
Napoleon, *N. Dak., U.S.A.* 40 B5
Napoleon, *Ohio, U.S.A.* 42 E3
Nápoli 14 D6
Nara Visa 41 H3
Naracoorte 32 C3
Naradhan 32 B4
Narbonne 12 E5
Narooma 32 C5
Narrabri 32 B4
Narran → 32 A4
Narrandera 32 B4
Narromine 32 B4
Narvik 7 D7
Naseby 33 L3
Naser, Buheirat en 27 D12
Nashua, *Mont., U.S.A.* 38 B10
Nashua, *N.H., U.S.A.* 42 D10
Nashville, *Ark., U.S.A.* 41 J8
Nashville, *Ga., U.S.A.* 43 K4
Nashville, *Tenn., U.S.A.* 43 G2
Nasik 25 D6
Nassau 45 B9
Nasser, L. = Naser, Buheirat en 27 D12
Natal 47 E11
Natashquan 37 C13
Natashquan → 37 C13
Natchez 41 K9
Natchitoches 41 K8
Nathalia 32 C4
Natimuk 32 C3
Natuna Besar, Kepulauan 23 C2
Natuna Selatan, Kepulauan 23 C2
Naturaliste, C. 32 D4
Nauru ■ 34 H8
Navajo Reservoir 39 H10
Navan = An Uaimh 11 C5
Navarra □ 13 A5
Navasota 41 K6
Naver → 10 C4
Navojoa 44 B3
Nawabshah 24 C5
Náxos 15 F11
Nazas → 44 B4
Naze, The 9 F9
Ndjamena 27 F8
Ndola 29 G5
Neagh, Lough 11 B5
Neah Bay 38 B1
Near Is. 36 C1
Neath 9 F4
Nebine Cr. → 32 A4
Nebraska □ 40 E5
Nebraska City 40 E7
Necedah 40 C9
Neches → 41 L8
Neckar → 16 D4
Needles 39 J6
Needles, The 9 G6
Neenah 42 C1
Neepawa 36 C10
Nefyn 8 E3
Negaunee 42 B2
Negrais C. = Maudin Sun 25 D8
Negril 44 a
Negro →, *Argentina* 48 E4
Negro →, *Brazil* 46 D7
Negros 23 C4
Nei Monggol Zizhiqu □ 21 B6
Neijiang 20 D5
Neilingding Dao 21 G10
Neillsville 40 C9
Neilton 38 C2
Neiva 46 C3
Neligh 40 D5
Nellore 25 D6
Nelson, *Canada* 36 D8
Nelson, *N.Z.* 31 J13
Nelson, *U.K.* 8 D5
Nelson, *U.S.A.* 39 J7
Nelson → 36 C10
Nelson, C. 32 C3
Nelspruit 29 K6
Neman → 18 D3
Nemunas = Neman → 18 D3
Nen Jiang → 21 B7
Nenagh 11 D3
Nene → 9 E8
Nenjiang 21 B7
Neodesha 41 G7
Neosho 41 G7
Neosho → 41 H7
Nepal ■ 25 C7
Nephi 38 G8
Nephin 11 B2
Nerang 32 A5
Ness, L. 10 D4
Ness City 40 F5
Netherlands ■ 16 C2
Netherlands Antilles ■ 45 E11
Nettilling L. 37 B12
Neuchâtel 12 C7
Neuchâtel, Lac de 12 C7
Neuse → 43 H7
Neusiedler See 16 E8
Neva → 7 E10
Nevada, *Iowa, U.S.A.* 40 D8
Nevada, *Mo., U.S.A.* 41 G7
Nevada □ 38 G5
Nevada City 38 G3
Nevers 12 C5
Nevertire 32 B4
Nevinnomyssk 17 B6
New → 42 F5
New Albany, *Ind., U.S.A.* 42 F3
New Albany, *Miss., U.S.A.* 41 H10
New Amsterdam 46 B7
New Angledool 32 A4
New Baltimore 42 D4
New Bedford 42 E10
New Bern 43 H7
New Boston 41 J7
New Braunfels 41 L5
New Brighton 33 K4
New Britain, *Papua N. G.* 34 H7
New Britain, *U.S.A.* 42 E9
New Brunswick 42 E8
New Brunswick □ 37 D13
New Caledonia ■ 34 K8
New Castle, *Ind., U.S.A.* 42 F3
New Castle, *Pa., U.S.A.* 42 E5
New Delhi 25 C6
New England 40 B3
New England Ra. 32 B5
New Forest 9 G6
New Galloway 10 F4
New Georgia Is. 31 B10
New Glasgow 37 D13
New Guinea 34 H5
New Hampshire □ 42 D10
New Hampton 40 D8
New Haven 42 E9
New Hebrides = Vanuatu ■ 34 J8
New Iberia 41 K9
New Ireland 34 H7
New Jersey □ 42 E8
New Lexington 42 F4
New Liskeard 37 D12
New London, *Conn., U.S.A.* 42 E9
New London, *Wis., U.S.A.* 40 C10
New Madrid 41 G10
New Martinsville 42 F5
New Meadows 38 D5
New Mexico □ 39 J10
New Norfolk 32 D4
New Orleans 41 L9
New Philadelphia 42 E5
New Plymouth, *N.Z.* 31 H13
New Plymouth, *U.S.A.* 38 E5
New Port Richey 43 L4
New Providence 45 B9
New Quay 9 E3
New Radnor 9 E4
New Richmond 40 C8
New Roads 41 K9
New Rockford 40 B5
New Romney 9 G8
New Ross 11 D5
New Salem 40 B4
New Scone 10 E5
New Siberian Is. = Novosibirskiye Ostrova 19 B15
New Smyrna Beach 43 L5
New South Wales □ 30 G8
New Town 40 B3
New Tredegar 9 F4
New Ulm 40 C7
New York 42 E9
New York □ 42 D8
New York Mts. 39 J6
New Zealand ■ 34 M9
Newark, *Del., U.S.A.* 42 F8
Newark, *N.J., U.S.A.* 42 E8
Newark, *N.Y., U.S.A.* 42 D7
Newark, *Ohio, U.S.A.* 42 E4
Newark-on-Trent 8 D7
Newberg 38 D2
Newberry, *Mich., U.S.A.* 42 B3
Newberry, *S.C., U.S.A.* 43 H5
Newburgh 42 E8
Newbury 9 F6
Newburyport 43 D10
Newcastle, *Australia* 30 G9
Newcastle, *U.K.* 11 B6
Newcastle, *U.S.A.* 40 D2
Newcastle Emlyn 9 E3
Newcastle-under-Lyme 8 D5
Newcastle-upon-Tyne 8 C6
Newcastle West 11 D2
Newell 40 C3
Newfoundland & Labrador □ 37 C14
Newhaven 9 G8
Newkirk 41 G6
Newlyn 9 G2
Newman 30 E2
Newmarket, *Ireland* 11 D2
Newmarket, *U.K.* 9 E8
Newnan 43 J3
Newport, *Ireland* 11 C2
Newport, *I. of W., U.K.* 9 G6
Newport, *Newp., U.K.* 9 F5
Newport, *Ark., U.S.A.* 41 H9
Newport, *Ky., U.S.A.* 42 F3
Newport, *N.H., U.S.A.* 42 D9
Newport, *Oreg., U.S.A.* 38 D1
Newport, *R.I., U.S.A.* 42 E10
Newport, *Tenn., U.S.A.* 43 H4
Newport, *Vt., U.S.A.* 42 C9
Newport, *Wash., U.S.A.* 38 B5
Newport Beach 39 K5
Newport News 42 G7
Newport Pagnell 9 E7
Newquay 9 G2
Newry 11 B5
Newton, *Ill., U.S.A.* 40 F10
Newton, *Iowa, U.S.A.* 40 E8
Newton, *Kans., U.S.A.* 41 F6
Newton, *Mass., U.S.A.* 42 D10
Newton, *Miss., U.S.A.* 41 J10
Newton, *N.C., U.S.A.* 43 H5
Newton, *N.J., U.S.A.* 42 E8
Newton, *Tex., U.S.A.* 41 K8
Newton Abbot 9 G4
Newton Aycliffe 8 C6
Newton Stewart 10 G4
Newtonmore 10 D4
Newtown 9 E4
Newtownabbey 11 B6
Newtownards 11 B6
Newtownstewart 11 B4
Nezperce 38 C5
Ngapara 33 L3
Ngoring Hu 20 C4
Nha Trang 23 B2
Nhill 32 C3
Niagara Falls, *Canada* 37 D12
Niagara Falls, *U.S.A.* 42 D6
Niamey 26 F6
Nias 23 C1
Nicaragua ■ 44 E7
Nicaragua, L. de 44 E7
Nice 12 E7
Niceville 43 K2
Nicholasville 42 G3
Nicobar Is. 25 E8
Nicosia 17 C4
Nicoya, Pen. de 44 F7
Nidd → 8 D6
Niedersachsen □ 16 B4
Niemen = Neman → 18 D3
Niger ■ 26 E7
Niger → 26 G7
Nigeria ■ 26 G7
Nightcaps 33 L2
Niigata 22 E6
Nijmegen 16 C2
Nikolayev = Mykolayiv 17 A4
Nikolayevsk-na-Amur 19 D15
Nīl, Nahr en → 27 B12
Nīl el Abyad → 27 E12
Nīl el Azraq → 27 E12
Nile = Nīl, Nahr en → 27 B12
Niles 42 E2
Nîmes 12 E6
Nimmitabel 32 C4
Nindigully 32 A4
Ninepin Group 21 G11
Ningbo 21 D7
Ningjing Shan 20 D4
Ningxia Huizu Zizhiqu □ 20 C5
Niobrara 40 D6
Niobrara → 40 D6
Niort 12 C3
Nipawin 36 C9
Nipigon, L. 37 D11
Nipissing, L. 37 D12
Nipomo 39 J3
Niš 15 C9
Nishinomiya 22 F4
Nistru = Dnister → 18 E4
Niterói 47 H10
Nith → 10 F5
Nitra 16 D9
Nitra → 16 E9
Niuafo'ou 31 D15
Niue 35 J11
Nivernais 12 C5
Nixon 41 L6
Nizamabad 25 D6
Nizhnevartovsk 18 C8
Nizhniy Novgorod 18 D5
Nizhniy Tagil 18 D6
Nízké Tatry 16 D9
Nkongsamba 28 D1
Nobeoka 22 G2
Noblesville 42 E3
Nocona 41 J6
Nogales, *Mexico* 44 A2
Nogales, *U.S.A.* 39 L8
Noirmoutier, Î. de 12 C2
Nome 36 B3
Nord-Ostsee-Kanal 16 A4
Nordfriesische Inseln 16 A4
Nordkapp 7 C9
Nordrhein-Westfalen □ 16 C3
Nordvik 19 B12
Nore → 11 D4
Norfolk, *Nebr., U.S.A.* 40 D6
Norfolk, *Va., U.S.A.* 42 G7
Norfolk □ 9 E8
Norfolk I. 34 K8
Norfork L. 41 G8
Norilsk 19 C9
Normal 40 E10
Norman 41 H6
Norman Wells 36 B7
Normandie 12 B4
Normandy = Normandie 12 B4
Normanton 30 D7
Norristown 42 E8
Norrköping 7 F7
Norrland 7 E7
Norseman 30 G3
North, C. 37 D13
North Adams 42 D9
North Augusta 43 J5
North Ayrshire □ 10 F4
North Battleford 36 C9
North Bay 37 D12
North Bend 38 E1
North Berwick 10 E6
North C. 31 G13
North Canadian → 41 H7
North Cape = Nordkapp 7 C9
North Carolina □ 43 H6
North Cascades Nat. Park 38 B3
North Channel 10 F3
North Charleston 43 J6
North Chicago 42 D2
North Dakota □ 40 B5
North Downs 9 F8
North East Lincolnshire □ 8 D7
North Esk → 10 E6
North Foreland 9 F9
North Fork Grand → 40 C3
North Fork Red → 41 H5
North Frisian Is. = Nordfriesische Inseln 16 A4
North I. 31 H14
North Korea ■ 21 C7
North Lanarkshire □ 10 F5
North Las Vegas 39 H6
North Lincolnshire □ 8 D7
North Little Rock 41 H8
North Loup → 40 E5
North Magnetic Pole 6 B1
North Minch 10 C3
North Myrtle Beach 43 J6
North Palisade 39 H4
North Platte 40 E4
North Platte → 40 E4
North Pole 6 A
North Powder 38 D5
North Pt. 45 g
North Ronaldsay 10 B6
North Saskatchewan → 36 C9
North Sea 3 B10
North Somerset □ 9 F5
North Taranaki Bight 33 H5
North Thompson → 36 C7
North Tonawanda 42 D6
North Truchas Pk. 39 J11
North Tyne → 8 B5
North Uist 10 D1
North Vernon 42 F3
North Walsham 8 E9
North West C. 30 E1
North West Christmas I. Ridge 35 G11
North West Frontier □ 25 B6
North West Highlands 10 D4
North West River 37 C13
North Wildwood 42 F8
North York Moors 8 C7
North Yorkshire □ 8 C6
Northallerton 8 C6
Northam 30 G2
Northampton, *U.K.* 9 E7
Northampton, *U.S.A.* 42 D9
Northamptonshire □ 9 E7
Northern Ireland □ 11 B5
Northern Marianas ■ 34 F6
Northern Territory □ 30 E5
Northfield 40 C8
Northland □ 33 F4
Northome 40 B7
Northport, *Ala., U.S.A.* 43 J2
Northport, *Wash., U.S.A.* 38 B5
Northumberland □ 8 B6
Northumberland, C. 32 C3
Northumberland Str. 37 D13
Northwest Territories □ 36 B9
Northwood, *Iowa, U.S.A.* 40 D8
Northwood, *N. Dak., U.S.A.* 40 B6
Norton 40 F5
Norton Sd. 36 B3
Norwalk, *Conn., U.S.A.* 42 E9
Norwalk, *Iowa, U.S.A.* 40 E8
Norwalk, *Ohio, U.S.A.* 42 E4
Norway, *Maine, U.S.A.* 43 C10
Norway, *Mich., U.S.A.* 42 C2
Norway ■ 7 E6
Norway House 36 C10
Norwegian Sea 4 A9
Norwich, *U.K.* 9 E9
Norwich, *Conn., U.S.A.* 42 E9
Norwich, *N.Y., U.S.A.* 42 D8
Noss Hd. 10 C5
Nossob → 29 K4
Notre Dame B. 37 D14
Nottaway → 37 C12
Nottingham 8 E6
Nottingham I. 37 B12
Nottinghamshire □ 8 D6
Nottoway → 42 G7
Nouâdhibou 26 D2
Nouâdhibou, Ras 26 D2
Nouakchott 26 E2
Nouméa 34 K8
Nouvelle-Amsterdam, I. 5 F13
Nova Friburgo 47 H10
Nova Iguaçu 48 A8
Nova Scotia □ 37 D13
Novara 12 D8
Novaya Zemlya 18 B6
Novgorod 18 D4
Novi Sad 15 B8
Novocherkassk 17 A6
Novokuznetsk 18 D9
Novomoskovsk 18 D4
Novorossiysk 17 B5
Novoshakhtinsk 17 A5
Novosibirsk 18 D9
Novosibirskiye Ostrova 19 B15
Novotroitsk 18 D6
Nowata 41 G7
Nowra 32 B5
Noxon 38 C6
Nu Jiang → 20 D4
Nu Shan 20 D4
Nubian Desert = Nûbîya, Es Sahrâ en 27 D12
Nûbîya, Es Sahrâ en 27 D12
Nueces → 41 M6
Nueltin L. 36 B10
Nueva Rosita 44 B4
Nuevitas 45 C9
Nuevo Laredo 44 B5
Nugget Pt. 33 M2
Nuhaka 33 H6
Nukey Bluff 32 B2
Nuku'alofa 34 K10
Nukulaelae 31 B14
Nukus 18 E6
Nullarbor Plain 30 G4
Numalla, L. 32 A3
Numazu 22 F6
Numurkah 32 C4
Nunap Isua 37 C15
Nunavut □ 37 B11
Nunivak I. 36 B3
Nuremberg = Nürnberg 16 D5
Nuriootpa 32 B2
Nürnberg 16 D5
Nushki 24 C5
Nuuk 37 B14
Nuweveldberge 29 L4
Nuyts Arch. 32 B1
Nyainqentanglha Shan 20 D4
Nyasa, L. 29 G6
Nymagee 32 B4
Nyngan 32 B4
Nyoman = Neman → 18 D3
Nysa 16 C8
Nyssa 38 E5

O

Oa, Mull of 10 F2
Oacoma 40 D5
Oahe, L. 40 C4
Oahe Dam 40 C4
Oak Harbor 38 B2
Oak Hill 42 G5
Oak Ridge 43 G3
Oakdale 41 K8
Oakes 40 B5
Oakesdale 38 C5
Oakey 32 A5
Oakham 9 E7
Oakland 39 H2
Oakley, *Idaho, U.S.A.* 38 E7
Oakley, *Kans., U.S.A.* 40 F4
Oakridge 38 E2
Oamaru 33 L3
Oates Land 6 D15
Oatlands 32 D4
Oaxaca 44 D5
Ob → 18 C7
Oba 37 D11
Oban 10 E3
Obbia 24 E3
Oberhausen 16 C3
Oberlin, *Kans., U.S.A.* 40 F4
Oberlin, *La., U.S.A.* 41 K8
Oberon 32 B4
Obi 23 D4
Obihiro 22 B8
Obskaya Guba 18 C8
Ocala 43 L4
Ocanomowoc 40 D10
Occidental, Cordillera 46 C3
Ocean City, *Md., U.S.A.* 42 F8
Ocean City, *N.J., U.S.A.* 42 F8
Ocean Park 38 C1
Oceanside 39 K5
Ochil Hills 10 E5
Ocho Rios 44 a
Ocilla 43 K4
Ocmulgee → 43 K4
Oconee → 43 K4
Oconto 42 C2
Oconto Falls 42 C1
Odawara 22 F6
Odense 7 F6
Oder → 16 B7
Odesa 17 A4
Odessa = Odesa 17 A4
Odessa, *Tex., U.S.A.* 41 K3
Odessa, *Wash., U.S.A.* 38 C4
O'Donnell 41 J4
Odra = Oder → 16 B7
Oelrichs 40 D3
Oelwein 40 D9
Offa 26 G6
Offaly □ 11 C4
Offenbach 16 C4
Ogaden 24 E3
Ōgaki 22 F5
Ogallala 40 E4
Ogasawara Gunto 34 E6
Ogbomosho 26 G6
Ogden 38 F7
Ogdensburg 42 C8
Ogeechee → 43 K5
Ogooué → 28 E1
Ogowe = Ogooué → 28 E1
Ohai 33 L2
Ohakune 33 H5
Ohau, L. 33 L2
Ohio □ 42 E3
Ohio → 42 G1
Ohře → 16 C7
Ohridsko Jezero 15 D9
Oil City 42 E6
Oise → 12 B5
Oistins 45 g
Oistins B. 45 g
Ōita 22 G2
Ojai 39 J4
Ojos del Salado, Cerro 48 B3
Oka → 18 D5
Okahandja 29 J3
Okanogan 38 B4
Okanogan → 38 B4
Okavango Delta 29 H4
Okayama 22 F3
Okazaki 22 F5
Okeechobee 43 M5
Okeechobee, L. 43 M5
Okefenokee Swamp 43 K4
Okehampton 9 G4
Okha 19 D15
Okhotsk 19 D15
Okhotsk, Sea of 19 D15
Okinawa-Jima 21 D7
Oklahoma □ 41 H6
Oklahoma City 41 H6
Okmulgee 41 H7
Okolona 41 J10
Oktyabrskoy Revolyutsii, Ostrov 19 B10
Okuru 33 K2
Ola 41 H8
Olancha 39 H4
Öland 7 F7
Olary 32 B3
Olathe 40 F7
Old Crow 36 B6
Old Town 43 C11
Oldbury 9 F5
Oldcastle 11 C4
Oldenburg 16 B4
Oldham 8 D5
Oldmeldrum 10 D6
Olean 42 D6
Olekminsk 19 C13
Olenek → 19 B13
Oléron, Î. d' 12 D3
Ölgiy 20 B3
Ólimbos, Óros 15 D10
Olinda 47 E12
Olney, *Ill., U.S.A.* 42 F1
Olney, *Tex., U.S.A.* 41 J5
Olomouc 16 D8
Olsztyn 16 B10
Olt → 15 C11
Olton 41 H3
Olympia 38 C2
Olympic Dam 32 B2
Olympic Mts. 38 C2
Olympic Nat. Park 38 C2
Olympus, Mt. = Ólimbos, Óros 15 D10
Olympus, Mt. 38 C2
Omagh 11 B4
Omagh □ 11 B4
Omaha 40 E7
Omak 38 B4
Oman ■ 24 C4
Oman, G. of 24 C4
Omaruru 29 J3
Ombai, Selat 23 D4
Omdurmân 27 E12
Ometepec 44 D5
Omsk 18 D8
Ōmuta 22 G2
Onaga 40 F6
Onalaska 40 D9
Onancock 42 G8
Onawa 40 D6
One Tree 32 B3
Onega, L. = Onezhskoye Ozero 7 E11
Oneida 42 D8
Oneida L. 42 D8
O'Neill 40 D5
Oneonta 42 D8
Onezhskoye Ozero 7 E11
Ongarue 33 H5
Onida 40 C4
Onitsha 26 G7
Onslow B. 43 H7
Ontario, *Calif., U.S.A.* 39 J5
Ontario, *Oreg., U.S.A.* 38 D5
Ontario □ 37 C11
Ontario, L. 42 D7
Ontonagon 40 B10
Oodnadatta 32 A2
Opava 16 D8
Opelika 43 J3
Opelousas 41 K8
Opheim 38 B10
Opole 16 C8
Oporto = Porto 13 B1
Opotiki 33 H6
Opp 43 K2
Opportunity 38 C5
Opua 33 F5
Opunake 33 H4
Oracle 39 K8
Oradea 17 A2
Öræfajökull 7 B2
Oral = Zhayyq → 18 E6
Oral 18 D6
Oran 26 A5
Orange, *Australia* 30 G8
Orange, *France* 12 D6
Orange, *Tex., U.S.A.* 41 K8
Orange, *Va., U.S.A.* 42 F6
Orange → 29 K3
Orange, C. 47 C8
Orange Grove 41 M6
Orangeburg 43 J5
Orbost 32 C4
Orchard City 39 G10
Ord 40 E5
Orderville 39 H7
Ordos = Mu Us Shamo 21 C5
Ordway 40 F3
Ore Mts. = Erzgebirge 16 C6
Örebro 7 F7
Oregon 40 D10
Oregon □ 38 E3
Oregon City 38 D2
Orel 18 D4
Orem 38 F8

St-Martin, C.

Orenburg 18 D6
Orense = Ourense 13 A2
Orepuki 33 M1
Orford Ness 9 E9
Orhon Gol → 20 A5
Oriental, Cordillera 46 B4
Orinoco → 46 B6
Orissa □ 25 D7
Oristano 14 E3
Orizaba 44 D5
Orizaba, Pico de 44 D5
Orkney Is. 10 B6
Orland 38 G2
Orlando 43 L5
Orléanais 12 C5
Orléans 12 C4
Ormara 24 C5
Ormoc 23 B4
Ormond 33 H6
Ormond Beach 43 L5
Ormskirk 8 D5
Örnsköldsvik 7 E7
Oro Valley 39 K8
Orofino 38 C5
Orono 43 C11
Oronsay 10 E2
Oroqen Zizhiqi 21 A7
Oroville, *Calif., U.S.A.* 38 G3
Oroville, *Wash., U.S.A.* 38 B4
Orroroo 32 B2
Orsha 18 D4
Orsk 18 D6
Ortonville 40 C6
Orūmīyeh, Daryācheh-ye 24 B3
Oruro 46 G5
Orwell → 9 F9
Osage 40 D8
Osage → 40 F9
Osage City 40 F7
Ōsaka 22 F4
Osawatomie 40 F7
Osborne 40 F5
Osceola, *Ark., U.S.A.* 41 H10
Osceola, *Iowa, U.S.A.* 40 E8
Oscoda 42 C4
Osh 18 E8
Oshawa 37 D12
Oshkosh, *Nebr., U.S.A.* 40 E3
Oshkosh, *Wis., U.S.A.* 40 C10
Oshogbo 26 G6
Osijek 15 B8
Osipenko = Berdyansk 17 A5
Osizweni 29 K6
Oskaloosa 40 E8
Oskarshamn 7 F7
Öskemen 18 E9
Oslo 7 F6
Oslofjorden 7 F6
Osnabrück 16 B4
Osorno 48 E2
Ossa, Mt. 30 J8
Ossabaw I. 43 K5
Østerdalälven 7 E6
Östersund 7 E6
Ostfriesische Inseln 16 B3
Ostrava 16 D9
Ostrów Wielkopolski 16 C8
Oswego 42 D7
Oswestry 8 E4
Otago □ 33 L2
Otago Harbour 33 L3
Otaki 33 J5
Otaru 22 B7
Othello 38 C4
Otjiwarongo 29 J3
Otorohanga 33 H5
Otranto 15 D8
Otranto, Str. of 15 D8
Ōtsu 22 F4
Ottawa = Outaouais → 37 D12
Ottawa, *Canada* 37 D12
Ottawa, *Ill., U.S.A.* 40 E10
Ottawa, *Kans., U.S.A.* 40 F7
Ottawa Is. 37 C11
Ottery St. Mary 9 G4
Ottumwa 40 E8
Otway, C. 32 C3
Ouachita → 41 K9
Ouachita, L. 41 H8
Ouachita Mts. 41 H7
Ouagadougou 26 F5
Ouahran = Oran 26 A5
Oubangi → 28 E3
Oudtshoorn 29 L4
Ouessant, Î. d' 12 B1
Oughterard 11 C2
Oujda 26 B5
Oulu 7 D9
Oulujärvi 7 E9
Oulujoki → 7 D9
Ouray 39 G10
Ourense 13 A2
Ouse →, *E. Susx., U.K.* 9 G8
Ouse →, *N. Yorks., U.K.* 8 D7
Outaouais → 37 D12
Outer Hebrides 10 D1
Outjo 29 J3
Ouyen 32 C3
Ovalau 33 C8
Overland Park 40 F7
Overton 39 H6
Oviedo 13 A3
Owaka 33 M2
Owatonna 40 C8
Owen Sound 37 D11
Owen Stanley Ra. 30 B8
Owens L. 39 H5
Owensboro 42 G2
Owo 26 G7
Owosso 42 D3
Owyhee 38 F5
Owyhee → 38 E5
Owyhee, L. 38 E5
Ox Mts. = Slieve Gamph 11 B3
Oxford, *N.Z.* 33 K4
Oxford, *U.K.* 9 F6
Oxford, *Miss., U.S.A.* 41 H10
Oxford, *N.C., U.S.A.* 43 G6
Oxford, *Ohio, U.S.A.* 42 F3
Oxfordshire □ 9 F6
Oxnard 39 J4
Oxus = Amudarya → 18 E6
Oyama 22 E6
Oykel → 10 D4
Oyo 26 G6
Ozark, *Ala., U.S.A.* 43 K3
Ozark, *Ark., U.S.A.* 41 H8
Ozark, *Mo., U.S.A.* 41 G8
Ozark Plateau 41 G9
Ozarks, L. of the 40 F8
Ozona 41 K4

P

Paamiut 37 B15
Paarl 29 L3
Pabbay 10 D1
Pacaraima, Sa. 46 C6
Pachuca 44 C5
Pacific-Antarctic Ridge 35 M16
Pacific Grove 39 H3
Pacific Ocean 35 G14
Padang 23 D2
Padangsidempuan 23 C1
Paderborn 16 C4
Pádova 14 B4
Padre I. 41 M6
Padstow 9 G3
Padua = Pádova 14 B4
Paducah, *Ky., U.S.A.* 42 G1
Paducah, *Tex., U.S.A.* 41 H4
Paeroa 33 G5
Pagadian 23 C4
Page 39 H8
Pago Pago 33 B13
Pagosa Springs 39 H10
Pahiatua 33 J5
Pahokee 43 M5
Pahrump 39 H6
Paignton 9 G4
Painted Desert 39 J8
Paintsville 42 G4
País Vasco □ 13 A4
Paisley, *U.K.* 10 F4
Paisley, *U.S.A.* 38 E3
Pak Tam Chung 21 G11
Pakistan ■ 24 C5
Pakxe 23 B2
Palacios 41 L6
Palana 32 C4
Palanpur 25 C6
Palapye 29 J5
Palatka 43 L5
Palau ■ 23 C5
Palawan 23 C3
Palembang 23 D2
Palencia 13 A3
Palermo, *Italy* 14 E5
Palermo, *U.S.A.* 38 G3
Palestine 41 K7
Palghat 25 D6
Palikir 34 G7
Palisades Reservoir 38 E8
Palk Strait 25 E6
Palm Bay 43 L5
Palm Beach 43 M6
Palm Coast 43 L5
Palm Springs 39 K5
Palma de Mallorca 13 C7
Palmas, C. 26 H4
Palmdale 39 J4
Palmer 36 B5
Palmer Lake 40 F2
Palmer Land 6 E4
Palmerston 33 L3
Palmerston North 31 J14
Palmetto 43 M4
Palmira 46 C3
Palmyra 40 F9
Palmyra Is. 35 G11
Palopo 23 D4
Palu 23 D3
Pamiers 12 E4
Pamir 18 F8
Pamlico → 43 H7
Pamlico Sd. 43 H8
Pampa 41 H4
Pampas 48 D4
Pamplona 13 A5
Pana 40 F10
Panaca 39 H6
Panaji 25 D6
Panamá 45 F9
Panama ■ 45 F9
Panamá, G. de 45 F9
Panama Canal 45 F9
Panama City 43 K3
Panamint Range 39 H5
Panay 23 B4
Pančevo 15 B9
Panevėžys 7 F8
Pangkajene 23 D3
Pangkalpinang 23 D2
Pangnirtung 37 B13
Panguitch 39 H7
Panhandle 41 H4
Pantar 23 D4
Pantelleria 14 F4
Paola 40 F7
Paonia 39 G10
Papa Stour 10 A7
Papa Westray 10 B6
Papakura 33 G5
Papantla 44 C5
Papeete 35 J13
Papua □ 23 D5
Papua, G. of 30 B7
Papua New Guinea ■ 34 H6
Pará = Belém 47 D9
Pará □ 47 D8
Paracel Is. 23 B3
Parachilna 32 B2
Paradise 38 G3
Paradise Valley 38 F5
Paragould 41 G9
Paraguay ■ 46 H7
Paraguay → 48 B5
Paraíba = João Pessoa 47 E12
Paramaribo 47 B7
Paraná 48 C4
Paraná → 48 C5
Paraparaumu 33 J5
Parbatipur 25 C7
Pardubice 16 C7
Parecis, Serra dos 46 F7
Parepare 23 D3
Paris, *France* 12 B5
Paris, *Idaho, U.S.A.* 38 E8
Paris, *Ky., U.S.A.* 42 F3
Paris, *Tenn., U.S.A.* 43 G1
Paris, *Tex., U.S.A.* 41 J7
Park City 41 G6
Park Falls 40 C9
Park Hills 41 G9
Park Range 38 G10
Park Rapids 40 B7
Park River 40 A6
Parker 39 J6
Parker Dam 39 J6
Parkersburg 42 F5
Parkes 32 B4
Parkston 40 D6
Parma, *Italy* 12 D9
Parma, *Idaho, U.S.A.* 38 E5
Parma, *Ohio, U.S.A.* 42 E5
Parnaíba → 47 D10
Paroo → 32 B3
Parowan 39 H7
Parrett → 9 F4
Parris I. 43 J5
Parry Is. 6 B1
Parry Sound 37 D12
Parsons 41 G7
Pasadena, *Calif., U.S.A.* 39 J4
Pasadena, *Tex., U.S.A.* 41 L7
Pascagoula 41 K10
Pascagoula → 41 K10
Pasco 38 C4
Pascua, I. de 35 K17
Pasni 24 C5
Paso Robles 39 J3
Passage West 11 E3
Passau 16 D6
Passo Fundo 48 B6
Pasto 46 C3
Patagonia, *Argentina* 48 F3
Patagonia, *U.S.A.* 39 L8
Patchewollock 32 C3
Patchogue 42 E9
Patea 33 H5
Pateros 38 B4
Paterson 42 E8
Pathfinder Reservoir 38 E10
Patiala 25 B6
Patna 25 C7
Patos, L. dos 48 C6
Pátrai 15 E9
Patras = Pátrai 15 E9
Patten 43 C11
Patterson, *Calif., U.S.A.* 39 H3
Patterson, *La., U.S.A.* 41 L9
Pau 12 E3
Paulatuk 36 B7
Pauls Valley 41 H6
Pavia 12 D8
Pavlodar 18 D8
Pavlograd = Pavlohrad 17 A5
Pavlohrad 17 A5
Pawhuska 41 G6
Pawnee 41 G6
Pawnee City 40 E6
Pawtucket 42 E10
Paxton, *Ill., U.S.A.* 42 E1
Paxton, *Nebr., U.S.A.* 40 E4
Payakumbuh 23 D2
Payette 38 D5
Payne L. 37 C12
Paynesville 40 C7
Payson 39 J8
Paz, B. de la 44 C2
Pazardzhik 15 C11
Peace → 36 C8
Peace River 36 C8
Peach Springs 39 J7
Peachtree City 43 J3
Peak District 8 D6
Peak Hill 32 B4
Peake Cr. → 32 A2
Peale, Mt. 39 G9
Pearl → 41 K10
Pearsall 41 L5
Pease → 41 H5
Peawanuck 37 C11
Pechora → 18 C6
Pecos 41 K3
Pecos → 41 L3
Pécs 16 E9
Pedder, L. 32 D4
Pedirka 32 A2
Pee Dee → 43 J6
Peebinga 32 B3
Peebles 10 F5
Peekskill 42 E9
Peel 8 C3
Peel →, *Australia* 32 B5
Peel →, *Canada* 36 B6
Peel Sound 36 A10
Peera Peera Poolanna L. 32 A2
Pegasus Bay 33 K4
Pegu 25 D8
Pegu Yoma 25 D8
Peipus, L. = Chudskoye, Ozero 7 F9
Pekalongan 23 D2
Pekanbaru 23 C2
Pekin 40 E10
Peking = Beijing 21 C6
Pelée, Mt. 44 c
Peleng 23 D4
Pella 40 E8
Pelly → 36 B6
Pelly Bay 37 B11
Peloponnese = Pelopónnisos □ 15 F10
Pelopónnisos □ 15 F10
Pelorus Sd. 33 J4
Pelotas 48 C6
Pelvoux, Massif du 12 D7
Pematangsiantar 23 C1
Pemba I. 28 F7
Pembina 40 A6
Pembroke, *Canada* 37 D12
Pembroke, *U.K.* 9 F3
Pembrokeshire □ 9 F3
Pen-y-Ghent 8 C5
Penarth 9 F4
Penas, G. de 48 F2
Pend Oreille → 38 B5
Pend Oreille, L. 38 C5
Pendleton 38 D4
Peng Chau 21 G11
Penguin 32 D4
Penicuik 10 F5
Peninsular Malaysia □ 23 C2
Penkridge 8 E5
Penmarch, Pte. de 12 C1
Penn Hills 42 E6
Penn Yan 42 D7
Pennines 8 C5
Pennsylvania □ 42 E7
Penobscot → 43 C11
Penobscot B. 43 C11
Penola 32 C3
Penong 30 G5
Penrith, *Australia* 32 B5
Penrith, *U.K.* 8 C5
Penryn 9 G2
Pensacola 43 K2
Pensacola Mts. 6 F5
Penshurst 32 C3
Penticton 36 D8
Pentland Firth 10 C5
Pentland Hills 10 F5
Penza 18 D5
Penzance 9 G2
Peoria, *Ariz., U.S.A.* 39 K7
Peoria, *Ill., U.S.A.* 40 E10
Perabumulih 23 D2
Perdido, Mte. 13 A6
Perdu, Mt. = Perdido, Mte. 13 A6
Pereira 46 C3
Perham 40 B7
Péribonca → 37 D12
Périgueux 12 D4
Perm 18 D6
Pernambuco = Recife 47 E12
Pernatty Lagoon 32 B2
Perpendicular Pt. 32 B5
Perpignan 12 E5
Perry, *Fla., U.S.A.* 43 K4
Perry, *Ga., U.S.A.* 43 J4
Perry, *Iowa, U.S.A.* 40 E7
Perry, *Okla., U.S.A.* 41 G6
Perryton 41 G4
Perryville 41 G10
Persian Gulf = Gulf, The 24 C4
Perth, *Australia* 30 G2
Perth, *U.K.* 10 E5
Perth & Kinross □ 10 E5
Perth Amboy 42 E8
Peru 42 E2
Peru ■ 46 D4
Peru Basin 35 J18
Peru-Chile Trench 35 K20
Perúgia 14 C5
Pervouralsk 18 D6
Pescara 14 C6
Peshawar 25 B6
Peshtigo 42 C2
Petaluma 38 G2
Peter I. 45 e
Peterborough, *Australia* 32 B2
Peterborough, *Canada* 37 D12
Peterborough, *U.K.* 9 E7
Peterculter 10 D6
Peterhead 10 D7
Peterlee 8 C6
Petersburg, *Alaska, U.S.A.* 36 C6
Petersburg, *Va., U.S.A.* 42 G7
Petersburg, *W. Va., U.S.A.* 42 F6
Petersfield 9 F7
Petit-Canal 44 b
Petit Piton 45 f
Petite Terre, Iles de la 44 b
Petitot → 36 B7
Petitsikapau L. 37 C13
Peto 44 C7
Petone 33 J5
Petoskey 42 C3
Petrified Forest Nat. Park 39 J9
Petrograd = Sankt-Peterburg 18 D4
Petropavl 18 D7
Petropavlovsk-Kamchatskiy 19 D16
Petrópolis 47 H10
Petrovsk-Zabaykalskiy 19 D11
Petrozavodsk 7 E10
Pforzheim 16 D4
Phan Rang 23 B2
Phan Thiet 23 B2
Pharr 41 M5
Phenix City 43 J3
Philadelphia, *Miss., U.S.A.* 41 J10
Philadelphia, *Pa., U.S.A.* 42 F8
Philip 40 C4
Philippi 42 F5
Philippines ■ 23 B4
Philipsburg 38 C7
Phillip I. 32 C4
Phillips 40 C9
Phillipsburg 40 F5
Philomath 38 D2
Phitsanulok 23 B2
Phnom Penh 23 B2
Phnum Penh = Phnom Penh 23 B2
Phoenix 39 K7
Phoenix Is. 34 H10
Phra Nakhon Si Ayutthaya 23 B2
Phuket 23 C1
Piacenza 12 D8
Pian Cr. → 32 B4
Picardie 12 B5
Picardy = Picardie 12 B5
Picayune 41 K10
Pickering 8 C7
Pickering, Vale of 8 C7
Pickwick L. 43 H1
Picton, *Australia* 32 B5
Picton, *N.Z.* 33 J5
Pidurutalagala 25 E7
Piedmont = Piemonte □ 12 D7
Piedmont 43 J3
Piedras Negras 44 B4
Piemonte □ 12 D7
Pierre 40 C4
Piet Retief 29 K6
Pietermaritzburg 29 K6
Piggott 41 G9
Pikes Peak 40 F2
Pikeville 42 G4
Pilcomayo → 48 B5
Pilliga 32 B4
Pilot Point 41 J6
Pilot Rock 38 D4
Pilsen = Plzeň 16 D6
Pima 39 K9
Pimba 32 B2
Pinar del Río 45 C8
Pinckneyville 40 F10
Pindos Óros 15 E9
Pindus Mts. = Pindos Óros 15 E9
Pine Bluff 41 H9
Pine Bluffs 40 E2
Pine City 40 C8
Pine Point 36 B8
Pine Ridge 40 D3
Pine River 40 B7
Pinedale 38 E9
Pinetop 39 J9
Pineville 41 K8
Ping → 23 B2
Pingdingshan 21 C6
Pingdong 21 D7
Pingliang 20 C5
P'ingtung 21 D7
Pingxiang 20 D5
Pinnaroo 32 C3
Pinos Pt. 39 H3
Pinsk 18 D3
Pioche 39 H6
Piotrków Trybunalski 16 C9
Pipestone 40 D6
Piqua 42 E3
Piracicaba 47 H9
Piræus = Piraiévs 15 F10
Piraiévs 15 F10
Pirmasens 16 D3
Pisa 14 C4
Pishan 20 C2
Pistóia 14 C4
Pit → 38 F2
Pitarpunga, L. 32 B3
Pitcairn I. 35 K14
Piteå 7 D8
Piteşti 15 B11
Pitlochry 10 E5
Pittsburg, *Kans., U.S.A.* 41 G7
Pittsburg, *Tex., U.S.A.* 41 J7
Pittsburgh 42 E6
Pittsfield, *Ill., U.S.A.* 40 F9
Pittsfield, *Maine, U.S.A.* 43 C11
Pittsfield, *Mass., U.S.A.* 42 D9
Pittsworth 32 A5
Piura 46 E2
Placentia 37 D14
Placentia B. 37 D14
Placerville 38 G3
Placetas 45 C9
Plainfield 42 E8
Plains, *Mont., U.S.A.* 38 C6
Plains, *Tex., U.S.A.* 41 J3
Plainview, *Nebr., U.S.A.* 40 D6
Plainview, *Tex., U.S.A.* 41 H4
Plainwell 42 D3
Plano 41 J6
Plant City 43 M4
Plaquemine 41 K9
Plata, Río de la 48 C5
Platte 40 D5
Platte →, *Mo., U.S.A.* 40 F7
Platte →, *Nebr., U.S.A.* 40 E7
Platteville 40 D9
Plattsburgh 42 C9
Plattsmouth 40 E7
Plauen 16 C6
Pleasanton 41 L5
Pleasantville 42 F8
Plenty, B. of 31 H14
Plentywood 40 A2
Pleven 15 C11
Płock 16 B9
Ploieşti 15 B12
Plovdiv 15 C11
Plover Cove Res. 21 G11
Plummer 38 C5
Plymouth, *U.K.* 9 G3
Plymouth, *Ind., U.S.A.* 42 E2
Plymouth, *N.C., U.S.A.* 43 H7
Plymouth, *Wis., U.S.A.* 42 D2
Plynlimon = Pumlumon Fawr 9 E4
Plzeň 16 D6
Po → 14 B5
Po Toi 21 G11
Pocahontas, *Ark., U.S.A.* 41 G9
Pocahontas, *Iowa, U.S.A.* 40 D7
Pocatello 38 E7
Pocomoke City 42 F8
Podgorica 15 C8
Pohnpei 34 G7
Point Hope 36 B3
Point L. 36 B8
Point Pleasant 42 F4
Pointe-à-Pitre 44 b
Pointe-Noire, *Congo* 28 E2
Pointe Noire, *Guadeloupe* 44 b
Poitiers 12 C4
Poitou 12 C3
Pojoaque 39 J11
Pokataroo 32 A4
Pokhara 25 C7
Pokrovsk = Engels 18 D5
Polacca 39 J8
Poland ■ 7 G7
Polesye = Pripet Marshes 7 G9
Polokwane 29 J5
Polson 38 C6
Poltava 18 E4
Polynesia 35 J11
Pomeroy, *Ohio, U.S.A.* 42 F4
Pomeroy, *Wash., U.S.A.* 38 C5
Pomona, *Australia* 32 A5
Pomona, *U.S.A.* 39 J5
Pompano Beach 43 M5
Pompeys Pillar 38 D10
Ponca 40 D6
Ponca City 41 G6
Ponce 45 d
Ponchatoula 41 K9
Pond Inlet 37 A12
Pondicherry 25 D6
Ponta Grossa 48 B6
Pontarlier 12 C7
Pontchartrain L. 41 K10
Pontevedra 13 A1
Pontiac, *Ill., U.S.A.* 40 E10
Pontiac, *Mich., U.S.A.* 42 D4
Pontianak 23 D2
Pontivy 12 B2
Pontypool 9 F4
Poochera 32 B1
Poole 9 G6
Poona = Pune 25 D6
Pooncarie 32 B3
Poopelloe L. 32 B3
Poopó, L. de 46 G5
Popayán 46 C3
Popilta L. 32 B3
Popio L. 32 B3
Poplar 40 A2
Poplar Bluff 41 G9
Poplarville 41 K10
Popocatépetl, Volcán 44 D5
Porbandar 25 C5
Porcupine → 36 B5
Pori 7 E8
Port Alberni 36 D7
Port Allegany 42 E6
Port Allen 41 K9
Port Angeles 38 B2
Port Antonio 44 a
Port Aransas 41 M6
Port Arthur, *Australia* 32 D4
Port Arthur, *U.S.A.* 41 L8
Port-au-Prince 45 D10
Port Augusta 30 G6
Port Austin 42 C4
Port Blair 25 D8
Port Broughton 32 B2
Port-Cartier 37 C13
Port Chalmers 33 L3
Port Charlotte 43 M4
Port Chester 42 E9
Port Clinton 42 E4
Port Davey 32 D4
Port-de-Paix 45 D10
Port Elizabeth 29 L5
Port Ellen 10 F2
Port Erin 8 C3
Port Fairy 32 C3
Port-Gentil 28 E1
Port Germein 32 B2
Port Gibson 41 K9
Port Glasgow 10 F4
Port Harcourt 26 H7
Port Hawkesbury 37 D13
Port Hedland 30 E2
Port Henry 42 C9
Port Hope Simpson 37 C14
Port Huron 42 D4
Port Jefferson 42 E9
Port Kenny 32 B1
Port Lairge = Waterford 11 D4
Port Laoise 11 C4
Port Lavaca 41 L6
Port Lincoln 30 G6
Port-Louis 44 b
Port MacDonnell 32 C3
Port McNeill 36 C7
Port Macquarie 30 G9
Port Maria 44 a
Port Morant 44 a
Port Moresby 34 H6
Port Neches 41 L8
Port Nolloth 29 K3
Port of Spain 46 A6
Port Orange 43 L5
Port Orford 38 E1
Port Pegasus 33 M1
Port Phillip B. 32 C3
Port Pirie 30 G6
Port Said = Bûr Sa'îd 27 B12
Port St. Joe 43 L3
Port St. Lucie 43 M5
Port Shepstone 29 L6
Port Stanley = Stanley 48 G5
Port Sudan = Bûr Sûdân 27 E13
Port Sulphur 41 L10
Port Talbot 9 F4
Port Townsend 38 B2
Port Vila 34 J8
Port Wakefield 32 B2
Port Washington 42 D2
Portadown 11 B5
Portaferry 11 B6
Portage 40 D10
Portage La Prairie 36 D10
Portageville 41 G10
Portales 41 H3
Portarlington 11 C4
Porterville 39 H4
Porthcawl 9 F4
Porthill 38 B5
Porthmadog 8 E3
Portile de Fier 15 B10
Portishead 9 F5
Portknockie 10 D6
Portland, *N.S.W., Australia* 32 B5
Portland, *Vic., Australia* 32 C3
Portland, *Maine, U.S.A.* 37 D12
Portland, *Mich., U.S.A.* 42 D3
Portland, *Oreg., U.S.A.* 38 D2
Portland, *Tex., U.S.A.* 41 M6
Portland, I. of 9 G5
Portland B. 32 C3
Portland Bight 44 a
Portland Bill 9 G5
Portland Pt. 44 a
Portmadoc = Porthmadog 8 E3
Portmore 44 a
Porto 13 B1
Pôrto Alegre 48 C6
Porto-Novo 26 G6
Porto-Vecchio 12 F8
Pôrto Velho 46 E6
Portola 38 G3
Portoviejo 46 D2
Portpatrick 10 G3
Portree 10 D2
Portrush 11 A5
Portsmouth, *U.K.* 9 G6
Portsmouth, *N.H., U.S.A.* 43 D10
Portsmouth, *Ohio, U.S.A.* 42 F4
Portsmouth, *Va., U.S.A.* 42 G7
Portsoy 10 D6
Portstewart 11 A5
Porttipahtan tekojärvi 7 D9
Portugal ■ 13 C1
Portumna 11 C3
Posadas 48 B5
Possum Kingdom L. 41 J5
Post 41 J4
Post Falls 38 C5
Postmasburg 29 K4
Potchefstroom 29 K5
Poteau 41 H7
Poteet 41 L5
Potenza 14 D6
Poteriteri, L. 33 M1
Potomac → 42 G7
Potosí 46 G5
Potsdam, *Germany* 16 B6
Potsdam, *U.S.A.* 42 C8
Pottstown 42 E8
Pottsville 42 E7
Poughkeepsie 42 E9
Poulaphouca Res. 11 C5
Poulsbo 38 C2
Poulton-le-Fylde 8 D5
Poverty B. 33 H7
Powder → 40 B2
Powder River 38 E10
Powell 38 D9
Powell, L. 39 H8
Powell River 36 D7
Powers 42 C2
Powys □ 9 E4
Poyang Hu 21 D6
Poza Rica 44 C5
Poznań 16 B8
Prague = Praha 16 C7
Praha 16 C7
Prairie City 38 D4
Prairie Dog Town Fork → 41 H5
Prairie du Chien 40 D9
Prato 14 C4
Pratt 41 G5
Prattville 43 J2
Praya 23 D3
Premont 41 M5
Prentice 40 C9
Prescott, *Ariz., U.S.A.* 39 J7
Prescott, *Ark., U.S.A.* 41 J8
Prescott Valley 39 J7
Preservation Inlet 33 M1
Presho 40 D4
Presidente Prudente 47 H8
Presidio 41 L2
Prespansko Jezero 15 D9
Presque Isle 43 B12
Prestatyn 8 D4
Presteigne 9 E5
Preston, *U.K.* 8 D5
Preston, *Idaho, U.S.A.* 38 E8
Preston, *Minn., U.S.A.* 40 D8
Prestonburg 42 G4
Prestwick 10 F4
Pretoria 29 K5
Pribilof Is. 36 C2
Price 38 G8
Prichard 43 K1
Prieska 29 K4
Priest L. 38 B5
Priest River 38 B5
Prime Seal I. 32 D4
Prince Albert 36 C9
Prince Albert Pen. 36 A8
Prince Albert Sd. 36 A8
Prince Charles I. 37 B12
Prince Charles Mts. 6 E10
Prince Edward I. □ 37 D13
Prince Edward Is. 5 G11
Prince George 36 C7
Prince of Wales I., *Canada* 36 A10
Prince of Wales I., *U.S.A.* 36 C6
Prince Patrick I. 6 B1
Prince Rupert 36 C6
Princeton, *Ill., U.S.A.* 40 E10
Princeton, *Ind., U.S.A.* 42 F2
Princeton, *Ky., U.S.A.* 42 G2
Princeton, *Mo., U.S.A.* 40 E8
Princeton, *N.J., U.S.A.* 42 E8
Princeton, *W. Va., U.S.A.* 42 G5
Principe, I. de 5 D10
Prineville 38 D3
Pripet = Prypyat → 18 D4
Pripet Marshes 7 G9
Pripyat Marshes = Pripet Marshes 7 G9
Priština 15 C9
Privas 12 D6
Prizren 15 C9
Probolinggo 23 D3
Progreso 44 C7
Prokopyevsk 18 D9
Prosser 38 C4
Proston 32 A5
Provence 12 E6
Providence, *Ky., U.S.A.* 42 G2
Providence, *R.I., U.S.A.* 42 E10
Providencia, I. de 45 E8
Provins 12 B5
Provo 38 F8
Prudhoe Bay 36 A5
Prut → 15 B13
Pryor 41 G7
Prypyat → 18 D4
Pskov 18 D3
Puebla 44 D5
Pueblo 40 F2
Puerca, Pta. 45 d
Puerco → 39 J10
Puerto Barrios 44 D7
Puerto Cabezas 45 E8
Puerto Cortés 44 D7
Puerto La Cruz 46 A6
Puerto Montt 48 E2
Puerto Plata 45 D10
Puerto Princesa 23 C3
Puerto Rico ■ 45 d
Puffin I. 11 E1
Puget Sound 38 C2
Pukaki, L. 33 L3
Pukapuka 35 J11
Pukekohe 33 G5
Pulaski, *N.Y., U.S.A.* 42 D7
Pulaski, *Tenn., U.S.A.* 43 H2
Pulaski, *Va., U.S.A.* 42 G5
Pullman 38 C5
Pulog, Mt. 23 B4
Pumlumon Fawr 9 E4
Pune 25 D6
Punjab □, *India* 25 B6
Punjab □, *Pakistan* 25 B6
Punta, Cerro de 45 d
Punta Arenas 48 G2
Punta Gorda 43 M5
Punto Fijo 46 A4
Punxsatawney 42 E6
Purbeck, Isle of 9 G6
Purcell 41 H6
Puri 25 D7
Purus → 46 D6
Purvis 41 K10
Pusan 21 C7
Putaruru 33 H5
Puttalam 25 E6
Putumayo → 46 D5
Puvirnituq 37 B12
Puy-de-Dôme 12 D5
Puyallup 38 C2
Pwllheli 8 E3
Pyapon 25 D8
Pyatigorsk 17 B6
P'yŏngyang 21 C7
Pyote 41 K3
Pyramid L. 38 G4
Pyrénées 12 E4

Q

Qaanaaq 6 B3
Qahremānshahr = Bākhtarān 24 B3
Qaidam Pendi 20 C4
Qamdo 20 C4
Qandahār 24 B5
Qaqortoq 37 B6
Qaraghandy 18 E8
Qarqan He → 20 C3
Qarshi 18 F7
Qatar ■ 24 C4
Qattâra, Munkhafed el 27 C11
Qattâra Depression = Qattâra, Munkhafed el 27 C11
Qazvin 24 B4
Qena 27 C12
Qeqertarsuaq, *Greenland* 37 B5
Qeqertarsuaq, *Greenland* 37 B14
Qeshm 24 C4
Qian Hai 21 F10
Qianshan 21 G10
Qi'ao 21 G10
Qi'ao Dao 21 G10
Qikiqtarjuaq 37 B13
Qilian Shan 20 C4
Qingdao 21 C7
Qinghai □ 20 C4
Qinghai Hu 20 C5
Qinhuangdao 21 C6
Qinzhou 20 D5
Qiqihar 19 E13
Qitai 20 B3
Qom 24 B4
Qoraqalpoghistan □ 18 E6
Qostanay 18 D7
Quambatook 32 C3
Quambone 32 B4
Quanah 41 H5
Quang Ngai 23 B2
Quantock Hills 9 F4
Quanzhou 21 D6
Quaqtaq 37 B13
Quartzsite 39 K6
Queanbeyan 32 C4
Québec 37 D12
Québec □ 37 C13
Queen Charlotte Is. 36 C6
Queen Charlotte Sd. 36 C7
Queen Elizabeth Is. 4 A5
Queen Maud G. 36 B9
Queen Maud Land 6 E7
Queenscliff 32 C3
Queensland □ 30 E7
Queenstown, *Australia* 32 D4
Queenstown, *N.Z.* 31 K12
Queenstown, *S. Africa* 29 L5
Quemado, *N. Mex., U.S.A.* 39 J9
Quemado, *Tex., U.S.A.* 41 L4
Querétaro 44 C4
Quesnel 36 C7
Quesnel L. 36 C7
Questa 39 H11
Quetta 24 B5
Quezaltenango 44 E6
Quezon City 23 B4
Qui Nhon 23 B2
Quilon 25 E6
Quilpie 30 F7
Quimper 12 B1
Quincy, *Calif., U.S.A.* 38 G3
Quincy, *Fla., U.S.A.* 43 K3
Quincy, *Ill., U.S.A.* 40 F9
Quincy, *Mass., U.S.A.* 42 D10
Quincy, *Wash., U.S.A.* 38 C4
Quirindi 32 B5
Quitman 43 K4
Quito 46 D3
Quixadá 47 D11
Quorn 32 B2
Qŭqon 18 E8
Quzhou 21 D6
Qyzylorda 18 E7

R

Raahe 7 E8
Raasay 10 D2
Raasay, Sd. of 10 D2
Raba 23 D3
Rabat 26 B4
Rabaul 34 H7
Rābigh 24 C2
Race, C. 37 D14
Rach Gia 23 B2
Racine 42 D2
Radcliff 42 G3
Radford 42 G5
Radnor Forest 9 E4
Radstock, C. 32 B1
Rae 36 B8
Rae Isthmus 37 B11
Raetihi 33 H5
Ragged Pt. 45 g
Raglan 33 G5
Ragusa 14 F6
Railton 32 D4
Rainbow Lake 36 C8
Rainier 38 C2
Rainier, Mt. 38 C3
Rainy L. 36 D10
Raipur 25 C7
Rajahmundry 25 D7
Rajang → 23 C3
Rajasthan □ 25 C6
Rajkot 25 C6
Rajshahi 25 C7
Rakaia 33 K4
Rakaia → 33 K4
Raleigh 43 H6
Ralls 41 J4
Rame Hd. 32 C4
Râmnicu Vâlcea 15 B11
Ramona 39 K5
Rampur 25 C6
Ramree I. 25 D8
Ramsey 8 C3
Ramsgate 9 F9
Rancagua 48 C2
Ranchester 38 D10
Ranchi 25 C7
Randalstown 11 B5
Randers 7 F6
Randolph, *Utah, U.S.A.* 38 F8
Randolph, *Vt., U.S.A.* 42 D9
Rangaunu B. 33 F4
Rangeley 42 C10
Rangely 38 F9
Ranger 41 J5
Rangiora 33 K4
Rangitaiki → 33 G6
Rangitata → 33 K3
Rangoon 25 D8
Rangpur 25 C7
Rankin 41 K4
Rankin Inlet 36 B10
Rankins Springs 32 B4
Rannoch, L. 10 E4
Rannoch Moor 10 E4
Rantemario 23 D3
Rantoul 42 E1
Rapa 35 K13
Raper, C. 37 B13
Rapid City 40 D3
Rapid River 42 C2
Rarotonga 35 K12
Ra's al Khaymah 24 C4
Rasht 24 B3
Rat Islands 36 C1
Rath Luirc 11 D3
Rathdrum 11 D5
Rathkeale 11 D3
Rathlin I. 11 A5
Rathmelton 11 A4
Raton 41 G2
Rattray Hd. 10 D7
Raukumara Ra. 33 H6
Raurkela 25 C7
Ravalli 38 C6
Ravenna, *Italy* 14 B5
Ravenna, *U.S.A.* 40 E5
Ravenswood 42 F5
Rawalpindi 25 B6
Rawene 33 F4
Rawlins 38 F10
Ray 40 A3
Ray, C. 37 D14
Rayleigh 9 F8
Raymond 38 C2
Raymondville 41 M6
Rayong 23 B2
Rayville 41 J9
Raz, Pte. du 12 C1
Ré, Î. de 12 C3
Reading, *U.K.* 9 F7
Reading, *U.S.A.* 42 E8
Reay Forest 10 C4
Recife 47 E12
Red →, *La., U.S.A.* 41 K9
Red →, *N. Dak., U.S.A.* 36 C10
Red Bluff 38 F2
Red Bluff L. 41 K3
Red Cliffs 32 B3
Red Cloud 40 E5
Red Deer 36 C8
Red Lake 36 C10
Red Lake Falls 40 B6
Red Lodge 38 D9
Red Oak 40 E7
Red Rock, L. 40 E8
Red Sea 24 C2
Red Wing 40 C8
Redcar 8 C6
Redcar & Cleveland □ 8 C7
Redcliffe 32 A5
Redding 38 F2
Redditch 9 E6
Redfield 40 C5
Redmond 38 D3
Redon 12 C2
Redruth 9 G2
Redwood City 39 H2
Redwood Falls 40 C7
Redwood Nat. Park 38 F1
Ree, L. 11 C3
Reed City 42 D3
Reedley 39 H4
Reedsburg 40 D9
Reedsport 38 E1
Reefton 33 K3
Reese → 38 F5
Refugio 41 L6
Regensburg 16 D6
Réggio di Calábria 14 E6
Réggio nell'Emília 14 B4
Regina 36 C9
Rehoboth 29 J3
Reichenbach 16 C6
Reidsville 43 G6
Reigate 9 F7
Reims 12 B6
Reindeer L. 36 C9
Reinga, C. 33 F4
Remarkable, Mt. 32 B2
Renfrewshire □ 10 F4
Renmark 32 B3
Rennell 31 C11
Rennes 12 B3
Reno 38 G4
Rensselaer 42 E2
Renton 38 C2
Republic, *Mo., U.S.A.* 41 G8
Republic, *Wash., U.S.A.* 38 B4
Republican → 40 F6
Repulse Bay 37 B11
Reserve 39 K9
Resistencia 48 B5
Resolution I., *Canada* 37 B13
Resolution I., *N.Z.* 33 L1
Retford 8 D7
Réthímnon 15 G11
Réunion ■ 5 F12
Reval = Tallinn 18 D3
Revelstoke 36 C8
Revillagigedo, Is. de 35 F16
Rexburg 38 E8
Rey Malabo 28 D1
Reykjavík 7 B1
Reynosa 44 B5
Rhayader 9 E4
Rhein → 16 C3
Rheine 16 B3
Rheinland-Pfalz □ 16 D3
Rhin = Rhein → 16 C3
Rhine = Rhein → 16 C3
Rhineland-Palatinate = Rheinland-Pfalz □ 16 D3
Rhinelander 40 C10
Rhinns Pt. 10 F2
Rhode Island □ 42 E10
Rhodes = Ródhos 15 F13
Rhodopi Planina 15 D11
Rhön 16 C4
Rhondda 9 F4
Rhondda Cynon Taff □ 9 F4
Rhône → 12 E6
Rhum 10 E2
Rhyl 8 D4
Riau, Kepulauan 23 C2
Ribble → 8 D5
Ribeirão Prêto 47 H9
Riccarton 33 K4
Rice Lake 40 C9
Richards Bay 29 K6
Richardson Lakes 42 C10
Richey 40 B2
Richfield 39 G8
Richland, *Ga., U.S.A.* 43 J3
Richland, *Wash., U.S.A.* 38 C4
Richland Center 40 D9
Richlands 42 G5
Richmond, *N.Z.* 33 J4
Richmond, *U.K.* 8 C6
Richmond, *Calif., U.S.A.* 38 H2
Richmond, *Ind., U.S.A.* 42 F3
Richmond, *Ky., U.S.A.* 42 G3
Richmond, *Mo., U.S.A.* 40 F8
Richmond, *Tex., U.S.A.* 41 L7
Richmond, *Utah, U.S.A.* 38 F8
Richmond, *Va., U.S.A.* 42 G7
Richmond Ra. 32 A5
Richwood 42 F5
Ridgecrest 39 J5
Ridgeland 43 J5
Ridgway 42 E6
Rifle 38 G10
Rīga 18 D3
Rigby 38 E8
Riggins 38 D5
Rigolet 37 C14
Rijeka 14 B6
Riley 38 E4
Rímini 14 B5
Rimouski 37 D13
Rio Branco 46 E5
Rio de Janeiro 47 H10
Río Gallegos 48 G3
Rio Grande = Grande, Rio → 41 N6
Rio Grande, *Brazil* 48 C6
Río Grande, *Nic.* 45 E8
Rio Grande, *Puerto Rico* 45 d
Rio Grande City 41 M5
Río Grande de Santiago → 44 C3
Rio Grande do Norte □ 47 E11
Río Muni □ 28 D2
Rio Rancho 39 J10
Ríobamba 46 D3
Ripley, *Tenn., U.S.A.* 41 H10
Ripley, *W. Va., U.S.A.* 42 F5
Ripon, *U.K.* 8 C6
Ripon, *U.S.A.* 42 D1
Rison 41 J8
Rita Blanca Cr. → 41 H3
Ritzville 38 C4
Riverhead 42 E9
Riverside 39 K5
Riverton, *Australia* 32 B2
Riverton, *N.Z.* 33 M2
Riverton, *U.S.A.* 38 E9
Rivière-du-Loup 37 D13
Rivière-Pilote 44 c
Rivière-Salée 44 c
Rivne 18 D3
Rivoli B. 32 C3
Riyadh = Ar Riyāḍ 24 C3
Road Town 45 e
Roan Plateau 38 G9
Roanne 12 C6
Roanoke, *Ala., U.S.A.* 43 J3
Roanoke, *Va., U.S.A.* 42 G6
Roanoke → 43 H7
Roanoke I. 43 H8
Roanoke Rapids 43 G7
Robbins I. 32 D4
Robert Lee 41 K4
Robertstown 32 B2
Roberval 37 D12
Robinson 42 F2
Robinvale 32 B3
Robson, Mt. 36 C8
Robstown 41 M6
Roca, C. da 13 C1
Rochdale 8 D5
Rochefort 12 D3
Rochelle 40 E10
Rochester, *U.K.* 9 F8
Rochester, *Ind., U.S.A.* 42 E2
Rochester, *Minn., U.S.A.* 40 C8
Rochester, *N.H., U.S.A.* 42 D10
Rochester, *N.Y., U.S.A.* 42 D7
Rock Falls 40 E10
Rock Hill 43 H5
Rock Island 40 E9
Rock Rapids 40 D6
Rock Springs, *Mont., U.S.A.* 38 C10
Rock Springs, *Wyo., U.S.A.* 38 F9
Rock Valley 40 D6
Rockdale 41 K6
Rockford 40 D10
Rockhampton 30 E9
Rockingham 43 H6
Rocklake 40 A5
Rockland, *Idaho, U.S.A.* 38 E7
Rockland, *Maine, U.S.A.* 43 C11
Rockland, *Mich., U.S.A.* 40 B10
Rockmart 43 H3
Rockport, *Mo., U.S.A.* 40 E7
Rockport, *Tex., U.S.A.* 41 L6
Rocksprings 41 K4
Rockville 42 F7
Rockwall 41 J6
Rockwell City 40 D7
Rockwood, *Maine, U.S.A.* 43 C11
Rockwood, *Tenn., U.S.A.* 43 H3
Rocky Ford 40 F3
Rocky Mount 43 H7
Rocky Mountain Nat. Park 38 F11
Rocky Mts. 36 C7
Rodez 12 D5
Ródhos 15 F13
Rodney, C. 33 G5
Rodriguez 5 E13
Roe → 11 A5
Roes Welcome Sd. 37 B11
Rogers 41 G7
Rogers City 42 C4
Rogue → 38 E1
Rojo, C. 44 C5
Rolla 41 G9
Roma, *Australia* 30 F8
Roma, *Italy* 14 D5
Roma, *U.S.A.* 41 M5
Romain C. 43 J6
Romaine → 37 C13
Romania ■ 15 B10
Romans-sur-Isère 12 D6
Rome = Roma 14 D5
Rome, *Ga., U.S.A.* 43 H3
Rome, *N.Y., U.S.A.* 42 D8
Romney 42 F6
Romney Marsh 9 F8
Romorantin-Lanthenay 12 C4
Romsey 9 G6
Rona 10 D3
Ronan 38 C6
Rondônia □ 46 F6
Ronge, L. la 36 C9
Ronne Ice Shelf 6 E4
Roof Butte 39 H9
Roosevelt 38 F8
Roosevelt → 46 E6
Roosevelt I. 6 E16
Roraima □ 46 C6
Roraima, Mt. 46 B6
Rosalia 38 C5
Rosario, *Argentina* 48 C4
Rosario, *Mexico* 44 C3
Roscommon 11 C3
Roscommon □ 11 C3
Roscrea 11 D4
Roseau, *Domin.* 45 D12
Roseau, *U.S.A.* 40 A7
Rosebery 32 D4
Rosebud, *S. Dak., U.S.A.* 40 D4
Rosebud, *Tex., U.S.A.* 41 K6
Roseburg 38 E2
Rosedale 41 J9
Rosenberg 41 L7
Rosenheim 16 E6
Rosetown 36 C9
Roseville 38 G3
Rosewood 32 A5
Ross, *Australia* 32 D4
Ross, *N.Z.* 33 K3
Ross Ice Shelf 6 F16
Ross L. 38 B3
Ross-on-Wye 9 F5
Ross River 36 B6
Ross Sea 6 E15
Rossall Pt. 8 D4
Rossan Pt. 11 B3
Rosses, The 11 A3
Rosslare 11 D5
Rostock 16 A6
Rostov 17 A5
Roswell, *Ga., U.S.A.* 43 H3
Roswell, *N. Mex., U.S.A.* 41 J2
Rotan 41 J4
Rother → 9 G8
Rotherham 8 D6
Rothes 10 D5
Rothesay 10 F3
Roto 32 B4
Rotoroa, L. 33 J4
Rotorua 31 H14
Rotorua, L. 33 H6
Rotterdam 16 C2
Rotuma 34 J9
Roubaix 12 A5
Rouen 12 B4
Round Mountain 38 G5
Round Mt. 30 G9
Round Rock 41 K6
Roundup 38 C9
Rousay 10 B5
Roussillon 12 E5
Rouyn-Noranda 37 D12
Rovaniemi 7 D9
Rovno = Rivne 18 D3
Rowena 32 A4
Roxas 23 B4
Roxboro 43 G6
Roxburgh 33 L2
Roy, *Mont., U.S.A.* 38 C9
Roy, *N. Mex., U.S.A.* 41 H2
Roy, *Utah, U.S.A.* 38 F7
Royal Canal 11 C4
Royal Leamington Spa 9 E6
Royal Tunbridge Wells 9 F8
Royale, Isle 40 B10
Royan 12 D3
Royston 9 E7
Ruahine Ra. 33 H6
Ruapehu 33 H5
Ruapuke I. 33 M2
Rub' al Khālī 24 D3
Rubh a' Mhail 10 F2
Rubha Hunish 10 D2
Rubtsovsk 18 D9
Ruby L. 38 F6
Ruby Mts. 38 F6
Rudall 32 B2
Rudyard 42 B3
Rufling Pt. 45 e
Rugby, *U.K.* 9 E6
Rugby, *U.S.A.* 40 A5
Ruhr → 16 C3
Ruidoso 39 K11
Rum = Rhum 10 E2
Rumania = Romania ■ 15 B10
Rumford 43 C10
Runanga 33 K3
Runaway, C. 33 G6
Runaway Bay 44 a
Runcorn 8 D5
Ruoqiang 20 C3
Rupat 23 C2
Rupert 38 E7
Rupert → 37 C12
Ruse 15 C12
Rush 11 C5
Rushden 9 E7
Rushmore, Mt. 40 D3
Rushville, *Ill., U.S.A.* 40 E9
Rushville, *Ind., U.S.A.* 42 F3
Rushville, *Nebr., U.S.A.* 40 D3
Russell 40 F5
Russellville, *Ala., U.S.A.* 43 H2
Russellville, *Ark., U.S.A.* 41 H8
Russellville, *Ky., U.S.A.* 43 G2
Russia ■ 19 C11
Rustavi 17 B7
Rustenburg 29 K5
Ruston 41 J8
Ruteng 23 D4
Rutland 42 D9
Rutland □ 9 E7
Rutland Water 9 E7
Ruwenzori 28 D5
Rwanda ■ 28 E5
Ryan, L. 10 G3
Ryazan 18 D4
Rybinsk 18 D4
Ryde 9 G6
Rye 9 G8
Rye → 8 C7
Rye Bay 9 G8
Rye Patch Reservoir 38 F4
Ryegate 38 C9
Rylstone 32 B4
Ryūkyū Is. = Ryūkyū-rettō 21 D7
Ryūkyū-rettō 21 D7
Rzeszów 7 G8

S

Saale → 16 C5
Saar → 12 B7
Saarbrücken 16 D3
Sabadell 13 B7
Sabah □ 23 C3
Sabinal 41 L5
Sabinas 44 B4
Sabinas Hidalgo 44 B4
Sabine → 41 L8
Sabine L. 41 L8
Sabine Pass 41 L8
Sable, C. 37 D13
Sable I. 37 D14
Sac City 40 D7
Sachsen □ 16 C6
Sachsen-Anhalt □ 16 C6
Saco, *Maine, U.S.A.* 43 D10
Saco, *Mont., U.S.A.* 38 B10
Sacramento 38 G3
Sacramento → 38 G3
Sacramento Mts. 39 K11
Safford 39 K9
Saffron Walden 9 E8
Safi 26 B4
Saga 22 G2
Sagar 25 C6
Saginaw 42 D4
Saginaw → 42 D4
Saginaw B. 42 D4
Sagua la Grande 45 C8
Saguache 39 G10
Saguaro Nat. Park 39 K8
Sahara 26 D6
Saharanpur 25 C6
Saharien, Atlas 26 B6
Sahiwal 25 B6
Sahuarita 39 L8
Sai Kung 21 G11
Sa'īdābād 24 C4
Saigon = Thanh Pho Ho Chi Minh 23 B2
St. Abb's Head 10 F6
St. Albans, *U.K.* 9 F7
St. Albans, *Vt., U.S.A.* 42 C9
St. Albans, *W. Va., U.S.A.* 42 F5
St. Alban's Head 9 G5
St. Andrews 10 E6
St. Ann's Bay 44 a
St. Anthony, *Canada* 37 C14
St. Anthony, *U.S.A.* 38 E8
St. Arnaud 32 C3
St-Augustin-Saguenay 37 C14
St. Augustine 43 L5
St. Austell 9 G3
St-Barthélemy 45 D12
St. Bees Hd. 8 C4
St. Brides B. 9 F2
St-Brieuc 12 B2
St. Catherines I. 43 K5
St. Catherine's Pt. 9 G6
St. Charles, *Ill., U.S.A.* 42 E1
St. Charles, *Mo., U.S.A.* 40 F9
St. Charles, *Va., U.S.A.* 42 F7
St. Christopher-Nevis = St. Kitts & Nevis ■ 45 D12
St. Cloud, *Fla., U.S.A.* 43 L5
St. Cloud, *Minn., U.S.A.* 40 C7
St. Croix 45 D12
St. Croix → 40 C8
St. Croix Falls 40 C8
St. David's 9 F2
St. David's Head 9 F2
St-Denis 12 B5
St-Dizier 12 B6
St. Elias, Mt. 36 B5
St. Elias Mts. 36 C6
St-Étienne 12 D6
St-Flour 12 D5
St. Francis 40 F4
St. Francis → 41 H9
St. Francisville 41 K9
St-Gaudens 12 E4
St. George, *Australia* 32 A4
St. George, *S.C., U.S.A.* 43 J5
St. George, *Utah, U.S.A.* 39 H7
St. George, C. 43 L3
St. George's 45 E12
St. Georges Basin 32 C5
St. George's Channel 11 E6
St. Georges Hd. 32 C5
St. Gotthard P. = San Gottardo, P. del 12 C8
St. Helena, *Atl. Oc.* 4 E9
St. Helena, *U.S.A.* 38 G2
St. Helena B. 29 L3
St. Helens, *Australia* 32 D4
St. Helens, *U.K.* 8 D5
St. Helens, *U.S.A.* 38 D2
St. Helens, Mt. 38 C2
St. Helier 9 H5
St-Hyacinthe 37 D12
St. Ignace 42 C3
St. Ignatius 38 C6
St. Ives 9 G2
St. James 40 D7
St-Jean, L. 37 D12
St. John, *Canada* 37 D13
St. John, *U.S.A.* 41 G5
St. John → 43 C12
St. John I. 45 e
St. John's, *Antigua & B.* 45 D12
St. John's, *Canada* 37 D14
St. Johns, *Ariz., U.S.A.* 39 J9
St. Johns, *Mich., U.S.A.* 42 D3
St. Johns → 43 K5
St. John's Pt. 11 B3
St. Johnsbury 42 C9
St-Joseph 44 c
St. Joseph, *La., U.S.A.* 41 K9
St. Joseph, *Mo., U.S.A.* 40 F7
St. Joseph → 42 D2
St. Joseph, L. 37 C10
St. Kitts & Nevis ■ 45 D12
St. Lawrence → 37 D13
St. Lawrence, Gulf of 37 D13
St. Lawrence I. 36 B3
St-Lô 12 B3
St.-Louis, *Guadeloupe* 44 b
St. Louis, *Senegal* 26 E2
St. Louis, *U.S.A.* 40 F9
St. Louis → 40 B8
St. Lucia ■ 45 f
St. Magnus B. 10 A7
St-Malo 12 B2
St-Marc 45 D10
St. Maries 38 C5
St-Martin 45 D12
St-Martin, C. 44 c

St. Martins

St. Martins 45 g
St. Mary Pk. 32 B2
St. Marys, *Australia* 32 D4
St. Mary's, *Corn., U.K.* 9 H1
St. Mary's, *Orkney, U.K.* 10 C6
St. Marys, *Ga., U.S.A.* 43 K5
St. Marys, *Pa., U.S.A.* 42 E6
St. Matthew I. 36 B2
St-Nazaire 12 C2
St. Neots 9 E7
St-Omer 12 A5
St. Paul, *Minn., U.S.A.* 40 C8
St. Paul, *Nebr., U.S.A.* 40 E5
St. Paul, I. 5 F13
St. Peter 40 C8
St. Peter Port 9 H5
St. Petersburg = Sankt-Peterburg 18 D4
St. Petersburg 43 M4
St-Pierre 44 c
St-Pierre et Miquelon □ 37 D14
St-Quentin 12 B5
St. Regis 38 C6
St. Simons I. 43 K5
St. Simons Island 43 K5
St. Thomas I. 45 e
St-Tropez 12 E7
St. Vincent, G. 30 G6
St. Vincent & the Grenadines ■ 45 E12
Ste-Anne 44 b
Ste. Genevieve 40 G9
Ste-Marie 44 c
Ste-Rose 44 b
Saintes 12 D3
Saintes, I. des 44 b
Saintfield 11 B6
Saintonge 12 D3
Saipan 34 F6
Sakakawea, L. 40 B4
Sakarya 17 B4
Sakata 22 D6
Sakha □ 19 C13
Sakhalin 19 D15
Sala 7 F7
Sala-y-Gómez 35 K17
Salado →, *Argentina* 48 C4
Salado →, *Mexico* 41 M5
Salālah 24 D4
Salamanca, *Spain* 13 B3
Salamanca, *U.S.A.* 42 D6
Salayar 23 D4
Salcombe 9 G4
Saldanha 29 L3
Sale, *Australia* 30 H8
Sale, *U.K.* 8 D5
Salekhard 18 C7
Salem, *India* 25 D6
Salem, *Ill., U.S.A.* 42 F1
Salem, *Ind., U.S.A.* 42 F2
Salem, *Mass., U.S.A.* 42 D10
Salem, *Mo., U.S.A.* 41 G9
Salem, *N.J., U.S.A.* 42 F8
Salem, *Ohio, U.S.A.* 42 E5
Salem, *Oreg., U.S.A.* 38 D2
Salem, *S. Dak., U.S.A.* 40 D6
Salem, *Va., U.S.A.* 42 G5
Salerno 14 D6
Salford 8 D5
Salina, *Kans., U.S.A.* 40 F6
Salina, *Utah, U.S.A.* 39 G8
Salina Cruz 44 D5
Salinas 39 H3
Salinas → 39 H3
Salinas Grandes 48 C4
Saline →, *Ark., U.S.A.* 41 J8
Saline →, *Kans., U.S.A.* 40 F6
Salisbury, *U.K.* 9 F6
Salisbury, *Md., U.S.A.* 42 F8
Salisbury, *N.C., U.S.A.* 43 H5
Salisbury I. 37 B12
Salisbury Plain 9 F6
Salliq 37 B11
Sallisaw 41 H7
Salluit 37 B12
Salmon 38 D7
Salmon → 38 D5
Salmon Arm 36 C8
Salmon River Mts. 38 D6
Salome 39 K7
Salon-de-Provence 12 E6
Salonica = Thessaloníki 15 D10
Salt → 39 K7
Salt Lake City 38 F8
Salta 48 A3
Saltash 9 G3
Saltburn by the Sea 8 C7
Saltcoats 10 F4
Saltee Is. 11 D5
Saltillo 44 B4
Salton Sea 39 K6
Saluda → 43 J5
Salvador 47 F11
Salvador, L. 41 L9
Salween → 25 D8
Salzburg 16 E6
Salzgitter 16 B5
Sam Rayburn Reservoir 41 K7
Samar 23 B4
Samara 18 D6
Samarinda 23 D3
Samarkand = Samarqand 18 F7
Samarqand 18 F7
Samoa ■ 34 J10
Sámos 15 F12
Samsun 17 B5
Samut Prakan 23 B2
San Agustin, C. 23 C4
San Ambrosio 35 K20
San Andreas 38 G3
San Andrés, I. de 45 E8
San Andres Mts. 39 K10
San Andrés Tuxtla 44 D5
San Angelo 41 K4
San Antonio, *N. Mex., U.S.A.* 39 K10
San Antonio, *Tex., U.S.A.* 41 L5
San Antonio → 41 L6
San Augustine 41 K7
San Benito 41 M6
San Bernardino 39 J5
San Bernardino Str. 23 B4
San Blas, C. 43 L3
San Carlos, *Phil.* 23 B4
San Carlos, *U.S.A.* 39 K8
San Carlos L. 39 K8
San Clemente 39 K5
San Clemente I. 39 K4
San Cristóbal, *Solomon Is.* 31 C11
San Cristóbal, *Venezuela* 46 B4
San Cristóbal de la Casas 44 D6
San Diego, *Calif., U.S.A.* 39 K5
San Diego, *Tex., U.S.A.* 41 M5
San Félix 35 K20
San Francisco 39 H2
San Francisco → 39 K9
San Francisco de Macorís 45 D10
San German 45 d
San Gottardo, P. del 12 C8
San Joaquin → 39 G3
San Jon 41 H3
San Jorge, G. 48 F3
San José, *Costa Rica* 45 F8
San Jose, *Phil.* 23 B4
San Jose, *U.S.A.* 39 H3
San Jose → 39 J10
San Juan, *Argentina* 48 C3
San Juan, *Dom. Rep.* 45 D10
San Juan, *Puerto Rico* 45 d
San Juan →, *Nic.* 45 E8
San Juan →, *U.S.A.* 39 H8
San Juan Mts. 39 H10
San Lucas, C. 44 C3
San Luis, *Ariz., U.S.A.* 39 K6
San Luis, *Colo., U.S.A.* 39 H11
San Luis Obispo 39 J3
San Luis Potosí 44 C4
San Manuel 39 K8
San Marcos 41 L6
San Marino ■ 14 C5
San Mateo 39 H2
San Matías, G. 48 E4
San Miguel, *El Salv.* 44 E7
San Miguel, *U.S.A.* 39 J3
San Miguel de Tucumán 48 B3
San Miguel I. 39 J3
San Nicolas I. 39 K4
San Pedro → 39 K8
San Pedro de las Colonias 44 B4
San Pedro de Macorís 45 D11
San Pedro Sula 44 D7
San Rafael, *Calif., U.S.A.* 38 H2
San Rafael, *N. Mex., U.S.A.* 39 J10
San Remo 12 E7
San Saba 41 K5
San Salvador 44 E7
San Salvador de Jujuy 48 A4
San Salvador I. 45 C10
San Sebastián = Donostia-San Sebastián 13 A5
San Sebastian 45 d
San Simon 39 K9
Sana' 24 D3
Sancti Spíritus 45 C9
Sancy, Puy de 12 D5
Sand Hills 40 D4
Sand Springs 41 G6
Sandakan 23 C3
Sanday 10 B6
Sanders 39 J9
Sanderson 41 K3
Sandersville 43 J4
Sandpoint 38 B5
Sandray 10 E1
Sandringham 8 E8
Sandusky, *Mich., U.S.A.* 42 D4
Sandusky, *Ohio, U.S.A.* 42 E4
Sandy 38 F8
Sandy C. 32 D3
Sandy Cr. → 38 F9
Sandy L. 36 C10
Sanford, *Fla., U.S.A.* 43 L5
Sanford, *Maine, U.S.A.* 43 D10
Sanford, *N.C., U.S.A.* 43 H6
Sanford, Mt. 36 B5
Sanger 39 H4
Sangihe, Pulau 23 C4
Sangli 25 D6
Sangre de Cristo Mts. 41 G2
Sanibel 43 M4
Sanirajak 37 B11
Sankt Gallen 12 C8
Sankt Moritz 12 C8
Sankt-Peterburg 18 D4
Sankuru → 28 E4
Sanliurfa 17 C5
Sanmenxia 21 C6
Sanming 21 D6
Sanquhar 10 F5
Santa Ana, *El Salv.* 44 E7
Santa Ana, *U.S.A.* 39 K5
Santa Barbara 39 J4
Santa Catalina, Gulf of 39 K5
Santa Catalina I. 39 K4
Santa Clara, *Cuba* 45 C9
Santa Clara, *U.S.A.* 39 H7
Santa Coloma de Gramenet 13 B7
Santa Cruz, *Bolivia* 46 G6
Santa Cruz, *U.S.A.* 39 H2
Santa Cruz de Tenerife 26 C2
Santa Cruz I. 39 K4
Santa Cruz Is. 34 J8
Santa Cruz Mts. 44 a
Santa Fe, *Argentina* 48 C4
Santa Fe, *U.S.A.* 39 J11
Santa Inés, I. 48 G2
Santa Isabel = Rey Malabo 28 D1
Santa Isabel 31 B10
Santa Lucia Range 39 J3
Santa Maria, *Brazil* 48 B6
Santa Maria, *U.S.A.* 39 J3
Santa María → 44 A3
Santa Marta 46 A4
Santa Marta, Sierra Nevada de 46 A4
Santa Monica 39 K4
Santa Rita 39 K10
Santa Rosa, *Calif., U.S.A.* 38 G2
Santa Rosa, *N. Mex., U.S.A.* 41 H2
Santa Rosa I., *Calif., U.S.A.* 39 K3
Santa Rosa I., *Fla., U.S.A.* 43 K2
Santa Rosa Range 38 F5
Santai 20 C5
Santander 13 A4
Santaquin 38 G8
Santarém, *Brazil* 47 D8
Santarém, *Portugal* 13 C1
Santee → 43 J6
Santiago 48 C2
Santiago → 46 D3
Santiago de Compostela 13 A1
Santiago de Cuba 45 D9
Santiago de los Cabelleros 45 D10
Santiago del Estero 48 B4
Santo Domingo 45 D11
Santo Domingo Pueblo 39 J10
Santorini = Thíra 15 F11
Santos 48 A7
Sanxiang 21 G9
São Bernardo do Campo 48 A7
São Francisco → 47 F11
São José do Rio Prêto 47 H9
São Lourenço 47 H9
São Luís 47 D10
São Paulo 48 A7
São Paulo, I. 4 D8
São Roque, C. de 47 E11
São Tomé & Principe ■ 5 D10
Saône → 12 D6
Sapelo I. 43 K5
Sapporo 22 B7
Sapulpa 41 H6
Saraburi 23 B2
Saragossa = Zaragoza 13 B5
Sarajevo 15 C8
Saran, Gunung 23 D3
Saranac Lake 42 C8
Sarangani B. 23 C4
Saransk 18 D5
Sarapul 18 D6
Sarasota 43 M4
Saratoga 38 F10
Saratoga Springs 42 D9
Saratov 18 D5
Sarawak □ 23 C3
Sardegna □ 14 D3
Sardinia = Sardegna □ 14 D3
Sargasso Sea 35 D20
Sarita 41 M6
Sark 9 H5
Sarlat-la-Canéda 12 D4
Sarnia 37 D11
Sarre = Saar → 12 B7
Sarreguemines 12 B7
Sarthe → 12 C3
Sasebo 22 G1
Saskatchewan □ 36 C9
Saskatchewan → 36 C9
Saskatoon 36 C9
Sássari 14 D3
Sassnitz 16 A6
Satilla → 43 K5
Satpura Ra. 25 C6
Satu Mare 17 A2
Saudi Arabia ■ 24 C3
Saugerties 42 D9
Sauk Centre 40 C7
Sauk Rapids 40 C7
Sault Ste. Marie, *Canada* 37 D11
Sault Ste. Marie, *U.S.A.* 37 D11
Saumur 12 C3
Saunders, C. 33 L3
Sava → 15 B9
Savage 40 B2
Savage River 32 D4
Savai'i 31 C16
Savanna 40 D9
Savanna-la-Mar 44 a
Savannah, *Ga., U.S.A.* 43 J5
Savannah, *Mo., U.S.A.* 40 F7
Savannah, *Tenn., U.S.A.* 43 H1
Savannah → 43 J5
Savannakhet 23 B2
Savoie □ 12 D7
Savona 12 D8
Savoy = Savoie □ 12 D7
Sawatch Range 39 G10
Sawel Mt. 11 B4
Sawtooth Range 38 E6
Sawu 23 E4
Sawu Sea 23 D4
Saxmundham 9 E9
Saxony = Sachsen □ 16 C6
Sayan, Zapadnyy 19 D10
Saydā 17 D5
Sayhūt 24 D4
Saynshand 21 B6
Sayre, *Okla., U.S.A.* 41 H5
Sayre, *Pa., U.S.A.* 42 E7
Sázava → 16 D7
Scafell Pike 8 C4
Scalloway 10 A7
Scalpay 10 D3
Scandinavia 7 E6
Scapa Flow 10 C5
Scarba 10 E3
Scarborough 8 C7
Scariff I. 11 E1
Scarp 10 C1
Scebeli, Wabi → 24 E3
Schaffhausen 12 C8
Schefferville 37 C13
Schelde → 16 C2
Schell Creek Ra. 38 G6
Schenectady 42 D9
Schleswig 16 A4
Schleswig-Holstein □ 16 A4
Schœlcher 44 c
Schouten I. 32 D4
Schurz 38 G4
Schuyler 40 E6
Schwäbische Alb 16 D4
Schwaner, Pegunungan 23 D3
Schwarzwald 16 D4
Schwerin 16 B5
Schwyz 12 C8
Scilly, Isles of 9 H1
Scioto → 42 F4
Scobey 40 A2
Scone 32 B5
Scotia 38 F1
Scotland □ 10 E5
Scott City 40 F4
Scottish Borders □ 10 F6
Scottsbluff 40 E3
Scottsboro 43 H3
Scottsburg 42 F3
Scottsdale, *Australia* 32 D4
Scottsdale, *U.S.A.* 39 K7
Scottsville 43 G2
Scottville 42 D2
Scranton 42 E8
Scunthorpe 8 D7
Seaford, *U.K.* 9 G8
Seaford, *U.S.A.* 42 F8
Seaforth, L. 10 D2
Seagraves 41 J3
Seaham 8 C6
Seal → 36 C10
Sealy 41 L6
Searchlight 39 J6
Searcy 41 H9
Searles L. 39 J5
Seascale 8 C4
Seaside, *Calif., U.S.A.* 39 G3
Seaside, *Oreg., U.S.A.* 38 D2
Seaspray 32 C4
Seattle 38 C2
Sebastián Vizcaíno, B. 44 B2
Sebastopol = Sevastopol 17 B4
Sebewaing 42 D4
Sebring 43 M5
Sebuku, Teluk 23 C3
Secretary I. 33 L1
Security-Widefield 40 F2
Sedalia 40 F8
Sedan, *France* 12 B6
Sedan, *U.S.A.* 41 G6
Seddon 33 J5
Seddonville 33 J4
Sedona 39 J8
Sedro Woolley 38 B2
Segovia 13 B3
Seguin 41 L6
Seil 10 E3
Seiling 41 G5
Seine → 12 B4
Sekondi-Takoradi 26 H5
Selah 38 C3
Selaru 23 D5
Selby, *U.K.* 8 D6
Selby, *U.S.A.* 40 C4
Selden 40 F4
Selenge Mörön → 20 A5
Seligman 39 J7
Selkirk, *Canada* 36 C10
Selkirk, *U.K.* 10 F6
Selkirk Mts. 36 C8
Sells 39 L8
Selma, *Ala., U.S.A.* 43 J2
Selma, *Calif., U.S.A.* 39 H4
Selma, *N.C., U.S.A.* 43 H6
Selmer 43 H1
Selsey Bill 9 G7
Selvas 46 E5
Selwyn L. 36 B9
Selwyn Mts. 36 B6
Semarang 23 D3
Semey 18 D9
Seminoe Reservoir 38 F10
Seminole, *Okla., U.S.A.* 41 H6
Seminole, *Tex., U.S.A.* 41 J3
Seminole Draw → 41 J3
Semipalatinsk = Semey 18 D9
Senatobia 41 H10
Sendai 22 D7
Seneca 43 H4
Seneca Falls 42 D7
Seneca L. 42 D7
Senegal ■ 26 F3
Sénégal → 26 E2
Senja 7 D7
Senlis 12 B5
Sens 12 B5
Sentinel 39 K7
Seoul = Sŏul 21 C7
Sept-Îles 37 C13
Sequim 38 B2
Sequoia Nat. Park 39 H4
Seram 23 D4
Seram Sea 23 D4
Serang 23 D2
Serbia □ 15 C9
Serbia & Montenegro ■ 15 B9
Seremban 23 C2
Serov 18 D7
Serowe 29 J5
Serpukhov 18 D4
Sète 12 E5
Sétif 26 A7
Settat 26 B4
Settle 8 C5
Settlement Pt. 43 M6
Setúbal 13 C1
Seul, Lac 36 C10
Sevastopol 17 B4
Severn →, *Canada* 37 C11
Severn →, *U.K.* 9 F5
Severnaya Zemlya 19 B10
Severodvinsk 18 C4
Sevier 39 G7
Sevier → 39 G7
Sevier Desert 38 G7
Sevier L. 38 G7
Sevilla 13 D2
Seville = Sevilla 13 D2
Seward, *Alaska, U.S.A.* 36 B5
Seward, *Nebr., U.S.A.* 40 E6
Seward Peninsula 36 B3
Seychelles ■ 5 E12
Seymour, *Australia* 32 C4
Seymour, *Ind., U.S.A.* 42 F3
Seymour, *Tex., U.S.A.* 41 J5
Sfântu Gheorghe 15 B11
Sfax 27 B8
Sha Tau Kok 21 F11
Sha Tin 21 G11
Shaanxi □ 21 C5
Shaba = Katanga □ 28 F4
Shache 20 C2
Shafter 39 J4
Shaftesbury 9 F5
Shahjahanpur 25 C6
Shajing 21 F10
Shakhty 17 A6
Shaki 26 G6
Shaluli Shan 20 C4
Shām, Bādiyat ash 24 B3
Shamo = Gobi 21 B5
Shamokin 42 E7
Shamrock 41 H4
Shan □ 25 C8
Shandong □ 21 C6
Shanghai 21 C7
Shangqiu 21 C6
Shangrao 21 D6
Shangshui 21 C6
Shannon 33 J5
Shannon → 11 D2
Shannon, Mouth of the 11 D2
Shannon Airport 11 D3
Shantar, Ostrov Bolshoy 19 D14
Shantou 21 D6
Shanxi □ 21 C6
Shaoguan 21 D6
Shaoxing 21 D7
Shaoyang 21 D6
Shap 8 C5
Shapinsay 10 B6
Shaqrā' 24 D3
Sharjah = Ash Shāriqah 24 C4
Shark B. 30 F1
Sharon 42 E5
Sharon Springs 40 F4
Shashi 21 C6
Shasta, Mt. 38 F2
Shasta L. 38 F2
Shatt al'Arab → 24 C3
Shawano 42 C1
Shawinigan 37 D12
Shawnee 41 H6
Shcherbakov = Rybinsk 18 D4
Sheberghān 24 B5
Sheboygan 42 D2
Sheelin, L. 11 C4
Sheep Haven 11 A4
Sheerness 9 F8
Sheffield, *U.K.* 8 D6
Sheffield, *U.S.A.* 43 H2
Shekou 21 G10
Shelby, *Mich., U.S.A.* 42 D2
Shelby, *Miss., U.S.A.* 41 J9
Shelby, *Mont., U.S.A.* 38 B8
Shelby, *N.C., U.S.A.* 43 H5
Shelbyville, *Ill., U.S.A.* 40 F10
Shelbyville, *Ind., U.S.A.* 42 F3
Shelbyville, *Ky., U.S.A.* 42 F3
Shelbyville, *Tenn., U.S.A.* 43 H2
Sheldon 40 D7
Shelikhova, Zaliv 19 D16
Shellharbour 32 B5
Shelton 38 C2
Shenandoah, *Iowa, U.S.A.* 40 E7
Shenandoah, *Pa., U.S.A.* 42 E7
Shenandoah, *Va., U.S.A.* 42 F6
Shenandoah → 42 F7
Shenandoah Nat. Park 42 F6
Shenyang 21 B7
Shenzhen 21 F10
Shenzhen Shuiku 21 F11
Shenzhen Wan 21 G10
Shepparton 30 H8
Sheppey, I. of 9 F8
Shepton Mallet 9 F5
Sherborne 9 G5
Sherbrooke 37 D12
Sheridan, *Ark., U.S.A.* 41 H8
Sheridan, *Wyo., U.S.A.* 38 D10
Sheringham 8 E9
Sherkin I. 11 E2
Sherman 41 J6
Sherwood Forest 8 D6
Shetland Is. 10 A7
Sheung Shui 21 F11
Sheyenne → 40 B6
Shibām 24 D3
Shiel, L. 10 E3
Shihezi 20 B3
Shijiazhuang 21 C6
Shikarpur 24 C5
Shikoku □ 22 G3
Shiliguri 25 C7
Shillelagh 11 D5
Shimoga 25 D6
Shimonoseki 22 G2
Shin, L. 10 C4
Shiping 20 D5
Shippensburg 42 E7
Shiprock 39 H9
Shīrāz 24 C4
Shire → 29 H7
Shiyan 21 F10
Shiyan Shuiku 21 F10
Shizuoka 22 F6
Shkodër 15 C8
Shoreham by Sea 9 G7
Shoshone 38 E6
Shoshone L. 38 D8
Shoshone Mts. 38 G5
Shoshoni 38 E9
Show Low 39 J9
Shreveport 41 J8
Shrewsbury 9 E5
Shropshire □ 9 E5
Shuangliao 21 B7
Shuangyashan 21 B8
Shule 20 C2
Shumagin Is. 36 C4
Shwebo 25 C8
Shymkent 18 E7
Si Kiang = Xi Jiang → 21 D6
Sialkot 25 B6
Siam = Thailand ■ 23 B2
Šiauliai 7 F8
Siberia 3 A14
Siberut 23 D1
Sibi 24 C5
Sibiu 15 B11
Sibley 40 D7
Sibolga 23 C1
Sibu 23 C3
Sibuyan Sea 23 B4
Siccus → 32 B2
Sichuan □ 20 C5
Sicilia 14 F6
Sicily = Sicilia 14 F6
Sidi-bel-Abbès 26 A5
Sidlaw Hills 10 E5
Sidmouth 9 G4
Sidney, *Mont., U.S.A.* 40 B2
Sidney, *N.Y., U.S.A.* 42 D8
Sidney, *Nebr., U.S.A.* 40 E3
Sidney, *Ohio, U.S.A.* 42 E3
Sidney Lanier, L. 43 H4
Sidon = Saydā 17 D5
Siegen 16 C4
Siena 14 C4
Sierra Blanca 39 L11
Sierra Blanca Peak 39 K11
Sierra Leone ■ 26 G3
Sierra Nevada, *Spain* 13 D4
Sierra Nevada, *U.S.A.* 38 G3
Sierra Vista 39 L8
Sikeston 41 G10
Sikhote Alin, Khrebet 19 E14
Sikkim □ 25 C7
Siler City 43 H6
Silesia = Śląsk 16 C8
Siling Co 20 C3
Silloth 8 C4
Siloam Springs 41 G7
Silsbee 41 K7
Silver City 39 K9
Silver Cr. → 38 E4
Silver Lake 38 E3
Silverton, *Colo., U.S.A.* 39 H10
Silverton, *Tex., U.S.A.* 41 H4
Silvies → 38 E4
Simbirsk 18 D5
Simeulue 23 C1
Simferopol 17 B4
Simi Valley 39 J4
Simplonpass 12 C8
Simpson Desert 30 F6
Simpson Pen. 37 B11
Sinai, Mt. = Mûsa, Gebel 27 C12
Sinclair 38 F10
Sinclair's B. 10 C5
Sind □ 25 C5
Sindh = Sind □ 25 C5
Singapore ■ 23 C2
Singaraja 23 D3
Singkawang 23 C2
Singleton 32 B5
Sinkiang Uighur = Xinjiang Uygur Zizhiqu □ 20 C3
Sinton 41 L6
Sion 12 C7
Sion Mills 11 B4
Sioux City 40 D6
Sioux Falls 40 D6
Sioux Lookout 36 C10
Siping 21 B7
Sipura 23 D1
Sir James MacBrien, Mt. 36 B7
Siracusa 14 F6
Siren 40 C8
Sisseton 40 C6
Sīstān, Daryācheh-ye 24 B5
Sisters 38 D3
Sitka 36 C6
Sittingbourne 9 F8
Sittwe 25 C8
Sivas 17 C5
Sīwa 27 C11
Six Cross Roads 45 g
Sixmilebridge 11 D3
Sjælland 7 F6
Skagerrak 7 F5
Skagway 36 C6
Skeena → 36 C6
Skegness 8 D8
Skellefte älv → 7 E8
Skellefteå 7 E8
Skerries, The 8 D3
Skíathos 15 E10
Skibbereen 11 E2
Skiddaw 8 C4
Skien 7 F5
Skikda 26 A7
Skipton 8 D5
Skopje 15 C9
Skowhegan 43 C11
Skull 11 E2
Skunk → 40 E9
Skye 10 D2
Skykomish 38 C3
Slaney → 11 D5
Śląsk 16 C8
Slatina 15 B11
Slaton 41 J4
Slave → 36 B8
Slave Coast 26 G6
Slave Lake 36 C8
Slavyansk = Slovyansk 17 A5
Sleaford 8 D7
Sleaford B. 32 B2
Sleat, Sd. of 10 D3
Sleeper Is. 37 C11
Sleepy Eye 40 C7
Slidell 41 K10
Slieve Aughty 11 C3
Slieve Bloom 11 C4
Slieve Donard 11 B6
Slieve Gamph 11 B3
Slieve Gullion 11 B5
Slieve Mish 11 D2
Slievenamon 11 D4
Sligo 11 B3
Sligo □ 11 B3
Sligo B. 11 B3
Sliven 15 C12
Slough 9 F7
Slovak Rep. ■ 16 D9
Slovakia = Slovak Rep. ■ 16 D9
Slovenia ■ 14 B6
Slovenské Rudohorie 16 D10
Slovyansk 17 A5
Slyne Hd. 11 C1
Smallwood Res. 37 C13
Smederevo 15 B9
Smerwick Harbour 11 D1
Smith Center 40 F5
Smith Sund 6 B3
Smithfield, *N.C., U.S.A.* 43 H6
Smithfield, *Utah, U.S.A.* 38 F8
Smithton 32 D4
Smithville 41 K6
Smoky → 36 C8
Smoky Bay 32 B1
Smoky Hill → 40 F6
Smoky Hills 40 F5
Smolensk 18 D4
Smyrna = İzmir 15 E12
Smyrna 42 F8
Snaefell 8 C3
Snake → 38 C4
Snake I. 32 C4
Snake Range 38 G6
Snake River Plain 38 E7
Snizort, L. 10 D2
Snøhetta 7 E5
Snohomish 38 C2
Snow Hill 42 F8
Snowdon 8 D3
Snowflake 39 J8
Snowshoe Pk. 38 B6
Snowtown 32 B2
Snowville 38 F7
Snowy → 32 C4
Snowy Mts. 30 H8
Snyder, *Okla., U.S.A.* 41 H5
Snyder, *Tex., U.S.A.* 41 J4
Sobral 47 D10
Soc Trang 23 C2
Socastee 43 J6
Sochi 17 B5
Société, Is. de la 35 J12
Society Is. = Société, Is. de la 35 J12
Socorro, *N. Mex., U.S.A.* 39 J10
Socorro, *Tex., U.S.A.* 39 L10
Socotra 24 D4
Soda L. 39 J5
Soda Springs 38 E8
Soddy-Daisy 43 H3
Söderhamn 7 E7
Sofia = Sofiya 15 C10
Sofiya 15 C10
Sognefjorden 7 E5
Sohâg 27 C12
Soissons 12 B5
Sokhumi 17 B6
Soko Islands 21 G10
Sokoto 26 F7
Solapur 25 D6
Soldotna 36 B4
Soledad 39 H3
Solent, The 9 G6
Solihull 9 E6
Solikamsk 18 D6
Solimões = Amazonas → 47 D9
Solingen 16 C3
Solomon, N. Fork → 40 F5
Solomon, S. Fork → 40 F5
Solomon Is. ■ 34 H7
Solomon Sea 30 B9
Solon 21 B7
Solon Springs 40 B9
Solothurn 12 C7
Solvang 39 J3
Solvay 42 D7
Solway Firth 8 C4
Somali Rep. ■ 24 E3
Sombrerete 44 C4
Somers 38 B6
Somerset, *Ky., U.S.A.* 42 G3
Somerset, *Pa., U.S.A.* 42 E6
Somerset □ 9 F5
Somerset I. 36 A10
Somerton 39 K6
Somme → 12 A4
Songgang 21 F10
Songhua Jiang → 21 B8
Songkhla 23 C2
Songpan 20 C5
Sonora, *Calif., U.S.A.* 39 H3
Sonora, *Tex., U.S.A.* 41 K4
Sonora → 44 B2
Sonoran Desert 39 K6
Sonoyta 44 A2
Sonsonate 44 E7
Soochow = Suzhou 21 C7
Sopot 16 A9
Soria 13 B4
Sorocaba 48 A7
Sorong 23 D5
Sørøya 7 C8
Sorrell 32 D4
Sosnowiec 16 C9
Soufrière, *Guadeloupe* 44 b
Soufrière, *St. Lucia* 45 f
Soufrière Bay 45 f
Sŏul 21 C7
Sound, The 9 G3
Souris → 36 D9
Sousse 27 A8
South Africa ■ 29 L4
South Australia □ 30 G6
South Ayrshire □ 10 F4
South Baldy 39 J10
South Bend 42 E2
South Boston 43 G6
South Carolina □ 43 J5
South Charleston 42 F5
South China Sea 23 C3
South Dakota □ 40 C5
South Downs 9 G7
South East C. 30 J8
South Esk → 10 E6
South Foreland 9 F9
South Fork Grand → 40 C3
South Fork Republican → 40 E4
South Georgia 48 G9
South Gloucestershire □ 9 F5
South Haven 42 D2
South Honshu Ridge 34 E6
South I. 31 J13
South Invercargill 33 M2
South Korea ■ 21 C7
South Lake Tahoe 38 G3
South Lanarkshire □ 10 F5
South Loup → 40 E5
South Magnetic Pole 6 D13
South Milwaukee 42 D2
South Molton 9 F4
South Nahanni → 36 B7
South Negril Pt. 44 a
South Orkney Is. 6 D4
South Pittsburg 43 H3
South Platte → 40 E4
South Pole 6 F
South Portland 43 D10
South Pt. 45 g
South Ronaldsay 10 C6
South Sandwich Is. 4 G8
South Saskatchewan → 36 C9
South Shetland Is. 6 D4
South Shields 8 C6
South Sioux City 40 D6
South Taranaki Bight 33 H5
South Tyne → 8 C5
South Uist 10 D1
South West C. 32 D4
South Yorkshire □ 8 D6
Southampton, *U.K.* 9 G6
Southampton, *U.S.A.* 42 E9
Southampton I. 37 B11
Southaven 41 H9
Southbridge 33 K4
Southend-on-Sea 9 F8
Southern Alps 31 J13
Southern Indian L. 36 C10
Southern Ocean 5 H13
Southern Pines 43 H6
Southern Uplands 10 F5
Southland □ 33 L1
Southport, *Australia* 32 A5
Southport, *U.K.* 8 D4
Southport, *U.S.A.* 43 K3
Southwest C. 33 M1
Southwest Nat. Park 32 D4
Southwold 9 E9
Soweto 29 K5
Spain ■ 13 B4
Spalding, *Australia* 32 B2
Spalding, *U.K.* 8 E7
Spanish Fork 38 F8
Spanish Town, *Br. Virgin Is.* 45 e
Spanish Town, *Jamaica* 44 a
Sparks 38 G4
Sparta, *Mich., U.S.A.* 42 D3
Sparta, *Wis., U.S.A.* 40 D9
Spartanburg 43 H5
Spartivento, C. 14 F7
Spean → 10 E4
Spearfish 40 C3
Spearman 41 G4
Speightstown 45 g
Spencer, *Idaho, U.S.A.* 38 D7
Spencer, *Iowa, U.S.A.* 40 D7
Spencer, *Nebr., U.S.A.* 40 D5
Spencer, C. 32 C2
Spencer G. 30 G6
Spennymoor 8 C6
Spenser Mts. 33 K4
Sperrin Mts. 11 B5
Spey → 10 D5
Spithead 9 G6
Spitzbergen = Svalbard 6 B7
Split 14 C7
Spofford 41 L4
Spokane 38 C5
Spooner 40 C9
Sprague 38 C5
Spratly Is. 23 C3
Spray 38 D4
Spree → 16 B6
Spring Creek 38 F6
Spring Hall 45 g
Spring Hill 43 L4
Spring Mts. 39 H6
Springdale 41 G7
Springer 41 G2
Springerville 39 J9
Springfield, *N.Z.* 33 K3
Springfield, *Colo., U.S.A.* 41 G3
Springfield, *Ill., U.S.A.* 40 F10
Springfield, *Mass., U.S.A.* 42 D9
Springfield, *Mo., U.S.A.* 41 G8
Springfield, *Ohio, U.S.A.* 42 F4
Springfield, *Oreg., U.S.A.* 38 D2
Springfield, *Tenn., U.S.A.* 43 G2
Springfield, *Vt., U.S.A.* 42 D9
Springhill 41 J8
Springs 29 K5
Springville 38 F8
Spur 41 J4
Spurn Hd. 8 D8
Srebrenica 15 B8
Sredinnyy Khrebet 19 D16
Srednekolymsk 19 C16
Srepok → 23 B2
Sri Lanka ■ 25 E7
Srinagar 25 B6
Staffa 10 E2
Stafford, *U.K.* 8 E5
Stafford, *U.S.A.* 41 G5
Staffordshire □ 8 E5
Staines 9 F7
Stalingrad = Volgograd 18 E5
Stalino = Donetsk 17 A5
Stalinogorsk = Novomoskovsk 18 D4
Stalybridge 8 D5
Stamford, *U.K.* 9 E7
Stamford, *Conn., U.S.A.* 42 E9
Stamford, *Tex., U.S.A.* 41 J5
Stamps 41 J8
Standish 42 D4
Stanford 38 C8
Stanislav = Ivano-Frankivsk 18 E3
Stanley, *Australia* 32 D4
Stanley, *China* 21 G11
Stanley, *Falk. Is.* 48 G5
Stanley, *U.K.* 8 C6
Stanley, *Idaho, U.S.A.* 38 D6
Stanley, *N. Dak., U.S.A.* 40 A3
Stanovoy Khrebet 19 D13
Stanthorpe 32 A5
Stanton 41 J4
Staples 40 B7
Stara Planina 15 C10
Stara Zagora 15 C11
Starbuck I. 35 H12
Starke 43 L4
Start Pt. 9 G4
State College 42 E7
Statesboro 43 J5
Statesville 43 H5
Staunton, *Ill., U.S.A.* 40 F10
Staunton, *Va., U.S.A.* 42 F6
Stavanger 7 F5
Staveley 33 K3
Stavropol 17 A6
Stawell 32 C3
Stayton 38 D2
Steamboat Springs 38 F10
Steele 40 B5
Steelton 42 E7
Steens Mt. 38 E4
Steiermark □ 16 E7
Steinkjer 7 E6
Steornabhaigh = Stornoway 10 C2
Stephens Creek 32 B3
Stephenville, *Canada* 37 D14
Stephenville, *U.S.A.* 41 J5
Sterling, *Colo., U.S.A.* 40 E3
Sterling, *Ill., U.S.A.* 40 E10
Sterling, *Kans., U.S.A.* 40 F5
Sterling City 41 K4
Sterling Heights 42 D4
Sterlitamak 18 D6
Stettin = Szczecin 16 B7
Stettler 36 C8
Steubenville 42 E5
Stevenage 9 F7
Stevens Point 40 C10
Stevensville 38 C6
Stewart 36 C7
Stewart → 36 B6
Stewart I. 31 K12
Stewartville 40 D8
Steyr 16 D7
Stigler 41 H7
Stikine → 36 C6
Stillwater, *N.Z.* 33 K3
Stillwater, *Minn., U.S.A.* 40 C8
Stillwater, *Okla., U.S.A.* 41 G6
Stillwater Range 38 G4
Stilwell 41 H7
Stirling 10 E5
Stirling □ 10 E4
Stockholm 7 F7
Stockport 8 D5
Stocksbridge 8 D6
Stockton, *Calif., U.S.A.* 39 H3
Stockton, *Kans., U.S.A.* 40 F5
Stockton, *Mo., U.S.A.* 41 G8
Stockton-on-Tees 8 C6
Stockton Plateau 41 K3
Stoer, Pt. of 10 C3
Stoke-on-Trent 8 D5
Stokes Pt. 32 D3
Stone 8 E5
Stonehaven 10 E6
Stonehenge 9 F6
Stora Lulevatten 7 D7
Storavan 7 D7
Store Bælt 7 F6
Storm B. 32 D4
Storm Lake 40 D7
Stornoway 10 C2
Storsjön 7 E6
Storuman 7 D7
Stour →, *Dorset, U.K.* 9 G6
Stour →, *Kent, U.K.* 9 F9
Stour →, *Suffolk, U.K.* 9 F9
Stourbridge 9 E5
Stowmarket 9 E9
Strabane 11 B4
Strahan 32 D4
Stralsund 16 A6
Strangford L. 11 B6
Stranraer 10 G3
Strasbourg 12 B7
Stratford, *N.Z.* 33 H5
Stratford, *U.S.A.* 41 G3
Stratford-upon-Avon 9 E6
Strath Spey 10 D5
Strathalbyn 32 C2
Strathaven 10 F4
Strathmore 10 E5
Strathpeffer 10 D4
Strathy Pt. 10 C4
Strawberry → 38 F8
Streaky B. 32 B1
Streaky Bay 32 B1
Streator 40 E10
Stroma 10 C5
Strómboli 14 E6
Stromeferry 10 D3
Stromness 10 C5
Stromsburg 40 E6
Stronsay 10 B6
Stroud 9 F5
Stroud Road 32 B5
Stryker 38 B6
Strzelecki Cr. → 32 A2
Stuart, *Fla., U.S.A.* 43 M5
Stuart, *Nebr., U.S.A.* 40 D5
Stuart L. 36 C7
Stuart Ra. 32 A1
Sturgeon Bay 42 C2
Sturgis, *Mich., U.S.A.* 42 E3
Sturgis, *S. Dak., U.S.A.* 40 C3
Stuttgart, *Germany* 16 D4
Stuttgart, *U.S.A.* 41 H9
Styria = Steiermark □ 16 E7
Subotica 15 A8
Suck → 11 C3
Sucre 46 G5
Sudan 41 H3
Sudan ■ 27 E11
Sudbury, *Canada* 37 D11
Sudbury, *U.K.* 9 E8
Sudeten Mts. = Sudety 16 C8
Sudety 16 C8
Suez = El Suweis 27 C12
Suffolk 42 G7
Suffolk □ 9 E9
Şuḩār 24 C4
Suihua 21 B7
Suir → 11 D4
Sukabumi 23 D2
Sukhumi = Sokhumi 17 B6
Sukkur 25 C5
Sulaiman Range 25 B5
Sulawesi □ 23 D4
Sulawesi Sea = Celebes Sea 23 C4
Sullivan, *Ill., U.S.A.* 40 F10
Sullivan, *Ind., U.S.A.* 42 F2
Sullivan, *Mo., U.S.A.* 40 F9
Sulphur, *La., U.S.A.* 41 K8
Sulphur, *Okla., U.S.A.* 41 H6
Sulphur Springs 41 J7
Sulu Arch. 23 C4
Sulu Sea 23 C4
Sumatera □ 23 C2
Sumatra = Sumatera □ 23 C2
Sumba 23 D3
Sumba, Selat 23 D3
Sumbawa 23 D3
Sumburgh Hd. 10 B7
Sumenep 23 D3
Sumgait = Sumqayıt 17 B7
Summer L. 38 E3
Summerside 37 D13
Summersville 42 F5
Summerville, *Ga., U.S.A.* 43 H3
Summerville, *S.C., U.S.A.* 43 J5
Summit Peak 39 H10
Sumner 40 D8
Sumqayıt 17 B7
Sumter 43 J5
Sumy 18 D4
Sun City 39 K7
Sun City Center 43 M4
Sun Lakes 39 K8
Sun Valley 38 E6
Sunart, L. 10 E3
Sunburst 38 B8
Sunbury, *Australia* 32 C3
Sunbury, *U.S.A.* 42 E7
Sunda, Selat 23 D2
Sunda Is. 34 H2
Sunda Str. = Sunda, Selat 23 D2
Sundance 40 C2
Sundarbans 25 C7
Sunderland 8 C6
Sundsvall 7 E7
Sungaipenuh 23 D2
Sunland Park 39 L10
Sunnyside 38 C3
Sunnyvale 39 H2
Supai 39 H7
Superior, *Ariz., U.S.A.* 39 K8
Superior, *Mont., U.S.A.* 38 C6
Superior, *Nebr., U.S.A.* 40 E5
Superior, *Wis., U.S.A.* 40 B8
Superior, L. 37 D11
Supiori 23 D5
Sur, Pt. 39 H3
Surabaya 23 D3
Surakarta 23 D3
Surat, *Australia* 32 A4
Surat, *India* 25 C6
Surgut 18 C8
Surigao 23 C4
Suriname ■ 47 C7
Surinam = Suriname ■ 47 C7
Surrey □ 9 F7
Susanville 38 F3
Susquehanna → 42 F7
Sussex, E. □ 9 G8
Sussex, W. □ 9 G7
Sutherland, *S. Africa* 29 L4
Sutherland, *U.S.A.* 40 E4
Sutherland Falls 33 L1
Sutherlin 38 E2
Sutlej → 25 C6
Sutton, *Nebr., U.S.A.* 40 E6
Sutton, *W. Va., U.S.A.* 42 F5
Sutton Coldfield 9 E6
Sutton in Ashfield 8 D6
Suva 34 J9
Suwannee → 43 L4
Suwarrow Is. 35 J11
Suzhou 21 C7
Svalbard 6 B7
Svealand □ 7 E7
Sverdlovsk = Yekaterinburg 18 D7
Sverdrup Is. 6 B2
Swabian Alps = Schwäbische Alb 16 D4
Swainsboro 43 J4
Swakopmund 29 J2
Swale → 8 C6
Swan Hill 30 H7
Swan Peak 38 C7
Swan Ra. 38 C7
Swan River 36 C9
Swanage 9 G6
Swansea, *Australia* 32 D4
Swansea, *U.K.* 9 F4
Swaziland ■ 29 K6
Sweden ■ 7 F7
Sweet Home 38 D2
Sweetgrass 38 B8
Sweetwater, *Tenn., U.S.A.* 43 H3
Sweetwater, *Tex., U.S.A.* 41 J4
Sweetwater → 38 E10
Swellendam 29 L4
Swift Current 36 C9
Swilly, L. 11 A4
Swindon 9 F6
Swinford 11 C3
Switzerland ■ 12 C8
Swords 11 C5
Sydney, *Australia* 30 G9
Sydney, *Canada* 37 D13
Sydprøven = Alluitsup Paa 37 B15
Syktyvkar 18 C6
Sylacauga 43 J2
Sylvania 43 J5
Sylvester 43 K4
Syracuse, *Kans., U.S.A.* 41 G4
Syracuse, *N.Y., U.S.A.* 42 D7
Syracuse, *Nebr., U.S.A.* 40 E6
Syrdarya → 18 E7
Syria ■ 24 B2
Syrian Desert = Shām, Bādiyat ash 24 B3
Syzran 18 D5
Szczecin 16 B7
Szechwan = Sichuan □ 20 C5
Szeged 16 E10
Székesfehérvár 16 E9
Szekszárd 16 E9
Szolnok 16 E10
Szombathely 16 E8

T

Ţabas 24 B4
Tablas I. 23 B4
Table Mt. 29 L3
Table Rock L. 41 G8
Tabora 28 F6
Tabrīz 24 B3
Tabuaeran 35 G12
Tabūk 24 C2
Tacheng 20 B3
Tacloban 23 B4
Tacna 46 G4
Tacoma 38 C2
Tacuarembó 48 C5
Tadmor 33 J4
Tadzhikistan = Tajikistan ■ 18 F8
Taegu 21 C7
Taejŏn 21 C7
Taft 39 J4
Taganrog 17 A5
Tagus = Tejo → 13 C1
Tahakopa 33 M2
Tahan, Gunong 23 C2
Tahiti 35 J13
Tahlequah 41 H7
Tahoe, L. 38 G3
Tahoe City 38 G3
Tahoka 41 J4
Tai Au Mun 21 G11
Tai Mo Shan 21 G11
Tai O 21 G10
Tai Pang Wan 21 F11
Tai Po 21 G11
Taibei = T'aipei 21 D7
T'aichung 21 D7
Taieri → 33 M3
Taihape 33 H5
Tailem Bend 32 C2
Taimyr Peninsula = Taymyr, Poluostrov 19 B11
Tain 10 D4
T'ainan 21 D7
Taínaron, Ákra 15 F10
Taipa 21 G10
T'aipei 21 D7
Taiping 23 C2
Taitao, Pen. de 48 F2
T'aitung 21 D7
Taiwan ■ 21 D7
Taiyuan 21 C6
Ta'izz 24 D3
Tajikistan ■ 18 F8
Tajo = Tejo → 13 C1
Tak 23 B1
Takaka 33 J4
Takamatsu 22 F4
Takaoka 22 E5
Takapuna 33 G5
Takasaki 22 E6
Taklamakan Shamo 20 C3
Talaud, Kepulauan 23 C4
Talbragar → 32 B4
Talca 48 D2
Talcahuano 48 D2
Taliabu 23 D4
Talihina 41 H7
Talladega 43 J2
Tallahassee 43 K3
Tallangatta 32 C4
Tallinn 18 D3
Tallulah 41 J9
Taloyoak 36 B10
Talwood 32 A4
Talyawalka Cr. → 32 B3
Tama 40 E8
Tamale 26 G5
Tamana 31 A13
Tamar → 9 G3
Tambov 18 D5
Tamil Nadu □ 25 D6
Tamo Abu, Pegunungan 23 C3
Tampa 43 M4
Tampa B. 43 M4
Tampere 7 E8
Tampico 44 C5
Tamworth, *Australia* 30 G9
Tamworth, *U.K.* 9 E6
Tana →, *Kenya* 28 E8
Tana →, *Norway* 7 C9
Tana, L. 27 F13
Tanami Desert 30 D5
Tanana → 36 B4
Tananarive = Antananarivo 29 H9
Tandou L. 32 B3
Tandragee 11 B5
Taneatua 33 H6
Tanga 28 F7
Tanganyika, L. 28 F6
Tanger 26 A4
Tanggula Shan 20 C4
Tangier = Tanger 26 A4
Tangjia 21 G10
Tangjia Wan 21 G10
Tangshan 21 C6
Tanimbar, Kepulauan 23 D5
Tanjungbalai 23 C1
Tanjungkarang Telukbetung 23 D2
Tanjungpandan 23 D2
Tanjungredeb 23 C3
Tanna 31 D12
Tanta 27 B12
Tantung = Dandong 21 B7
Tanunda 32 B2
Tanzania ■ 28 F6
Tanzhou 21 G9
Taos 39 H11
Tapachula 44 E6
Tapajós → 47 D8
Tapanui 33 L2
Tapuaenuku 33 K4
Tara 32 A5
Tarabagatay, Khrebet 18 E9
Tarābulus, *Lebanon* 17 D5
Tarābulus, *Libya* 27 B8
Tarakan 23 C3
Taranaki □ 33 H5
Taranaki, Mt. 33 H5
Taransay 10 D1
Táranto 14 D7
Táranto, G. di 14 D7
Tararua Ra. 33 J5
Tarawa 34 G9
Tarawera 33 H6
Tarawera, L. 33 H6
Taraz 18 E8
Tarbat Ness 10 D5
Tarbert, *Arg. & Bute, U.K.* 10 F3
Tarbert, *W. Isles, U.K.* 10 D2
Tarbes 12 E4
Tarboro 43 H7
Tarcoola 30 G5
Tarcoon 32 B4
Taree 30 G9
Târgovişte 15 B11
Târgu-Jiu 15 B10
Tarim He → 20 C3
Tarim Pendi 20 B3
Tarn → 12 E4
Tarnów 7 G8
Taroom 32 A4
Tarpon Springs 43 L4
Tarragona 13 B6
Tarraleah 32 D4
Tarsus 17 C4
Tartu 18 D3
Tashi Chho Dzong = Thimphu 25 C7
Tashkent = Toshkent 18 E7
Tasikmalaya 23 D2
Tasman B. 33 J4
Tasman Mts. 33 J4
Tasman Pen. 32 D4
Tasman Sea 34 L8
Tasmania □ 30 J8
Tassili n'Ajjer 26 C7
Tatarsk 18 D8
Tathra 32 C4
Tatnam, C. 37 C10
Tatra = Tatry 16 D10
Tatry 16 D10
Tatum 41 J3
Tat'ung = Datong 21 B6
Tauern 16 E6
Taumarunui 33 H5
Taunton, *U.K.* 9 F4
Taunton, *U.S.A.* 42 E10
Taunus 16 C4
Taupo 33 H6
Taupo, L. 33 H5
Tauranga 33 G6
Tauranga Harb. 33 G6
Taurus Mts. = Toros Dağları 17 C4
Taveuni 33 C9
Tavistock 9 G3
Tavoy 25 D8
Taw → 9 F3
Tawas City 42 C4
Tawau 23 C3
Tay → 10 E5
Tay, Firth of 10 E5
Tay, L. 10 E4
Taylor, *Nebr., U.S.A.* 40 E5
Taylor, *Tex., U.S.A.* 41 K6
Taylor, Mt. 39 J10
Taylorville 40 F10
Taymyr, Poluostrov 19 B11
Tayport 10 E6
Tbilisi 17 B6
Tchad = Chad ■ 27 F8
Te Anau, L. 33 L1
Te Aroha 33 G5
Te Awamutu 33 H5
Te Kuiti 33 H5
Te Puke 33 G6
Te Waewae B. 33 M1
Teague 41 K6
Tecumseh, *Mich., U.S.A.* 42 D4
Tecumseh, *Okla., U.S.A.* 41 H6
Tees → 8 C6
Tees B. 8 C6
Tegal 23 D2
Tegucigalpa 44 E7
Tehachapi 39 J4
Tehachapi Mts. 39 J4
Tehrān 24 B4
Tehuantepec 44 D5
Tehuantepec, G. de 44 D5
Tehuantepec, Istmo de 44 D6
Teifi → 9 E3
Teign → 9 G4
Teignmouth 9 G4
Tejo → 13 C1
Tekamah 40 E6
Tekapo, L. 33 K3
Tekoa 38 C5
Tel Aviv-Yafo 17 D4
Tela 44 D7
Telegraph Creek 36 C6
Teles Pires → 46 E7
Telescope Pk. 39 H5
Telford 9 E5
Tell City 42 G2
Telluride 39 H10
Teluk Intan 23 C2
Tema 26 G5
Teme → 9 E5
Temecula 39 K5
Temirtau 18 D8
Tempe 39 K8
Temple 41 K6
Templemore 11 D4
Temuco 48 D2
Temuka 33 L3
Ten Degree Channel 25 E8
Tenaha 41 K7
Tenasserim □ 25 D8
Tenby 9 F3
Tenerife 26 C2
Tengchong 20 D4
Tennant Creek 30 D5
Tennessee □ 43 H2
Tennessee → 42 G1
Tenterden 9 F8
Tenterfield 32 A5
Teófilo Otoni 47 G10
Tepic 44 C4
Teraina 35 G11
Téramo 14 C5
Terang 32 C3
Terek → 17 B7
Teresina 47 E10
Terewah, L. 32 A4
Teridgerie Cr. → 32 B4
Ternate 23 C4
Terni 14 C5
Terowie 32 B2
Terrace 36 C7
Terrassa 13 B7
Terre Haute 42 F2
Terrebonne B. 41 L9
Terrell 41 J6
Terry 40 B2
Teruel 13 B5
Teryaweyna L. 32 B3
Tesiyn Gol → 20 A4
Teslin 36 B6
Test → 9 G6
Teton → 38 C8
Tétouan 26 A4
Tetovo 15 C9
Teutoburger Wald 16 B4
Tevere → 14 D5
Teviot → 10 F6
Tewantin 32 A5
Tewkesbury 9 F5
Texarkana, *Ark., U.S.A.* 41 J8
Texarkana, *Tex., U.S.A.* 41 J7
Texas 32 A5
Texas □ 41 K5
Texas City 41 L7
Texel 16 B2
Texline 41 G3
Texoma, L. 41 J6
Tezpur 25 C8
Thabana Ntlenyana 29 K5
Thabazimbi 29 J5
Thailand ■ 23 B2
Thailand, G. of 23 B2
Thallon 32 A4
Thames 33 G5
Thames → 9 F8
Thames Estuary 9 F8
Thane 25 D6
Thanet, I. of 9 F9
Thanh Hoa 23 B2
Thanh Pho Ho Chi Minh 23 B2
Thar Desert 25 C6
Thargomindah 30 F7
Thatcher, *Ariz., U.S.A.* 39 K9
Thatcher, *Colo., U.S.A.* 41 G2
Thayer 41 G9
The Alberga → 32 A2
The Crane 45 g
The Dalles 38 D3
The Frome → 32 A2
The Hague = 's-Gravenhage 16 B2
The Hamilton → 32 A2
The Macumba → 32 A2
The Neales → 32 A2
The Pas 36 C9
The Rock 32 C4
The Salt L. 32 B3
The Settlement 45 e
The Stevenson → 32 A2
The Warburton → 32 A2
The Woodlands 41 K7
Thedford 40 E4
Theebine 32 A5
Theodore 43 K1
Theodore Roosevelt Nat. Memorial Park 40 B3
Theodore Roosevelt Res. 39 K8
Thermaïkós Kólpos 15 D10
Thermopolis 38 E9
Thessaloníki 15 D10
Thetford 9 E8
Thetford Mines 37 D12
Thevenard 32 B1
Thibodaux 41 L9
Thief River Falls 40 A6
Thiers 12 D5
Thiès 26 F2
Thikombia 33 B9
Thimphu 25 C7
Thionville 12 B7
Thíra 15 F11
Thirsk 8 C6
Thistle I. 32 C2
Thlewiaza → 36 C9
Thomas 41 H5
Thomas, L. 32 A2
Thomaston 43 J3
Thomasville, *Ala., U.S.A.* 43 K2
Thomasville, *Ga., U.S.A.* 43 K4
Thomasville, *N.C., U.S.A.* 43 H5
Thompson 36 C10

 **AFGHANISTAN**

 **ALBANIA**

 **ALGERIA**

 ANDORRA

 **ANGOLA**

 ANTIGUA & BARBUDA

 ARGENTINA

 **BARBADOS**

 BELARUS

 **BELGIUM**

 **BELIZE**

 **BENIN**

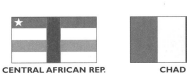 **BHUTAN**

 BOLIVIA

 **BURUNDI**

 **CAMBODIA**

 CAMEROON

 CANADA

 **CAPE VERDE**

 CENTRAL AFRICAN REP.

CHAD

 **CROATIA**

 CUBA

 CYPRUS

 **CZECH REPUBLIC**

 DENMARK

 DJIBOUTI

 DOMINICA

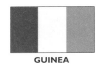 **ETHIOPIA**

 **FAROE ISLANDS**

 FIJI

 FINLAND

 **FRANCE**

 GABON

 GAMBIA

 GUINEA

 **GUINEA-BISSAU**

 **GUYANA**

 HAITI

 **HONDURAS**

 HUNGARY

 ICELAND

 **IVORY COAST**

 JAMAICA

 JAPAN

 **JORDAN**

 **KAZAKHSTAN**

 **KENYA**

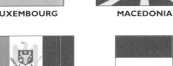 **KIRIBATI**

 **LESOTHO**

 **LIBERIA**

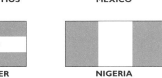 **LIBYA**

 LIECHTENSTEIN

 **LITHUANIA**

 **LUXEMBOURG**

 **MACEDONIA**

 MARSHALL ISLANDS

 **MAURITANIA**

 **MAURITIUS**

 MEXICO

 **MICRONESIA**

 **MOLDOVA**

 MONACO

 NEW ZEALAND

 NICARAGUA

 **NIGER**

 **NIGERIA**

 NORTHERN MARIANAS

 **NORWAY**

 OMAN

 PORTUGAL

 PUERTO RICO

 QATAR

 ROMANIA

 RUSSIA

 RWANDA

 SAMOA

 **SINGAPORE**

 SLOVAK REPUBLIC

SLOVENIA

SOLOMON ISLANDS

SOMALIA

SOUTH AFRICA

SPAIN

SWEDEN

SWITZERLAND

SYRIA

TAIWAN

TAJIKISTAN

TANZANIA

THAILAND

UGANDA

UKRAINE

UNITED ARAB EMIRATES

UNITED KINGDOM

UNITED STATES

URUGUAY

UZBEKISTAN